CU00793921

FIRST NIGHT FEVER

In 1975, at a concert in the Carnegie Hall, New York.

FIRST NIGHT FEVER

The Memoirs of
HERMAN PREY

Written with the help of Robert D. Abraham

Translated by Andrew Shackleton

JOHN CALDER · LONDON
RIVERRUN PRESS · NEW YORK

First published in Great Britain in 1986 by
John Calder (Publishers) Limited
18 Brewer Street, London W1R 4AS

And in the United States of America in 1986 by
Riverrun Press Inc.,
1170 Broadway, New York, NY 10001

Original German edition published as *Premierenfieber* in 1981 by
Kindler Verlag GmbH, Munich.

British Library Cataloguing in Publication Data

Prey, Herman
    First night fever: the memoirs of Herman Prey.
    1. Prey, Herman   2. Singers—Germany—Biography
    I. Title   II. Abraham, Robert D.
    III. Premierenfieber.   *English*
    782.1'092'4   ML420.P96/

    ISBN 0-7145-3998-8
        0-7145-4102-8 (pbk)

Library of Congress Cataloging in Publication Data

Prey, Hermann, 1929–
    First night fever.

    Translation of: Premierenfieber.
    Includes index.
    1. Prey, Hermann, 1929-   .   2. Singers—Germany
(West)—Biography.   3. Singing.   I. Abraham, Robert D.
II. Shackleton, Andrew.   III. Title.
ML420.P967A313 1986   784.3'0092'4 [B]   86-6491
ISBN 0-7145-3998-8
    0-7145-4102-8 (pbk)

Photoset in 11 on 12 point Baskerville
and printed in Great Britain by WBC Print Ltd, Bristol

CONTENTS

ILLUSTRATIONS

ABOUT THE CO-AUTHOR

Robert D. Abraham was born in Zürich in 1930. He studied
music and psychology in both London and Zürich. Since 1960
he has practised as a psychologist in Zürich, and has written
several books. He was also co-author of Maria Stader's
autobiography, *Nehmt meinen Dank* (*Accept my Thanks*).

CHAPTER 1

The 1980 *Orpheus* Première

My Experience with Directors

It is Monday 17th March 1980. The time is nine o'clock, and the sky is covered with grey clouds. I am on my way into town. Once on the motorway, I step on the accelerator and zoom off towards Munich, but by the time I reach the Fürstenriederstrasse I am forced to brake and progress becomes increasingly slow. I am just about to turn into the central ring-road when the car is forced to stop altogether. The traffic is now totally jammed for more than half a mile.

It must be that damned craft fair! Or is it the Munich Fashion Festival? It is already 9.50, so I have only an hour to reach the *Nationaltheater* and change into my costume before the rehearsal begins at eleven o'clock. I had originally intended to take my car to the garage first, which would mean crossing Munich and returning to the Opera by taxi. I shall never manage that!

I know Munich as well as my role in Karl Orff's *Orpheus*, which has its première next Saturday, 22nd March. I decide against going to the garage. In order to avoid the Donnersberg Bridge, I push my way across two lanes of stationary traffic, drive over a white-shaded area and thread onto the Heckenstallerstrasse slip-road. The southern by-pass route involves a considerable detour, but it is still better than sitting in a traffic jam on the Donnersberg Bridge. I eventually arrive in time for my rehearsal.

Munich has a chronic parking problem, but the *Nationaltheater* has its own carpark in Marstall Square for the use of staff and cast. Visiting singers are also allowed to use the carpark, provided they have obtained a small numbered triangle to stick on their windscreen. I am at present making a guest appearance in Munich, and although I have forgotten to ask for a yellow triangle, my face is well known to the carpark attendant, who waves me through without one.

There is exactly one parking-space left at the back. I squeeze the car in here, put my music under my arm and stroll gently across to the Maximilianstrasse. After all, it is only half past ten and there is plenty of time. I open the stage door, which is made of reinforced glass, and leads to the porters' lodge and opera workrooms. I greet the porter, who leans across towards me. 'Herr Prey! There you are at last! They're looking everywhere for you! The rehearsal's begun long since!'

I am amazed. 'What? Surely the rehearsal was planned for eleven o'clock!'

'No, ten o'clock.'

Good God! There has either been a misunderstanding, or else one of these last-minute changes which no one told me about. I hare up to the men's dressing-rooms on the second floor, taking three steps at a time. The stairway and corridors are empty. Normally full of activity, they are now strangely silent, like the bare, vaulted corridors of my old school in Berlin when I arrived late for lessons.

My dresser is waiting in the open doorway. The costume is lying ready. Thank goodness *Orpheus* does not require complicated make-up or costume. The hero wears nothing more than khaki battledress—a kind of guerrilla overall with large pockets on the chest and legs. These must be for carrying barbed wire or grenades or something. Orpheus finally hangs a thin metal chain around his neck. From it dangles an amulet in the form of a dark blue Maltese cross. I glance at it, and it occurs to me that it looks far too much like a carnival medal. It must be changed. I must definitely mention this to Pierre Jean. Pierre Jean is the young director of this enterprise, and I am working with him for the first time.

I now have about thirty years' experience of different opera directors. The first important director of my career was Günther Rennert, who invited me over to Hamburg in 1953. Rennert was manager of the Hamburg State Opera from 1946 to 1956. The only thing I have against him is that he frustrated me for a relatively long time in never giving me any of the roles I most wanted to sing: Mozart roles like the Count in *The Marriage of Figaro*, or Figaro in Rossini's *Barber of Seville*. Rennert had auditioned me for the Hamburg State Opera in 1952. The last note had scarcely died away when he called out from the auditorium, 'You have a dramatic voice.' He accordingly engaged me as Silvio in *Pagliacci*, and in the rather dramatic role of the happy broom-maker in *Hansel and Gretel*. Then in 1954, in only my second season, he gave me the great dramatic role of Don Carlos di Vargas, the avenger in Verdi's *Force of Destiny*. On the other hand he would never consider me for light baritone roles. 'Papageno? No, Prey,' he said, 'I can't see you in that role.'

Admittedly, he later changed his mind completely, particularly after he had actually seen me in a lighter role, as Giglio in Arthur Honegger's operetta *Roi Pausole* under the direction of Helmut Käutner. I appeared in a white suit and straw hat with a walking stick in my hand. Rennert was very taken with my performance, and gave me my first engagement as Guglielmo in *Così fan Tutte*. In 1959 he invited me to Salzburg to give my debut as the barber in Strauss' *Die schweigsame Frau* (*The Silent Woman*). Rennert was present at some of the triumphs of my career, including the 1967 performance of *The Magic Flute* at the Met. in New York, with Chagall's colourful stage-designs.

When asked which director I liked most, I always say Rennert. He was a real leader of singers, indeed, a leader of men in the truest sense of the word. With Rennert everything was organised with clockwork precision. Every single movement was carefully integrated to form a vital part of the whole, like a well-choreographed ballet.

There is a good example at the beginning of *The Barber of Seville*, in which Fiorillo and his musicians come in at night with lanterns, in order to 'accompany' Almaviva's serenade. Light and shade moved in time with the music, and during the serenade each musician played his instrument in exact unison with the corresponding player in the orchestra pit. Rennert prepared his production in the silence of his own room, like a general staff officer, planning his actors' every move in a carefully organised strategy before entering battle.

On the other hand, there are some directors who arrive with only a very general conception of the whole, and rely primarily on the inspiration of the moment. To develop their ideas, they need the atmosphere of the theatre, with all its bits and pieces—the props, the prop-man, the spotlights, the stage-dust, the wings; and of course the singers, preferably in costume, who can be moved round like chess pieces by means of stage directions. Such a director can create a kind of improvised drama of his own as he laughs, curses and engages in heated discussions.

'Now listen,' he might call out in despair, 'it's all rubbish! How the hell are we going to produce a drama if you can't think of anything sensible to do? You, Prey! You stand there under your weeping willow, you hold up Papageno's rope and you mumble, "One... two... " I can't stand it any longer!'

'If I might make a suggestion... ,' I say.

'Of course! Fire away!'

'Maybe Papageno could have his birds back,' I suggest, 'now that Sarastro and his men don't want him any more. And when he decides to end it all, it might be rather nice for him to let the birds go. So before I hang myself I could let the birds out one by one.'

'But how do you imagine we'd do that? With real birds? They'd fly all over the auditorium.'

'Perhaps you could solve the problem with stuffed birds. You could suspend them in the cage, on lengths of nylon thread hanging from the gridiron.'

'All right then,' says the director. 'Let's forget the technical details. Just mime the scene.'

So I do that, and he quite likes the idea. Next day, as we approach the same point in the opera, he calls out, 'Now listen, Prey. That idea of mine—I've thought it over again. I don't think it would be technically possible to produce anything decent in so short a time.'

What does he mean? *His* idea? It was *my* idea, after all, but I decide not to hold it against him. Hot-tempered characters like that always tend to attribute any decent ideas to themselves. And as this example shows, working with them is always stimulating and never boring.

I gave my first Papageno in Salzburg under Oscar Fritz Schuh. It was also under Schuh's direction that I sang my first Don Giovanni, in German. This was in March 1960 in Cologne. Wolfgang Sawallisch was conducting and Caspar Neher had created the marvellous stage-designs. Such a production was generally known as a *Schuhhaus Sawallisch* or 'Schuhhouse Sawallisch' production. Schuh's *Don Giovanni* involved an entirely new and interesting approach. Don Giovanni himself hardly moved throughout the performance, in this way forming a central focus for the rest of the drama. The spell which he seemed to cast over all those around him was demonstrated in the behaviour of the other characters towards him: Donna Anna, Donna Elvira, Don Ottavio and Masetto. Whenever Don Giovanni appeared, this produced a strange and exciting tension, without my having to do anything myself. Quite apart from this, Schuh was an expert in staging grandiose effects.

Full-blooded directors like Otto Schenk are often outstanding actors too, and they usually act far better than the singers. It is incredible, for example, how Schenk can feel his way into situations, always having a precise conception of what he wants. I once performed under him as the Count in *The Marriage of Figaro* at La Scala, Milan, with Claudio Abbado conducting. At the first rehearsal, Otti (as we all call him) said to me, 'Now, Hermann, you know the Count has a slight kink in his spine. It comes from having had too many women. He appears all blasé and elegant, but with a slight stoop, like a squire who's fallen off his horse once too often.' He demonstrated this to me, and I imitated his movements. 'Very slick,' he commented. I thus became, either consciously or unconsciously, yet another 'little Otti', like all those who work under him.

There are other directors who have no idea at all, such as a certain theatre buff from my youth, who simply gathered his singers around him and said, 'Right, lads! Off we go! Show me what you can do.' Everybody contributed what they could, and we eventually achieved a passable performance.

Researsals in Munich

There is no more inspiring figure on the opera stage than that of Orpheus, the ancient bard whose song could tame the animals and stop the splashing of the fountains. Countless composers have used the Orpheus legend in the course of the past four centuries. One of the first of these was Claudio Monteverdi in 1607. After centuries of neglect, this composer's works are now celebrating a considerable revival, which is in no small part due to the initiative of men such as Nikolaus Harnoncourt, Jean-Pierre Ponnelle and Claus Helmut Drese, manager of the Zürich Opera.

The best-known version of *Orpheus* is that of Christopher Willibald Gluck, who came, incidentally, from Bavaria like Carl Orff. The opera was first performed in 1762. The famous aria *Che farò senza Euridice?* (*What shall I do without Eurydice?*) belongs to the standard repertoire of every contralto. This is a sore point, to which I shall return later. I sang the part of Orpheus myself, at the *Nationaltheater*, Munich, in October 1967. Leonore Kirschstein sang Eurydice, Joseph Keilberth was conducting and Rennert directed the performance. Keilberth and Rennert were both great friends of mine. It was Rennert's first production in his capacity as Munich Opera's intendant and successor to Rudolf Hartmann.

Should the opera be given a happy ending? Should the beloved Eurydice return? Or should she perish for good before the curtain falls? Gluck chooses the happy ending, with the lovers reunited and Eros or Amor appearing in the final scene in the role of *deus ex machina*. Rennert, however, opted for the harder alternative by cutting the final scene. The opera begins with Orpheus mourning at Eurydice's grave. He falls asleep and dreams that he is descending into the underworld, that he returns with Eurydice and having rescued her loses her a second time. At the end he is lying by her grave, as at the beginning, but the dream is now over. This version was performed without an interval, which meant that I had to spend a whole two hours on stage.

About thirteen years later, in March 1980, Orpheus was to

return to the Munich stage, this time not in the form of Gluck's opera, but as Carl Orff's edited version of the Monteverdi work. Orff's *Orpheus* is too short for a whole evening, so it was to be performed together with another of Orff's works entitled *Die Kluge* (*The Wise Woman*). The composer protested about this, but in vain, so that Munich could expect a highly unusual evening's entertainment, particularly since the two operas had entirely separate casts. I was in *Orpheus*, while my fellow-baritone Wolfgang Brendel sang in *Die Kluge*. *Orpheus* was to be directed by the French director Pierre Jean Valentin, *Die Kluge* by Giancarlo del Monaco, son of Mario del Monaco. The conductor was to be Ferdinand Leitner.

I have already indicated some of my reservations about the title role in Gluck's *Orpheus*, and the same applies to the Monteverdi work. Both composers wrote the part for a contralto or, more precisely, for a castrato and thus for a male alto. Gluck did admittedly write a later Parisian version, which was for a tenor, but by the middle of the nineteenth century the part was firmly in the hands of women singers. With a contralto the voice lies in the range intended by the composer, whereas with a baritone it is a whole octave lower. Thirds become tenths, for example, which must affect the way the voice blends with the higher wind and strings, and with Eurydice's soprano line. A few minutes before the Gluck première with Rennert, Keilberth put his hands on my shoulder and said, 'You know, Prey, you sing the part beautifully, but it still sounds far better with a contralto.'

I did not exactly appreciate the remark at the time, but Keilberth was quite right.

The same problem crops up with Gustav Mahler's *Lieder eines fahrenden Gesellen* (*Songs of a wayfarer*), and his *Kindertotenlieder* (*Songs on the Death of Children*). The words are written for a man, but, in my opinion at least, the music sounds better with a mezzo or a contralto.

Orff's version of *Orpheus* is by no means easy to learn, and for months I travelled the world with the piano score under my arm, studying it at every free moment. I was, after all, under considerable pressure of time. The part was very difficult and

An extract from my *Orpheus* score.

trying, mainly because Orff had written out in full all the coloraturas and melismas—extensions and ornamentations of the melody on the vowels. These parts had, in their own period, been improvised by the singer himself. But instead of allowing him free rein, Orff forced the singer to keep strictly to the bars and note values in the score. And yet at the time it was supposed to sound like an improvisation. This was no easy task.

New roles are always a challenge to me, but at first I have considerable qualms and misgivings to overcome. Sometimes what I need most is someone to encourage me a little, and then I am ready to take the plunge.

It was August Everding, manager of the *Nationaltheater*, who asked me if I would like to do the title role in Carl Orff's Monteverdi arrangement, which was to be performed in honour of Orff's eighty-fifth birthday. In principle I was willing to do so, although in practice it had somehow to be squeezed into an already over-filled schedule. We are often asked to take on a role as many as three or four years in advance. In this case I had only twelve months' notice, so that I had to alter a number of dates in my diary. The role is musically extremely demanding, indeed it is one of the most difficult parts that has ever been written. I had so far only sung it on record, so I still had to learn it by heart. On top of all this, the production had been entrusted to a certain Pierre Jean Valentin, a young director who had previously specialised in stage-dramas. I could see problems ahead.

I had already heard the name Pierre Jean Valentin in connection with the Nancy Festival.

'Have you directed much opera before?' I asked him.

'I'm a qualified photographer and I came to stage-drama via films.' He spoke fluent German.

'Your first opera?' Disaster loomed.

'No,' he smiled back, 'I've done a variety of operas: Falla's *Master Pedro's Puppet Show*, and also some Henze and Stravinsky.' He seemed to sense my uneasiness and added, 'We'll get on alright. If there's anything you don't like, just let me know.'

I felt somewhat reassured.

Rehearsals were exhausting and full of arguments. I have a good general grasp of the meaning of the Orpheus story. It is a traditional interpretation, but nonetheless a flexible one. However, Valentin's ideas were decidedly idiosyncratic and by no means readily comprehensible. When I am singing in the title role, I always like to know what's going on, and preferably why. To this day I've never fully grasped what Valentin intended.

Similarly, it took some effort to make head or tail of Hubert
Monloup's stage-designs. He wanted to demonstrate the
dichotomy between ancient Greece and modern Russia. To the
right of the stage he placed a plain brick wall, and in front of it
the stumps of two doric columns. In front of these he scattered
more cornices and pieces of column, grouped in a casual yet
meaningful fashion. This was complemented by the blackened
skeleton of a factory or barracks which reared up on the left, its
entrance lit by an electric lamp. Why it was this lamp in
particular that so offended my senses I don't know. At any rate, I
could not get used to it. The opera was to be performed on a
foam-rubber floor, supposed to represent an ancient pavement.
In the background the outline of a bunker could just be seen,
long iron bars jutted threateningly into the air, like the
forefingers of Charon the ferryman. Behind the bunker the path
led down into the underworld.

My wife came to one of the rehearsals. 'What,' she asked, 'is
that crumpled flag over the bunker meant to signify?'

'I don't know what it is now, but at one time it was a Coca
Cola advert, like the ones you see on the motorway.'

Bärbel looked at me in disbelief. 'What on earth does a
motorway advert have to do with Orpheus?'

'You don't understand,' I said. 'It belongs to the motorway.'

'What motorway?'

'The motorway on the stage, of course.'

'But there isn't a motorway on stage.'

She was wrong on this point. Next to the bunker the paving
stones changed into asphalt, or that was how it was explained to
me, though I must say I would not have thought of it myself.
Was this the arcadian landscape which Monteverdi and Orff
had envisaged? Most certainly not!

Apart from odd mysterious details like this, the stage-design
struck me as both visually impressive and technically ingenious.
Not only could the tableau be quickly rolled up and carried
away to make way for *Die Kluge*, but thanks to the ingenious
lighting scheme it was possible to create some quite amazing
effects, though I only know this from hearsay as I was on stage for
most of the performance.

Valentin tried to impress on me the idea of the so-called visionary theatre. His apocalyptic vision of the Orpheus tale might best be summed up like this: in a world poisoned by nuclear explosions, the fulfilment of love becomes a mere memory, the ghostly echo of earlier times. Orpheus, a representative of the man in the street, rebels against this notion and spares no effort to regain his lost love, but in vain. At the end of the opera he simply stands there with clenched fists. What does this mean? Rebellion or despair?

What will the audience make of this final gesture? The problem with stage allegories is that their creators take far too much for granted. There is no single prop on stage which does not evoke in their minds a host of meaningful images and associations, but these are of interest to few apart from themselves. And so, regrettably, the public are none the wiser for it. Admittedly, anyone with a taste for the ethereal or the unearthly can simply let his mind be transported by the magical scenes on stage. But many in the audience will be totally confused by the strange birds which swagger around, the inhabitants of the underworld in their Martian costumes, and the corpse-bearers disguised in space-suits. They will ask, and not without reason, 'What's it all about?'

In Munich, the director's vision was also at odds with the realities of the production. We had a piano accompanist for the dress rehearsal. First the iron curtain rose, clanking and thundering like an omen from God. Next the stage was invaded by a poison-green cloud of 'atomic' dust, which thickened and billowed out everywhere. I wondered how I was supposed to breathe, let alone sing. The conductor, Ferdinand Leitner, stared in amazement as the green fog rolled implacably on, crossing the apron and plunging into the orchestra pit, completely engulfing the pianist as it reached the conductor's stand and he marched forward into the auditorium. 'Out of the question!' came Leitner's voice from the cloud. Fortunately now, as on previous occasions, both director and stage-designer proved willing to compromise, and the fog was reduced to the minimum.

Should Eurydice return?

It is 10.45 a.m. on Monday, 17th March 1980. After four weeks *Orpheus* rehearsals, I'm quite accustomed to moving in all spheres, both above and below the earth, but still have mixed feelings about the forthcoming première on Saturday. I am afraid that the public will protest, and must summon all my resources to produce a performance convincing enough to quell their dissention. At least I have learnt to get on with Messrs Valentin and Monloup, while Prof. Leitner and I are old friends, having cracked many a hard nut together.

Annoyed at having arrived forty-five minutes late, I throw on my battledress and race down to the stage, where the rehearsal is in full swing and the stage-design partially finished. My eye ranges over the vast empty spaces of the auditorium. A reading-lamp in the twelfth row reveals an improvised director's stand, behind which I can just make out the director. He comes forward and climbs onto the stage via a plank thrown across the orchestra pit; it is from here that I shall sing my ode to the forests.

This production of Orff's *Orpheus* contains four dramatic climaxes. The first of these is the entrance of a strange procession of fabulous and archetypal creatures, including artificial birds on perches, a war-god in a shining gold breastplate and maidens scattering confetti. They come up from the underworld and carry Eurydice away with them. As the procession appears, a black cloth is held beneath my nose, it is a symbol of death and the underworld. I am anaesthetised by it and fall unconscious, thus allowing the ceremony to pass over me. This cloth accompanies me for the rest of the performance, I usually hold it in my hand, though I have to blindfold myself with it before descending to the underworld. It signifies that Orpheus has been marked out by fate, though I doubt whether the audience are aware of this.

I remain lying by the column for the whole of the separation scene, while the chorus carries on the drama from the orchestra pit, to which it has been banished. This is highly effective from an acoustic point of view, but somewhat decreases the dramatic impact of the scene. However, I decide to keep quiet about this, as I am more interested in the next three big scenes. The first of these is the entrance of Fate (Cornelia Wulkopf) to announce Eurydice's death. Next I sing my duet with Cerberus, guardian of the underworld (Karl Christian Kohn).

We have spent a long time polishing up these two scenes. My altercation with Cerberus in his space-suit should really be one of the most effective scenes in the whole production. The giant strides towards me through the darkness with a miner's lamp tied round his waist, while I lie on the ground with my back turned, representing man's powerlessness against death.

The real climax of the work is the scene in which I disobey Hades' commands and turn back towards Eurydice, thus losing her for ever. This scene has caused us no end of headaches, and I am still not satisfied with the director's plans.

I arrive just as they finish rehearsing the procession scene. The last dancer stomps in on stilts and practises his steps on the foam-rubber floor. We now move on to the entrance of the messenger, Fate. The orchestra pit is still only occupied by the conductor and chorus. For the moment the orchestral part is played on the piano by a répétiteur. The stage is empty at last, so I wait for the spotlight to be directed on me, exchange a glance with the conductor and then we begin. Frau Wulkopf enters the stage from the right... 'Stop!' shouts the director. 'Better come in between the columns!' Frau Wulkopf disappears and comes back in again. She falls demonstratively on her knees and imparts her message of doom.

This is followed by my lament for the loss of Eurydice and my descent to the underworld. We finish these without a hitch, but there is an interruption when Karl Christian makes his entrance wearing his costume on stage for the very first time. It is made of inflated plastic, with a bright silver helmet on his head. As he comes trudging in, his costume protests with loud scrunching and crackling noises. Prof. Leitner raps his music stand: the noise is drowning the music. We scratch our heads and try to come up with a solution to this problem. Silvery Cerberus leaves the stage to loud crackles, and this time returns more cautiously. But as the guardian of Hades he cannot come in *too* gingerly. It occurs to me that he could really do with a pair of roller skates!

I sing to Kohn imploringly: 'I am Orpheus, and I seek Eurydice, the one desire of my life.' Vocally, this solo is one of the most difficult, consisting of only one sentence, but the melismas fill up two whole pages of the piano score. As Carl Orff put it to me, 'This where Orpheus hands in his visiting card.'

Kohn, a real giant in his Martian costume, eventually lets me in. Orpheus ventures forth into the shady realm to rescue his beloved from the clutches of Hades. As far as Valentin is concerned, Eurydice (Suzanne Sonnenschein) is no more than a mere symbol of forlorn love. She does not belong to Orpheus as Isolde does to Tristan, Juliet to Romeo, Mélisande to Pelléas, or Susanna to Figaro. She is not his wife, neither does her costume have any resemblance to Orpheus' khaki battledress, which prohibits a visual association of the kind seen between Papageno and Papagena in their feathered costumes. On the contrary, she alone of all the cast has the costume which most establishes her as an ancient Athenian. She stands with me on stage at the beginning of the opera, but then leaves me and goes down to the underworld. Should she return at the end of the opera? This is the thorny question which preoccupies us right up to the first night.

We carefully consider a variety of alternative solutions. The problem, from the production point of view, lies in the fact that Eurydice sings a duet with Orpheus immediately before his infringement of Hades' law causes her to disappear again. One solution would be for me to lead her up from the underworld myself, thus bringing her on stage. But this would mean that at the very moment I turn to look at her she must disappear from view. This effect would be difficult from a technical point of view. 'I'm supposed to look back,' I say, 'but she's still standing there while I sing of my despair at losing her.'

'Let's go back to my original idea,' suggests Valentin.

'Would that mean no more Eurydice?'

'Yes, that's right.'

But I am not happy about this: 'OK, Eurydice doesn't appear again. But then it looks as though Hades has betrayed me, which contradicts the story, and also weakens the effect of my suddenly losing her again. My disobedience would appear to have made no difference.'

A number of our colleagues have joined us during this conversation, and make some suggestions of their own. With Valentin, even those not directly involved have something to say on the matter. Someone suggests that we project Eurydice's shadow on the white backdrop, to which there is a mixed reaction. Then someone else speaks up more forcefully: 'Death itself is incomprehensible, so why should the audience expect to understand the end of the opera?'

That is the end of the matter, Eurydice no longer returns, and I must face the finale alone. This has a number of advantages. Firstly, I shall be able to sing the duet with Eurydice from behind the wings, where we can sing directly from the score. There are no problems with the orchestra: we can watch them on a television monitor placed behind the stage. Secondly, I will have the stage to myself at the end of the performance. As I am in the title role, I quite like this idea, since it means that all eyes are focused on me as the curtain falls.

On 21st March, the day before the première, Carl Orff is present at the rehearsal. Orff's wife, Luise Rinse, says of him that he is essentially an ancient Greek who was accidentally born in twentieth-century Bavaria. It is thus not surprising that he is unhappy with Valentin's interpretation. Neither does he agree that Eurydice should be excluded from the final scene, which for him would be to miss the climax of the whole tragedy. The opera manager August Everding intervenes and pleads with me to come an hour earlier next day, so that we can re-incorporate Eurydice's entrance and rehearse it before the performance. Thank goodness I know the duet by heart!

Only a few hours before the curtain rises, we are still rehearsing. But all is in vain: for technical reasons the finale can no longer be adapted. This provokes a number of fierce arguments, but at last I am able to retire to my room and sit down at the make-up table. I am already wearing my battledress; the medal hung round my neck is of a flaming sun, replacing the carnival medal. Now all I need is peace and quiet in order to collect myself.

Orff's *Orpheus* goes off as scheduled with Eurydice no longer returning from the underworld. The production is not as popular as I would have liked, for no one could know better than I the sincerity of its aims and the plethora of ideas which went into it.

My own performance, however, is to prove a great personal triumph, richly rewarding the considerable efforts which went into it. Karl Schumann's review in the *Süddeutsche Zeitung* runs thus: 'Orff's *Orpheus* rescued by a singer.'

CHAPTER 2

A singer's thoughts

Before a lieder recital in paris

The *Orpheus* première was on a Saturday, and the next day my wife and I flew to Paris. That afternoon I rehearsed with Irwin Gage at the beautiful Paris home of my fellow-baritone Tom Krause. It is now Monday evening, and I am due to give a Lieder recital at the *Théâtre Athenée*. I have exchanged my battledress for evening dress, and a glance at the clock tells me that it is nearly half past eight. Concerts begin at nine o'clock in France, so there is another half an hour to go. The programme includes Schumann's *Kerner-Lieder*, followed by a selection of songs by Richard Strauss.

Green-rooms are comfortable on only the rarest of occasions. They are usually sparsely furnished, windowless and fusty, and only intended for short stays. This one, in the *Théâtre Athenée*, is just about passable. I make myself as comfortable as possible and relax for the last few minutes before the concert. How many hundreds of times have I gone through this? Sometimes I feel like a travelling salesman dealing in romantic songs. The realities of the profession are decidedly un-romantic; every day I move on to a different town and sing in a different concert hall. My wife Bärbel accepts this nomadic existence with an air of serene resignation. She travels everywhere with me, and so I am able to discuss everything with her. She comforts me when things go wrong, and is always there beside me; I could never manage without her. She also keeps me company in the green-room. At a given point she repeats her reassuring 'There, there, there' for the umpteenth time, and I reply automatically, 'Will you come back in the interval?'

I go off into a daydream, and think back to 1949. I was only twenty at the time, an ambitious young music student. I could no longer hide my talents from the public, so I decided to give a concert. It was to be a solo recital, but with an accompanist, for nothing is possible without a pianist. I found a suitable room in the Platanenallee in Berlin-Charlottenburg. It was not too big, cheap to hire and had survived the bombs fairly well. I had a little experience of organising small concerts, so I already knew that publicity is extremely important. I rushed all over the place, pinning up home-made posters and trying to persuade shopkeepers to let me put my advertisements in their windows. Anybody who shopped within a mile or so of the planned venue would notice them immediately: 'Hermann Prey sings songs by Beethoven, Schubert, Brahms and Wolf. This Saturday at 3.00 p.m.' Friends had been invited with the following instructions: 'Always clap, even if you don't like the piece, but only when everyone else stops, otherwise there's no point.'

Then, as now, we sat waiting in the green-room, Martin Malzer and I. It was a small, windowless room behind the stage. I tried to look calm, but I was seething with excitement underneath. Martin had accompanied me at a number of private concerts. He fingered his music, while I looked at the clock every fifteen seconds. I pictured the audience in my mind's eye, and anticipated their applause.

On the stroke of three o'clock, we walked down the dark corridor which led to the stage, where the sudden brightness was dazzling. Someone was clapping: it was Aunt Dora. I blinked across the room, and was greeted by rows and rows of empty seats. It must be an optical illusion! Alas, it was not. Aunt Dora was not the only one present, for she had been joined by half a dozen faithful friends. they sat huddled together in the middle of the seventh and eighth rows, looking like the survivors of a shipwreck and surrounded by a yawning void. I tried to ignore this, and stood ready to sing.

As yet I did not have any tails, but that did not really matter. No one in Berlin did, it was too soon after the war and only a year after the currency reform. It was unbearably hot that afternoon, and before Martin had so much as finished the introduction I was sweating all over.

In the middle of Beethoven's *Adelaide* the sunlight flashed at me through the window and suddenly dazzled me. Even the sun was against me today, but I was determined to see this thing through.

As a young singer I usually sang with my hands clasped tight and my eyes shut. Not long after, following a concert in Schöneberg Town Hall in West Berlin, a friend told me, 'You know, somebody in front of me said to the person next to him, "He's a talented young man, it's a pity he's blind." ' I must have left a similar impression in Charlottenburg in 1949. At all events, I battled through the programme from start to finish. The takings amounted to six marks, so I treated everyone to a beer.

There is a knock on the door, which brings me back to the present. I open the door and receive an enormous bouquet of flowers. The room is suddenly filled with the babble of conversation, like the noise of the sea. The concert is sold out. In musical centres such as New York, London, Vienna and Moscow, I sing to audiences of two, three, sometimes even four thousand. In other places it might be less than a thousand since small towns are also included in my itinerary. I make no distinction whatsoever between important and less important concerts, I must give of my best at every single recital. I admit I'm not always in the best of moods, but this depends on factors over which I have no control. After years of experience, I am more than ever convinced that there *is* such a thing as a good or a bad audience. I have a strong sixth sense for the quality of my audience. As soon as I step on the platform, I begin to pick up the vibes, and know instinctively the sort of audience that waits before me. The atmosphere of the building itself also plays an important role. I prefer to sing in halls which were created exclusively for music, or in buildings with a long and interesting history.

A concert is less affected by the events of the previous day than one might imagine. The day can be fraught with problems: I argue with the hotel manager as I leave in the morning; I arrive in the early afternoon and ram the car into a post in the underground carpark; I cannot find my reading-glasses when I unpack, so that my wife has to ring the previous hotel to see if I have left them behind; I make a preliminary visit to the concert hall and find lighting problems on the stage; or the weather is atrocious, I am going down with a cold and, to cap it all, there is a dreadful draught in the green-room. Sometimes everything goes wrong at once, and then I want to cancel my performances and give it all up. I pace up and down the room like a lion in a cage. I storm onto the stage and... give a brilliant recital. At other times the day runs like clockwork, but the evening recital leaves a lot to be desired.

After this Paris concert, I asked Bärbel how she thought it went. 'Give yourself a pat on the back,' was her reply.

Fear is the watchword

Am I ever afraid of not being able to hold the audience's attention, or of disappointing them? I certainly am. Every concert brings new challenges.

An experienced recitalist can sense immediately when he is losing control. I like the hall to be dimmed, so that the programme and the words of the songs can barely be made out. I prefer the listeners to look at me rather than at their programme notes. The visual element is very important, and those who watch me will understand more of what I am trying to communicate.

It is always possible to suffer a lapse of memory and it is easy to mix up lines, especially in songs made up of stanzas. Leonard Hokanson, my chief accompanist for many years, claims that I am gifted with total recall. It is true that even pieces I have not sung for years I can polish up in a very short time. My wife says I have the memory of an elephant, yet it can still happen that I suddenly forget a line. I have on occasion been known to compose whole new stanzas, suitable in content and rhyming perfectly.

These days on the whole, I find it more difficult to remember new material. This is in spite of the fact that I have undergone a specific form of visual memory training. My memory is by nature a visual one. When I sing a particular work, I can picture my score in front of me: the page number, the order of the words, the notes of the music and the printed and pencilled instructions. When I reach the bottom of the page, I turn it over in my mind's eye. On one occasion, at a performance of *Winterreise* in America, someone on the front row was following a score in an edition different from my own. This meant that he turned the pages in different places from those in my visual memory, and thus wrongly from my point of view. I had to shut my eyes for the whole recital and sing 'blindly', just as I had done in my earliest concerts.

It is a considerable step from a visual memory to a photographic memory. Arturo Toscanini, for example, is said to have had a photographic memory. Dimitri Metropoulos was the same: he read a complicated modern orchestral score only once, and could then recall it like a photograph imprinted in his mind. I am similarly amazed at the feats of memory achieved by conductors such as Karl Richter, whose untimely death occurred earlier this year [1980]. On Good Friday we were performing together in Bach's *Matthew Passion* as we had many times before. I was singing the part of Christ. Richter sat at the harpsichord, playing and conducting this enormous work, with all its confusing rhythms and phrases, by heart from beginning to end. He still managed to leave his watch and baton behind in the green-room we shared. I returned his watch to him at the hotel, but kept the baton as a souvenir.

When musicians speak of fear, they are usually talking about stage fright. I suffer from ice-cold hands, which can sometimes become completely numb. It is fortunate that I am not a pianist! This numbness persists long after I have overcome concert nerves, and sometimes lasts into the second or third act of an opera. When I shake hands in the green-room afterwards, the frequent comment is, 'What cold hands you have!' Then I think to myself, I must have sung well today. For these cold hands are an outward sign of the inward tension which enables me to excel myself.

Surely I ought to be satisfied with myself by now? Professionally, I have achieved all I could possibly desire. I have travelled the world giving Lieder recitals; I have performed in the world's greatest opera houses in all my favourite roles: Papageno in *The Magic Flute*, Guglielmo in *Così fan Tutte*, Figaro in *The Barber of Seville* and Wolfram in *Tannhäuser*. Also, thanks to the medium of television, I cannot be seen anywhere without somebody asking, 'Excuse me, you wouldn't by any chance be Hermann Prey?' I sometimes receive a friendly pat on the shoulder, or somebody whispers to his neighbour, 'Look, there's...'

Can I possibly have any more worries? But of course I have! I've discovered that a life of continuing success becomes increasingly complicated, and that professional problems become ever more incalculable. As someone who has 'arrived', I must rack my brains over problems I could have previously dismissed with a flourish. Should I or should I not sing a particular role or song? Is the stress damaging my health? Will taking part in a television show affect my reputation as a recitalist? A singing career is rather like climbing a mountain. The ascent can be difficult, but moving along a crest from one summit to another can be even more difficult. And where do I go from there? I am reminded of the Brahms setting of Friedrich Rückert's poem:

Mit vierzig Jahren ist der Berg erstiegen.
Wir stehen still und schau'n zurück
Dort sehen wir der Kindheit stilles liegen,
Und dort der Jugend lautes Glück.

Noch einmal schau, und dann gekräftigt weiter,
Erhebe deinen Wanderstab!
Hindehnt ein Bergesrücken sich, ein breiter,
Und hier nicht, drüben geht's hinab.

Nicht atmend aufwärts brauchst du mehr zu steigen,
Die Eb'ne zieht von selbst sich fort;
Dann wird sie sich mit dir unmerklich neigen,
Und eh' du's denkst, bist du im Port.

At forty we have reached the summit.
We stand in silence and look back;
There we see the serenity of childhood,
And the utter happiness of youth.

Look back again and, thus strengthened,
Take up your staff and go forward!
The mountain stretches onward, sometimes broad,
Sometimes narrow, and over there drops sheer.

You need no longer climb upwards, panting:
The plateau stretches before you;
Then you will begin to move imperceptibly downwards,
And before you realise, you will have arrived in port.

The more problems I encounter as an artist, the more self-critical, the less satisfied, I become. I am no longer independent either. For like all fathers, I worry about my children's problems, and feel responsible even though I can do very little to help. The young want, indeed ought, to solve their problems for themselves. I used to think, in all seriousness, that adults did not have any real problems, and that life for them was one long holiday. I thought greater maturity would make problems easier to solve, in fact the opposite is the case. I also hoped that greater experience would mean fewer mistakes. Since then I have decided that it is more important to learn to deal with mistakes than to avoid making them altogether.

There are fewer and fewer people to whom I can turn for advice. I am more often the person to whom others come for advice. Naturally, I can always share my problems with Bärbel. At one time I could turn to my friend Fritz Wunderlich as well. I never had any inhibitions about confiding my worries to him. He knew that crises are part and parcel of our profession. He once tried to calm me down in the following conversation (in Berlin dialect):

'Get into yourself, man!' (*'Mensch, jeh in dir!'*)

'Been there before,' (*'War ick schon,'*) I replied, 'nothing doing either.' (*'ooch nischt los.'*)

Two empty seats

I always run from the green-room into the concert hall and in my mind I'm already there. I sometimes give a recital in an opera house, and here the route can be extremely long, leading up and down through silent, empty corridors. Suddenly a door springs open to reveal a dazzle of bright spotlights. As I stand there in the footlights, the audience applauds as if to say, 'Off you go, Wolfram von Eschenbach!'

I am as familiar with conditions in the world's great concert halls as an experienced pilot is familiar with airport runways. Countless obstacles are lying in wait: piano stools creak and pedals squeak; nails and planks protrude from old creaky stages. One accompanist of mine tends to aim for such phenomena, and always lands on his nose, preferably in full view of the audience. His comic turns can become quite annoying if they occur more than once in the same recital.

I have encountered stages so vast that the piano is thirty yards or more from the stage door. The accompanist and I must walk the whole distance under the full gaze of the public. I once had to point this out to a young and inexperienced pianist. 'Look here, old chap. It doesn't matter what you do this side of the door. Scratch yourself or pick your ears for all I care. But as soon as you've crossed the threshold, the audience will take note of every little thing you do.'

I stand by the piano and bow. At first I am unaware of any individuals in the audience. Only after a short interval can I discern any details, such as a white fur hat, a bright yellow evening gown, a red beard or a nun's habit. The man with the score in the front row gives me a questioning look. But I cannot see anything beyond the fifth row.

I always look out for Bärbel. Where is she tonight? Ah, there she is in the fourth row on the left. We exchange glances. I see two empty seats, and this sets me thinking again. How lovely it would have been to see my parents in those seats. Father witnessed my rise to fame, but Mother died in 1954 when my career was just beginning. Yet it was Mother who really believed in me, she had frequently put in a good word for me when Father opposed my musical aspirations. A realist and a practical man, he could not understand why his son could not think of anything more sensible than a singing career. In 1965 we invited him to Bayreuth to hear me sing Wolfram in *Tannhäuser*. The performance greatly affected him, and even moved him to tears. In the interval a friend of mine went up to him and praised my voice. He beamed at him, 'He got that from me,' he said proudly. When Bärbel told me about it afterwards, we just had to laugh. And yet I could not help taking it as a special compliment.

My first solos

Like all artists, singers must always be in the limelight, success and adulation can become addictive. After the performance we remove our false beards and take off our costumes, and become ordinary people again. Can we really change our mental attitudes? I suspect that very few people can easily achieve this, I myself can never fully switch off. Only when I get away to the island of Amrum for a few weeks' holiday can I fully cast off my professional identity.

A singing career requires constant attention, which is not always pleasant for those around me. Friends too often take second place. Another great danger is that of self-preoccupation. I might, for example, spend an agreeable evening with friends, only to realise as I go to bed, that all the conversation revolved around me. I firmly resolve to change this. But next time it is usually the same as before.

I am quite a good talker, but not a good listener. If my wife tells a story which involves me, it is not long before I chip in with my own version, which I always consider more accurate. If I find myself in company where I have nothing to say, where things do not happen the way I want, or where there are language barriers, I slip quietly away. Sometimes I even go to sleep in a corner.

Singers and actors have a need to entertain people, which for most of us begins in childhood. Such was the case with me, I always loved a chance to show off. Even if there was no audience, I would still perform to myself. I would paint on a moustache, don my father's bowler hat, take his stick in my hand and put a cigar in my mouth. Then I would strut out of the front door and come in disguised as a guest.

I can still remember an event which occurred when I was five. There was a folk festival, and a band was playing on stage. In the interval I climbed onto the stage and ventured across the apron to have a closer look at the lighting. Everything fascinated me: the boards, the lights, the rows of seats and the people in the audience. I must have looked as if I was going to bow for I heard someone clapping, and a voice called out, 'Come on, Hermi, sing us something!' I fled, but I was already stage-struck. I shall never forget that moment.

Another story came from Aunt Dora, my father's sister-in-law. Apparently the whole family was assembled at my grandparents' house, it was Christmas, and we were awaiting the arrival of Father Christmas. I could smell pine-needles, and the candles flickered in the drawing-room. 'Let's go in now,' said Mother, 'and Hermi will sing *O Tannenbaum*.'

'Haven't you noticed, Anni?' Aunt Dora commented to Mother afterwards. 'Your son sings quite differently from the other children. It isn't all chopped up, it's more like a violin with proper bowing.'

CHAPTER 3

My parental home

From a butcher's family

My childhood was an untroubled one, thanks to the effort and efficiency with which my father ran his business. I was born on 11th July 1929, on the eve of the great depression. Yet even in the terrible years of the 'thirties, and later during the war, the Prey family fared well in comparison with others in Germany. The family trade was a stable one, and there is always a market for meat.

Grandfather Prey had finished his apprenticeship when he moved to Berlin from Pomerania in around 1891. By the time my father was born in 1901, Grandfather had worked his way up to the status of master-butcher and shopkeeper. These were years of economic growth and as owner of the firm he was open to technical innovations, and soon bought a Mercedes van. By 1904 he was driving around Berlin on solid rubber tyres. Twenty years later, Grandfather was one of the first Berlin meat-importers to trade in frozen meat from Argentina. Had it not been for regulations which prevented this trade, he would have taken advantage of it before the First World War. He always considered this to be the only sensible way of providing good cheap meat for a city population. However, the import of frozen meat remained illegal in Germany up to 1922. The first steamers had brought frozen beef and lamb to Europe from overseas as early as 1880, but ever since then, vehement arguments had raged as to the quality of refrigerated meat. Importers like my grandfather had first to overcome the opposition and the prejudices of their fellow-countrymen. But gradually even the farmers began to realise the benefits of refrigeration, and took full advantage of it.

In the thirties my father was in his prime and lived only for his business, like his own father before him. My children might well add to this, 'Dad, *you're* only interested in your career.' And they would be quite correct.

On the other hand my mother, who was musically inclined, had little interest in the butcher's trade. In retrospect, I suspect she was considered an outsider in the business-minded Prey family. Nevertheless she dutifully went with Father 'to market' —to the wholesale market—and sat at the till, taking in the money with a friendly smile. The profit margins were small, but quite enough when you consider that sales of meat sometimes amounted to several tons. If the unavoidable happened and the accounts showed a deficit of one mark forty-two in a day, Mother was inconsolable. She would not let up until she had found where the mistake was. Father was just as fussy in such matters. Mother loved him dearly, and was always at great pains to please him. She also went with him to the Prey grandparents on Sundays, although I feel she never really felt at home there.

Before her marriage Mother had worked as a ladies' hairdresser in a high-class salon in the Kurfürstendamm. If she had been sufficiently encouraged, she could certainly have succeeded professionally if not artistically. She possessed all the necessary qualities: sensitivity, refinement of taste, a strong aesthetic sense and a steady hand. For example, who else could have decorated the dinner table so delightfully with the simplest of flowers: marguerites, cowslips, harebells and cuckoo-flowers? She inherited this ability from her father. Like Grandfather Prey, Oskar Senkbeil had finished his apprenticeship when he moved to Berlin. He came from West Prussia and had trained as a house-painter. Later he tried his hand as an artist, painting murals in people's houses in the Victorian style which was characteristic of the period. One or two of his creations may well have survived the war: perhaps a landscape or a flower arrangement, framed with stucco designs in the style which was then fashionable. The initials 'O.S.' will indicate if it is one of

Grandfather's creations. As the demand for murals decreased, he changed to varnishing furniture.

Whether as a painter or as a varnishing expert, Grandfather cannot have found it easy to support a family of seven children. I can no longer remember Grandfather Senkbeil, as he died at the relatively young age of fifty-two, but I can still picture my grandmother. She was the kind of granny you always find in picture-books: homely and motherly, sitting on the sofa knitting woollen stockings for my sister and me. In the twenties the Senkbeils lived in the Strassmannstrasse, not far from the Landsberger Allee and thus near to the abattoirs. The Preys also lived in this area, which is how my parents got to know each other.

Father had a hard outer shell, but it concealed a soft heart. He once remarked to me, 'You know, when I was your age I was a soft-hearted, dreamy lad, just like you. I'll never forget the look on the face of the first calf I slaughtered. But *somebody's* got to do it, haven't they? Everyone likes meat, but people are funny, they go into the shop and buy a joint, and at the same time they say, "That butcher, what a brute!" There's got to be somebody to kill the animal that's lying there so nicely prepared on the plate.'

Later, when I was not quite thirteen, Father took me to the abattoir to introduce me to his work. Here I saw pigs being slaughtered and carved up. I thought, 'This can't possibly be the life for me.'

I felt the same later when we were going for a Sunday walk together, which did not happen very often, and he started talking about my career. We had not yet decided whether I should apprentice as a butcher or go on to do my *Abitur* (school certificate) at the *Gymnasium* (grammar school). Father had never spoken about the matter directly. He had merely dropped odd hints like, 'Go and wash your hands—cleanliness is essential in our profession.'

Father was smoking his Sunday cigar. 'As far as I'm concerned,' he said, 'you can stay on at school. A good education never goes amiss.' We walked past a brewery. Father pointed out the enormous façade. 'In Chicago there are enormous meat factories with thousands of workers, but even

they started with only a handful of men. So when the war's over
we could build up something like that together.'

'Look, Dad,' I said, 'I don't think it's the right profession for
me.'

'What do you want to be then?'

'I don't know yet.'

'You can make something of yourself in any profession,' he
went on to explain. 'You can either waste your life away as the
cook on a trawler, or else you can become a king among chefs
and cook for kings, like Alfred Walterspiel.' We walked on
silently, but before we turned back he added, 'Well, finish school
first and then we'll see.'

Three years later, Germany was lying in ruins and Father's
business no longer existed. I had to find my own way in life.

A mother's dream

My mother was an outstandingly beautiful woman. I shall never
forget what her hair looked like. I can still picture her now as she
combed it in front of the mirror. Her light-brown hair was thick
and lustrous, and reached as far as her knees. Her movements
were graceful, and her voice was extraordinarily beautiful. She
was fond of singing, and must secretly have longed for the day
when my father might take her to a concert or the opera. Alas,
this was out of the question, as Father was on his feet the whole
day and never had any time for it.

She was particularly fond of the voice of Heinrich Schlusnus,
and loved to listen to records by him. She would put on
Schubert's *Ständchen* or Dapertutto's aria from *Tales of Hoffmann*,
so that when I came home from school and opened the front
door, I was often greeted by Schlusnus' gentle, sonorous voice. I
would creep into the living room and sit down by the
gramophone.

'I say, Mum,' I once asked, 'what do you have to do to be able
to sing like Schlusnus?'

'What should I say? You'd have to take singing lessons.'

'But what do you do in singing lessons?'

'I don't know exactly. Are you interested?'

'Yes, I am.'

'Well, when you're bigger, perhaps *you* can have singing lessons. Then you'll be able to find out for yourself.'

'That must be wonderful, standing on a stage and singing to people.'

'Would you like to become a singer eventually?'

'No. . . . or rather I'm not sure yet.'

Mother became thoughtful. 'There aren't any musicians in the Prey family,' she commented. 'And the Senkbeils? I don't think so. It should be in the blood, you know.'

'But Schlusnus—he was only a postman.'

'Really? How do you know that?'

'I read it somewhere.'

'Where on earth?'

Heinrich Schlusnus enjoyed a position of honour amongst the baritones of his time, like Richard Tauber among the tenors. He had reached the pinnacle of his profession, in spite of heavy competition in all German-speaking countries. In those days it was possible to hear as many as twenty outstanding baritones on the German stage. All of them distinguished themselves, and their names have entered the annals of operatic history. Their roles have covered the whole gamut, from the light, playful Papageno to the strong heroes of Wagner's musical dramas. With a little thought I can bring to mind about two dozen of my predecessors. Here they are in roughly chronological order:

Joseph Schwarz	1880—1926
Eduard Habich	1880—1960
Theodor Scheidl	1880—1959
Emil Schipper	1882—1957
Leo Schützendorf	1886—1931
Wilhelm Rode	1887—1959
Benno Ziegler	1887—1963
Heinrich Schlusnus	1888—1952
Friedrich Schorr	1888—1953
Alfred Jerger	1889—1976
Rudolf Burg	1890—1946

Hans Duhan	1890—1971
Jaro Prohaska	1891—1965
Rudolf Bockelmann	1892—1958
Herbert Janssen	1892—1965
Heinrich Rehkemper	1894—1949
Eugen Fuchs	1895—1971
Hans Reinmar	1895—1961
Karl Hammes	1896—1939
Hans-Hermann Nissen	1896—1980
Willi Domgraf-Fassbaender	1897—1978
Paul Schöffler	1897—1977
Karl Schmitt-Walter	1900—
Gerhard Hüsch	1901—

These baritons were all colleagues of Schlusnus. Of them, Habich, Scheidl, Schipper, Schorr, Prohaska, Bockelmann and Nissen were all outstanding Wagnerians. Schorr was internationally the most famous Sachs of his time. Janssen also sang in some difficult Wagner roles, though that of Wolfram was undeniably his best. Rode was a master of both character and declamatory roles, whose Scarpia was equally as stunning as his Wotan. Jerger, Duhan, Rehkemper, Hammes, Domgraf-Fassbaender and Hüsch were famous in Mozart roles; Schöffler was equally at home with Mozart, Wagner or Strauss; Schwarz, Schlusnus, Burg, Ziegler and Reinmar made names for themselves in Italian opera; Fuchs and Schmitt-Walter were masters in lyric baritone roles, as was Leo Schützendorf. Bremen once witnessed an original, indeed unique, event during the course of the First World War: namely a performance of *The Mastersingers* in which all four of the main bass and baritone roles were sung by Leo Schützendorf and his three brothers. Alfons, who was engaged in Hamburg, sang the role of Sachs; Leo, engaged in Darmstadt, sang Beckmesser; Gustav, who normally sang in Strasbourg, was Pogner; and Guido of Bremen was Kothner.

Duhan, Janssen, Rehkemper, Schmitt-Walter and Hüsch were all known as outstanding Lieder recitalists, but my mother's favorite, Heinrich Schlusnus, outshone all the others.

In his heyday he could pack the Berlin Philharmonic up to three times a year and could gauge the sympathies of his audience like no other recitalist. I can hear my mother talking of him as if it were only yesterday: 'Hermi, if ever you become a singer you must sing just like Heinrich Schlusnus.'

I never heard Schlusnus give a recital, though I have many times heard him on record. I did once see him in opera as Rigoletto, in the Admiral's Palace in Berlin. The power and intensity of his voice are with me still. I was sitting very near the back, but I could hear his voice, even in its softest whispers. I can remember his portrayal of a silent, suffering father, a court jester who, even in his greatest anguish, never seemed to become brutal or vulgar. His voice embraced every nuance from the mellowest softness to dramatic richness. I cannot imagine that Schlusnus would ever have been chosen for Rigoletto today. Most conductors and directors would consider him far too fine and lyrical.

Once, during the early fifties, I was giving a matinée recital at the house of Mrs. Lyon, wife of the American High Commissioner in Berlin-Dahlem. A lady came up to me afterwards and introduced herself as Annemay Schlusnus. I cautiously asked her if she was related to Heinrich Schlusnus. She smiled and told me she was his widow. I was surprised, as she looked young enough to be his daughter. She went on to explain that Wolf's *Anacreon's grave* had been one of her husband's favorite songs. 'He would certainly have been delighted to hear how beautifully you sang it today. What a shame that he can no longer hear it. I believe you have a great future ahead of you.'

Years afterwards, Frau Schlusnus told me I had looked quite flabbergasted at the time.

Mother's wish that I should sing like Heinrich Schlusnus has always remained with me. I was fascinated that he should have made such an impact and been so adored by the public. I wanted to be loved by the public in the same way. I kept in contact with Frau Schlusnus, and she watched my rise to fame with interest. She often expressed opinions on my singing, and was sometimes highly critical. She would have been happier for me to follow every nuance of Schlusnus' technique: his *tempi*, his choice of key, his phrasing and his breathing. But much as I honoured him, I had to go my own way in the end.

It was quite a surprise when, in 1962, Frau Schlusnus invited me to sing on the occasion of the tenth anniversary of her husband's death. The event was to take place in the Rittersaal in the Marksburg above Braubach am Main, which was Schlusnus' birthplace. My accompanist was to be Sebastian Peschko, who had accompanied Schlusnus for many years. Annemay had requested some of his best-known songs, such as *Freundliche Vision* ('Friendly vision') and *Traum durch die Dämmerung* ('Twilight dream') by Richard Strauss.

I was more nervous than ever before because a critical audience would be comparing my interpretations with those of Schlusnus himself. Also amongst the audience was Wilhelm Backhaus, who was to play a piece by Beethoven. It was to be one of the most difficult concerts of my whole career. Frau Schlusnus had hung an oil-painting of her husband on the wall behind the stage, and it felt very strange to be standing in front of it.

While rehearsing with Peschko, I decided to sacrifice a little of Prey for the sake of Schlusnus, and asked him questions like, 'What *tempo* did Schlusnus follow here?' or 'Did he breathe here as well?' Peschko was generous with his advice. I wanted to know what keys he had chosen for his songs, they turned out to be very high, as one might expect from a high baritone. Fortunately, I too am a high baritone. I usually sing *Traum durch die Dämmerung* in E major, though Schlusnus sang it even higher. Tonight, however, I decided to follow Schlusnus. I wanted to sound as much like him as possible, although this should not have been very difficult. As I stood by the piano at the concert my thoughts wandered back twenty years, to the time when I sat next to the gramophone and Mother said to me, 'Hermi, if ever you become a singer...'

The concert was followed by a wine-tasting in the vault of the Marksburg, where I recall having an interesting conversation with Wilhelm Backhaus about Schubert's Heine songs.

1. I always felt proud to be able to walk with my father, though this did not happen very often.

2. My mother encouraged my musical ambitions.

3. 'You can make something of yourself in any profession', was Father's motto.

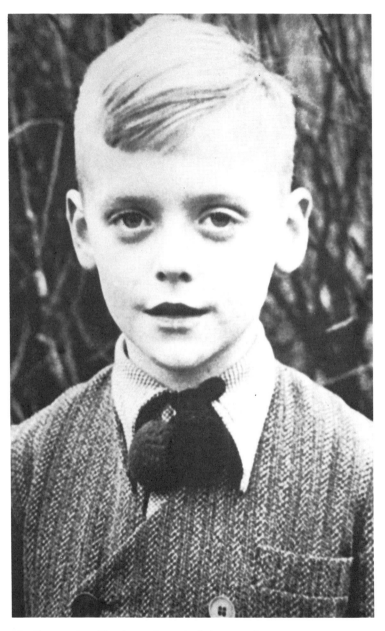

4. Even as a boy, I loved an audience. And when no audience was available, I would don a hat and false beard and perform to myself.

5.   With my mother and sister, who later cared for my mother at great personal sacrifice. Alas, only once did Mother have the pleasure of hearing me sing in public.

6.   The 'Rhythm Trio', with Alfred Hix (bass), myself (accordion) and Theodor Schnurbus (guitar). We soon became a regular feature of the night-life of post-war Berlin.

Life in the Treskowstrasse

I was born in the Oberseestrasse, which was in Hohenschönhausen in the north-eastern suburbs of Berlin. From 1934
onwards, and therefore for as far back as I can remember, I lived
with my parents and my sister at No.1 Treskowstrasse, on the
corner of the Berliner Strasse. Most of the streets in our area had
old-fashioned cobbled pavements. The Treskowstrasse was an
exception to this rule, as it was asphalted and well-suited for
roller-skating. Whenever our roller-skating club, known as
'Thunder and Lightning', was out training, it was impossible to
get through.

The Treskowstrasse is no longer to be found on a modern plan
of Berlin. It is now called the Manetstrasse, though it still forms
part of the route from the Berliner Strasse to a nearby lake called
the Orankesee, via the Oberseestrasse. In the same street, on the
left-hand side (coming from the Berliner Strasse) and not quite
half way along, stands the villa which used to belong to my
paternal grandfather. It is a two-storey affair, built in yellow
sandstone in the neo-classical style and supported by fluted
pillars on either side. The flat roof is bordered by a smart stone
balustrade, just like the State Opera building in Unter den
Linden. The drive runs in a semi-circle to the foot of a curved
staircase, which formerly led up between two stone lions to the
entrance on the upper ground floor. It was known in the area as
the *Löwenvilla* or 'Lion Villa', and remains there to this day
in East Berlin, although no longer guarded by aristocratic
lions.

A few years ago, I went to visit the house where I had spent
such an important part of my childhood. It looked sadly
neglected; the plaster was peeling off the walls; behind any
windows which had not been boarded up, I could see tattered
curtains and ragged carpets; and what had become of Grandfather's beloved garden? It was now no more than a rubbish
dump.

Our own home was somewhat less distinguished, being a flat
on the first floor of No.1 Treskowstrasse, which was a red-brick
building. However it was still comfortable enough. Apart from

the kitchen, bathroom and bedrooms, there was a living room and a room which was 'kept for best'. It had a bay window and was furnished as a dining room, but I can only vaguely remember eating there once or twice. It seemed to exist for its own sake, and tended to accumulate all the best furniture in the house: firstly the cabinet with all Mother's Hutschenreuth china; then a splendid sideboard, which was ten feet long, weighed a ton and was adorned by two bright silver candelabra; then the Schimmel piano, which was bought for me during the war (I had just about managed the first prelude from Bach's *Well-tempered Klavier* when the house was ripped apart by a bomb in 1943); and finally an oil-painting in a heavy gilded frame, which depicted a storm at sea.

In the society in which we lived, it was very common to collect objects like these, whose presence served little more than to show that you owned them. They were honoured as a symbol of *bourgeois* respectability, and would be cosseted and protected like museum exhibits. The sliding door separating the 'best room' from the living room boasted a brightly-coloured stained-glass panel, but was almost invariably locked. During the summer we were permitted to use the 'best room' to gain access to the balcony, which extended along the whole front of the house. It was occupied by Mother's geraniums, which once won first prize as the most beautiful flower decoration in the area. On hot Sundays we ate our meals under an awning, surrounded by magnificent flowers; on weekdays I preferred to do my homework here. There was also a deckchair on the balcony, which was reserved for Father when he was at home.

Although I considered my grandparents' house extremely high-class, we were 'respectable middle class' too. It was thanks to my father's profession that we kept up our standard of living through the depression and right up to 1943, when the house was destroyed. Nowadays it is difficult to imagine how bad things were in the thirties. When I first went to school in 1936, some of my classmates came barefoot. Their parents could not even afford to buy shoes for them. I can still remember my *Schultüte*—a special bag of goodies given to German children on their first day at school, and a tradition still practised today.

Mother filled it with only very few sweets out of consideration for less fortunate children.

I have another memory, this time from the severe winter of 1937, when I was eight. It was still dark as I trotted off through the snow to school. I was wearing a dark-blue coat and long woollen stockings which Grandmother Senkbeil had knitted by hand. Although most of my classmates wore them, I thought them extremely effeminate and they scratched horribly. No sooner had I rounded the corner than I rolled them down to several inches below the knee despite the snow and wind, just like all my classmates. This produced pink 'lifebelts' round our legs as we climbed the stone steps into school, pushed our way along the dim, musty corridors into the classroom and waited for the bell to ring. It had scarcely finished ringing when the door opened and in walked our teacher, Herr Stark. He wore a frock-coat and pin-stripe trousers, called 'Stresemann trousers' after a former German foreign minister. We stood quickly to attention. There followed a prayer and then the usual order to sit down.

Herr Stark stepped up onto the rostrum and sat down at his desk. He then took out his notebook and began to ply us with questions. Every now and then he took out a large red handkerchief, blew his nose in it with great ceremony and then draped it over the heater. Woe betide anyone who did not know his stuff, even if he did have a 'lifebelt'. He was summoned to the front of the class, and if he made further mistakes he was ordered to pull down his trousers and bend over the desk at the front. 'Old Yellowface' then administered a number of painful lashes.

CHAPTER 4

A schoolboy at Berlin's oldest school

The Grey Monastery

In 1939 I went on to Berlin's *Gymnasium zum Grauen Kloster* (Grey Monastery School). I am not exactly sure why my parents sent me to this classical school, which was situated in the Kloster-strasse, just south of Alexander Square in the city centre. To get there required three-quarters of an hour's journey by tram. Presumably, my mother wanted me to have the best possible education, while Father could proudly say to his relatives, 'Hermi's off to the Grey Monastery.'

It was not only Berlin's most famous school, but also its oldest *Gymnasium*. I ought perhaps to explain for the uninitiated that the school was protestant and not catholic, and had in former times been the prestigious establishment to which all the sons of the nobility had been sent. Former pupils had included Wilhelm Dilthey the philosopher, and Hans Delbrück and Johann Gustav Droysen, both historians and liberal politicians; also Carl Gotthard Langhans who built the Brandenburg Gate, and Johann Gottfried Schadow, creator of the Victory Monument which, until it was destroyed in the last war, formed the crowning glory of the Brandenburg Gate. One of the school's most famous 'old boys' was Prussia's greatest architect, Karl Friedrich Schinkel. I doubt whether my father knew this. On the other hand he was well aware of the fact that Bismarck, of whom he was a life-long admirer, had completed his *Abitur* at the Grey Monastery. He was delighted for his son to be going to the same school.

The school was called *Das Graue Kloster* ('The Grey Monastery'). The origin of this name can be traced back to the early history of the site, which was familiar to most scholars. The exact details remain engraved in my memory: the school was named after the Franciscan monastery which was the first building to be erected on the site. This was subsequently replaced by the Seminary of St Mary and St Nicholas. Then on 13th July 1574, Johann Georg, Elector of Brandenburg, founded Berlin's first *Gymnasium* on the same site in the Klosterstrasse. *Gymnasium* was the name given by the protestant reformers to the classics schools which had begun in the late Middle Ages, and corresponds to the English grammar school.

As scholars we had to learn by heart the motto which the Elector had given to the school. I can repeat it in my sleep: 'To be of use and service not only to this city, but to the entire youth of this electorate and of the Marches of Brandenburg, and also to boys in other countries, both rich and poor.'

The church authorities had never ceased to try to regain their influence over the school, though they had so far been unsuccessful. Today, however, the school has been refounded in West Berlin, in Grunewald, and is again subject to the authority of the Church. For it was only with the help of the Church that it was possible, in 1963, to found a successor to this ancient school. Since then the school has been known as the *Evangelisches Gymnasium zum Grauen Kloster in Berlin* ('Grey Monastery Protestant Grammar School, Berlin'). The old building had been bombed out in February 1945. After the end of the war, the school had moved into temporary premises in East Berlin, where it had continued to eke out a miserable existence until, in 1958, it was closed down by the city council and the old Grey Monastery was no more.

Vanilla or chocolate?

I was not a particularly good scholar. Our class teacher at the Grey Monastery, Dr. Lieben, did not use a cane like Herr Stark at the elementary school. He had his own teaching methods. For punishment he would offer a choice of two rulers: a yellow one

and a brown one. 'Now then, Porky!' he would ask. 'Which is it
to be? Vanilla or chocolate?' The victim could choose either
ruler, but whichever one he chose would then be rapped once,
twice or three times across both hands. For a serious offence he
would haul us up by the ears. 'Now I'll twist your little ears off
and send you back to Mummy like faulty goods,' he would
mock, shaking the victim so violently that he could no longer see
or hear.

I have hardly ever felt so wretched as on Monday mornings
when I was at school. We had Latin from eight to ten o'clock,
and there was often a test due. The alarm went off at six, and I
would smother it with my pillow to allow myself another minute
of rest.

Father would already be at work, having risen at four o'clock.
Meat wholesalers in Berlin started business at half past five.
Mondays, Wednesdays and Fridays were reserved for slaughter-
ing, and began with animal inspections. The remaining
weekdays were market days and it was then that meat was sold
to the retail butchers who came into the market to make their
selections. A completed transaction was sealed by a handshake
and was paid for in cash. Mother used to sit by the till and work
everything out.

I often went to school with a boy who lived nearby. He would
stand in the middle of the street and shout up to his mother,
'Mum! Throw my sandwiches down here!' The window would
open on cue, and a paper bag full of sandwiches would come
sailing through the air and land on the pavement at our feet. I
liked this, as it was a different way of doing things. Our servant
would have laid places at table for my sister and me, and we
would have to sit there and swallow down our bread and butter
and hot cocoa. Forebodings of doom and disaster at school
would rob me of any appetite.

In the tram on the way to school I always stood at the back,
holding on tight to the brake wheel. I would gaze enviously at
the grown-ups, smugly reading their newspapers. What did they
know of the cares of a schoolboy who had to choose between
vanilla and chocolate? The prospect of a 'blue letter' was not
very pleasant either. Such a letter was issued by Dr. Lieben to

report a particularly serious offence or a bad piece of work. A 'blue letter' had to be signed by your father and returned next day. This could have further unfortunate consequences.

When I received two of these dreadful documents within a week, I would have to keep out of Father's way or there would be a scene. So I went and called on my Aunt Dora, whom my sister and I used to call 'Tado'. 'But Hermi!' she called out in amazement as she opened the front door and saw my crushed figure standing there on the landing. 'What's the matter? Where've you come from?'

'From school.'

'Yes, but now? At three o'clock?' (German schools finish at one o'clock.)

'I had to stay behind, up in the library.'

'Well, come in then. What have you got in your hand?'

'Tado,' I pleaded, 'there's something I'd like you to do for me. Would you be so kind as to sign this letter for me?'

'What! A blue letter?'

'Yes, but the worst of it is that it's the second one I've had in only a few days. If Father sees it it'll be the end of the world.'

'No, Hermi! That won't do at all. That would be forgery.'

'Why! You only need to sign it with "Prey". Then nobody's lied.'

But Tado was not to be persuaded, though she did ring home and put in a good word for me. For the rest I had to face the music. Only one thought comforted me: the fact that one day I would be grown up. There would be no more school books, no more Latin and Greek, no more vanilla and chocolate, no more twisting of ears, no more blue letters and no more staying behind in that ancient library which smelled of yellow paper. Then I would be care-free and nothing would stand in the way of my happiness.

I have still to tell you about one of the school's traditions which had an early influence on my singing. The two seminaries from which the school had emerged over 400 years ago had been obliged to provide a choir to St Mary and St Nicholas. Our school had taken over this duty, thus choral singing was greatly encouraged, and I was naturally eager to take part. I can still remember how I once sang a small solo in St Nicholas' Church and was disappointed not to see my name on the printed programme.

I sang my first 'big' solo in 1941, when our school was visited by Count Ciano the Italian foreign minister and son-in-law to Mussolini. He sat on the front row, accompanied by his entourage and a whole crowd of party officials. I was to perform Mozart's *Komm lieber Mai*. I had previously sung only as part of a group. This time I was standing alone in the middle of this great hall, with the pianist just behind me (my class-mate Werner Schulze, who is now an organist in West Berlin), the choir in the background, and in front of me the assembled audience, which consisted of VIPs, teachers and fellow-schoolboys. I naturally had stage-fright, and was also afraid of forgetting my words. It was like a real Lieder recital for the first time.

The school had another tradition, which went back to 1821. Every Whitsun, all choir members, both young and old, undertook a three-day singing tour. The tradition continues to this day; for many years now, I have intended to take part in it, and just as soon as my diary allows, whether next year or the year after, I hope to carry out that intention. If they want me to sing a solo, I may well sing the song which was written for 'the monastery' by a school-leaver in 1822:

> *Graues Kloster, Berlin-Mitte—*
> *Alte Schule in der alten Stadt,*
> *Glücklich, wer in deinen Mauern*
> *Einstmals sich getummelt hat!*
>
> *Alte Sprachen, junge Lieder,*
> *Heisse Mühen und ein frohes Spiel,*
> *Ruderriege, Sängerfahrten—*
> *Segensreicher Klosterstil!*
>
> *Graues Kloster, du verbandest*
> *Uns mit Gegenwart und Altertum—*
> *Längst gebührte dir der Titel*
> *'Musisches Gymnasium'!*

Grey Monastery in central Berlin—
Ancient school in this ancient city,
Happy the man who once romped
Within these walls.

Ancient tongues and modern songs,
Zeal in work and joy in play,
Rowing squads and singing tours—
The happy monastic life!

Grey Monastery, you have bound us
Both to past and present—
You have long deserved the title of
'Musical school'!

As I have said, I was not particularly good at school, but the 'Grey Monastery' has left me with more than just vanilla and chocolate. Much of my eight years of Latin and three years of Greek has remained in my subconscious. I can still picture the school hall, which contained a marble bust of Friedrich Wilhelm III and a statue of the educationalist August Hermann Francke. However, I was most impressed by two Canalettos, one of the Rialto Square and the other of the Grand Canal. These were not copies but actual originals, and had been bequeathed to the school in the eighteenth century.

Whenever I am with my wife on one of our all-too-rare visits to Venice, I stop in the beautiful Rialto Square, shut my eyes for a moment, and visualise the school hall in the Grey Monastery. For a few seconds I am a schoolboy again, sitting in that solemn hall and longing to see Venice. Then I open my eyes and the dream has come true.

CHAPTER 5

When the bombs fell

Almost a child star

While I was at the Grey Monastery a friend told me about the Berlin Mozart Choir, which at the time enjoyed an unrivalled reputation. It had been founded in 1922 by a twenty-two-year-old teacher called Erich Steffen, in Berlin-Weissensee, and its members were schoolchildren. The concerts which they performed both in and around Berlin were so successful that the City of Berlin began to take an interest in the choir. As older members remained in the choir after their voices had broken, it gradually developed from a boys' choir into a mixed youth choir.

In 1929, the year in which I was born, Steffen was freed from ordinary teaching duties in order to devote himself entirely to running the choir. The City of Berlin took over the patronage, and the then Lord Mayor assumed the role of chairman. The choir began to undertake singing tours both in Germany and abroad. It was known as the Berlin Mozart Choir up until 1937, at which time Steffen was summoned to the Ministry of Propaganda. The presiding official explained to him: 'Herr Steffen, it would be of considerable advantage to the Berlin Mozart Choir if it were to become part of the Hitler Youth. We are sure you would not wish to forego this opportunity and give you until tomorrow to consider this offer.' Such was the way things were worded at the time: orders were disguised as informal requests. Günther Weissenborn, who was later to become my friend and accompanist for many years, and from whom I was to learn so much, received just such a request in

1942. This was at the time when German musicians were being recruited for opera-houses in France. 'We write,' they informed him, 'to inquire whether you would be willing to assume the post of chief conductor at the German Theatre in Lille. We request you to undertake the journey to Lille as soon as possible, within one week at the latest. A rail ticket is enclosed, *Heil Hitler!* Signed Hinkel.'

When Erich Steffen left the Ministry that day, he had been made a *Stammführer* in the Hitler Youth. Alas, he paid dearly for this after the war with a period in the Russian concentration camp in Sachsenhausen.

It was not easy to get into the choir, the competition was keen and the entrance examination was stiff. Steffen left nothing to chance, and thoroughly examined each candidate's musical achievement and ability. 'I'd very much like to join, you know,' I said to a schoolfriend whose father was a teacher and knew Steffen.

'Don't say I didn't warn you. That man is a real stickler,' he replied. But I was adamant: I passed the entrance examination, and in 1940 became a soprano in the Mozart Choir.

I thus escaped the usual stint in the Hitler Youth: the Mozart Choir itself was a part of it. We just played music instead of learning drill. We had a uniform, and appeared in concerts dressed in black double-breasted tunics with gold buttons, looking just like page-boys.

As a schoolboy I went on several concert tours with the Mozart Choir, one of which took us into the Sudetenland. Steffen was just as strict as my friend had predicted. He was a serious musician and a strong disciplinarian. Whenever the choir entered a competition, we invariably carried off one of the top prizes.

I sang soprano, as I mentioned before, and my voice could reach some extremely high notes. It is strange that most boy sopranos turn into baritones or basses, while boys with lower voices usually become tenors when their voices break. Enrico Caruso is said to have had a soft alto voice as a boy.

In 1942 the film director, Harald Braun, appeared at one of the choir's rehearsals and selected a small group of boys. He was looking for child actors for the film *Diesel*, which was to be produced by UFA (the Universal Film Company). He said to me, 'Show me the kind of face you would make if you had just discovered a hundred-mark note. Now pretend you've just been given a thrashing.' I pulled the required faces, and was given the part of Diesel's friend in an event from his childhood. I was quite sure I was going to be a star. For the more I heard about the film project, the more clear it became that it was going to be a really important affair. A trip to Prague had been arranged, which included a stay of several weeks in a first-class hotel, paid for, naturally, by UFA. I was due shortly to take an important Latin test at the Grey Monastery, which clashed with the filming sessions, but this made it all the more exciting.

The school was not altogether happy with this new development in my career, especially since my achievements in Latin left a lot to be desired. However, UFA was backed up by the Ministry of Propaganda, and to go against them would not be in the school's interests, so they reluctantly let me go. The evening arrived, and I climbed into the sleeper-carriage for Prague, together with two fellow singers from the Mozart Choir and the young lady who was to be our guardian for the duration of the trip. We were picked up by car on arrival at the station, and driven to the Hotel Flora, where the three of us were to share a room.

We first amused ourselves by pressing every switch and button in sight, thus summoning the chambermaid, the barman, the page and the bootboy respectively. Filming began on the following day. I was very much impressed with the work, and if Willy Birgel had dropped out of the title role, I should not have hesitated to offer myself for the part of Diesel. I smelt the scent of make-up for the very first time, a fragrance which since then has never ceased to give me pleasure. But the fun was not to last. A few days later at breakfast time, my guardian announced, 'The car will pick you up at midday today, Hermann. In the meantime I'll have packed your things, and I'll see you off from the station after lunch.'

I thought I had misheard. Packing? Station? We had hardly been a week in Prague, and were still in the middle of filming.

My guardian went on to explain: 'It's all been arranged with the school authorities so that you won't miss your Latin test. As soon as that's over you'll come back to Prague.' What! Just because of this stupid test I had to interrupt my important duties here and go back to Berlin! I was flabbergasted.

The world première of *Diesel* was due to take place at the UFA Palace at the Zoo, which was Berlin's largest cinema. I could talk of nothing else. My parents sighed, 'This UFA film has really gone to Hermi's head,' they said. And so the great day approached. My parents could not come as Mother was ill, but Tado came with me. We had already received complimentary tickets which, as we entered the vast auditorium, turned out to be good ones. We were sitting directly by the central aisle, and my heart was beating fast. The public came streaming in, here and there I glimpsed a familiar face: my maths teacher, my gym teacher and a few schoolfriends with their parents. Meanwhile I awaited the moment when the director of UFA would summon me with all my colleagues to the front, to acknowledge the applause which was due to us.

The performance began with a lengthy overture on the Wurlitzer organ, which I considered altogether superfluous as it only delayed the film. At last the film began, and I could see the story in chronological order for the first time. It seemed to be ages before I appeared on the screen. I was sitting on the edge of my seat, and kept thinking my moment had come. I tugged at Tado's arm and whispered in her ear, but in vain. The time seemed to tick away, until Tado suddenly nudged me. 'Look! There you are!'

Yes, that figure did look like me. He was sitting at the table, leaning on his left arm and fingering a model steam-engine with his right hand. I also recognised the velvet suit and the stiff collar, several of which I had needed to try on for size. But before I had finished musing on this, the sequence was over. It had lasted less than half a minute. The story-line changed and moved on to a different place. My scene was over.

I was livid. 'But that's outrageous! It wasn't even my voice.' The people nearby turned round to shush me. 'And they cut out the best scenes!' Tado tried to calm me down, but I was in despair. My dreams had collapsed. 'What's left for me now?' I groaned. 'All the people who know me, my teachers, my friends—all of them came to see me. They'll think I'm a fool!'

The people at UFA thought it was all quite wonderful. They talked to my parents and the people at school, suggesting that I might take up acting as a career. They wanted to make me into a child star, but Father and Mother were completely against it. UFA still had plans to cast me in a film of William Tell, with Heinrich George in the title role, and myself as Tell's son. But the war was worsening, Germany's future looked bleak, and the project was shelved. I was soon to be occupied with things other than apples balanced on my head, and my film career was over for the time being.

As a schoolboy at a classical school, I was most concerned with Latin, Greek and choir practice. I did not have much to do with Nazism, having other problems to worry about. I was no less sceptical of the older generation and the powers that be, than the youth of today. We did not believe all we were told—far from it. I remained in my own little world, almost oblivious of the fact that it was wartime, although this soon changed when the bombs began to fall on Hohenschönhausen.

Survival in Berlin

As far as I can recall, there were bombs in Berlin as early as 1941. It was great fun for a schoolboy, looking for bits of shrapnel and taking them to show everyone at school. We soon got used to the sirens and the air-raid shelters, though it was a different matter when it was the Preys' turn to be bombed. In 1943 the bombs hit the Treskowstrasse, destroying my parents' house. By this time Father was the only one left there. I had gone off to an evacuation camp at Landsberg an der Warthe, where the school had been temporarily re-sited. Father had then sent my mother and sister away to Silesia. He and the other residents had to wait a full twelve hours in the cellar before they could be rescued from the rubble. You can imagine how the loss of their home upset my parents, particularly my poor mother. This was the first of many blows from which she was never fully to recover.

The whole area was completely flattened, only Grandpa's Lion Villa survived, miraculously, amidst the smoking ruins. It was admittedly minus doors and windows, but it stood there, otherwise undamaged, in its little orchard which the owners had so lovingly maintained. We were not the only relatives to become homeless. As we were bombed out one by one, we all moved into the Lion Villa, where Grandma Prey had lived alone since Grandpa's death.

A girls' school had also been evacuated to Landsberg an der Warthe. It was Dorothy's Lyceum (or Secondary School for Girls) from Berlin-Steglitz. The girls also boasted a choir, and from time to time we held concerts together. I was particularly taken with one girl: a fair, gentle, ethereal creature. I had been aware of the delights of the fairer sex for some time now. As far as I can remember, it began at the age of eight when I was hired as a ball-boy for female tennis matches. In the evenings I came home exhausted, dragging red sand all over the house. 'Take your gym-shoes off!' shouted Mother. But I had to tell her all about it. 'Mum,' I said, 'There's a girl who plays there. She's got the most beautiful lips. I do like her.'

'Oh really, so you noticed?'

'Yes, and her hands are so soft. And her teeth!'

Mother looked into my eyes and sighed. 'Yes, I see.'

The choir in Landsberg was conducted by our music teacher, Herr Gütte. He also led the combined boys' and girls' choir in the cantata *Von Himmel hoch da komm ich her* ('I come down to earth from heaven'), in which I was to sing the soprano solo. We stood in lines on the stage in the Landsberg Hall. My beloved was standing immediately behind me, dressed in a dark-blue velvet dress; around her neck she wore a small cross on a gold chain. I had to step forward to sing my solo and felt extremely uncomfortable: my voice was just beginning to break, and might easily crack or 'mis-fire' during my solo. I was going to feel ridiculous, particularly in front of my loved-one for whom I must give of my best.

As it was I managed it, albeit with great difficulty. The top of my mouth ached from the strain. As I returned to my place her hand seemed to grope for mine. She gripped it hard as if to say, 'You sang that beautifully.' At that moment I went into ecstasies.

I stayed about eighteen months in Landsberg and shall never forget the last harrowing months there, during the autumn of 1944. We were made to kneel in rows in vast, ice-covered fields of potatoes, digging with our hands until they bled. No one spoke. The occasional cawing of a crow made a scene like that in Schubert's *Winterreise*.

We were allowed home for Christmas. My mother and sister had also returned from Silesia. Things looked bad on the Eastern Front, and Father refused to let me go back again afterwards. He thought we should stick together now.

Our family was still in a comparatively enviable position, although Christmas 1944 was a tragic time for most Germans. Food rations were now extremely short, but this was nothing compared to the personal suffering which most of us had to endure. Many families had been torn apart, husbands and sons had been lost or imprisoned. Women with small children had been evacuated, while many children had been sent away alone into the country. Most families mourned the loss of someone. Many could not celebrate Christmas at home as they no longer had a home to go to. Millions of houses and flats had been flattened.

The worst was yet to come: the 3rd of February 1945 saw the total destruction of Berlin by American bombers, in its worst air raid ever. Our capital was razed to the ground, and this time even air raid shelters could not withstand the flames. Old people and schoolboys were by now being conscripted into the army, and shirkers were publicly hanged from the nearest tree. 'We'll win before I hang!' soon became the standard phrase all over Berlin. To talk like this was not without its dangers, but we Berliners held on to our ironic sense of humour. Ede asks Paula, 'What's the latest joke?' To which she replies, 'A year in a concentration camp,' or 'Enjoy the war while you can—peace is going to be dreadful.'

In front of the Lion Villa stood two silver-firs, which seemed to me as a boy to reach as far as the sky. I loved to hide under their branches, surveying the world from beneath a shelter of needles. I felt safe there. As I grew up I soon realised that they did not reach the sky and were just common or garden firs. But that did not change things in my eyes because they were still the most beautiful trees for miles around.

A high-explosive bomb landed close by in the Treskowstrasse. It ripped the earth apart, badly damaging the two trees. In April 1945, only a few days before the war was over, I was standing in the living room, looking out into the garden. It was strangely quiet outside, but a stiff easterly breeze carried with it the distant rumble of the Eastern Front as it moved inexorably closer. I suddenly heard the sound of groaning and creaking; the silver-fir to the right of the drive began to tremble and sway; it bent forward and then came crashing to the ground, leaving behind it a tangle of twisted branches and twigs.

I have always had a strong sense of symbolism. The great turning point in my life was not the loss of our home, neither was it the coming defeat; it was the collapse of this fir tree which brought home to me the fact that my childhood was over.

CHAPTER 6

The war is over

The Lion Villa entertains guests

Life in Berlin was becoming grimmer by the day. The Russian advance could no longer be kept in check, and the last of the reserves had already been called up, so now they were recruiting schoolboys, arming them with anti-tank grenade launchers. The Berliners commented wryly, 'Now they're commandeering prams.'—'Why?'—'To take our toddlers to the front.'

I had already been enlisted and my call-up papers had been sent out. They had arrived in Landsberg an der Warthe long after I had returned to Berlin. They were eventually forwarded to Berlin after some considerable delay, but Father took them and hid them. Now that the war was nearly over he wanted his son to stay alive.

Though you could hardly call it living, life was fast becoming a living hell. We could only hope for a miracle. Goebbels' propaganda started a series of rumours about amazing secret weapons and a special reserve army which would change the course of the war and stop the Russians taking Berlin. People came up with some incredible suggestions. In the air raid shelters at night they talked of how the Western Allies would unite with Hitler's troops to help fight Russia.

The people of Berlin faced these disasters with their customary cheeky humour. A conversation heard on the metropolitan railway, which had been partially repaired after the bombs, went as follows: A train was once packed to bursting and a woman called out 'You're crushing my chest!' Someone was heard to reply, 'Don't worry, they'll rebuild it bigger and better when the war's over!'

Indeed, the war was nearly over as the battle raged around Berlin. Then in April the Russians suddenly arrived. Much to our own good fortune, the first to arrive were the elite troops. We were living in the cellar of the Lion Villa at the time. It had survived the bombs well, so much so that it soon attracted the attention of the occupying forces. It was not long before a detachment of armed soldiers invaded the premises, under the command of a young lieutenant.

'All of you stay down here,' ordered Father.

'But Dad, I want to come too.'

Father thought for a minute. 'Oh all right, come on.'

We climbed the cellar stairs and found ourselves face to face with loaded guns.

'You alone?' someone asked in a rough voice. Father replied, carefully enunciating every syllable. 'Four more people. Wife, mother and two ... old people.'

The man with the rough voice translated this. A soldier went down to the cellar, ran over it with a torch, came back up and whispered something to his superior. Then someone walked up to Father and shrieked at him 'You fascist swine!'

Father was not to be intimidated: 'Me German. Not fascist. Never have been.' The officer then nodded to us to follow him, we gathered from this that he wanted us to make a tour of the premises. Father led the way upstairs, followed by the soldiers. 'That,' he explained, pointing at an empty doorframe, 'was once my parents' bedroom. My father's dead now,' he added.

The officer poked his head in and hesitated. Father said to the one soldier who appeared to speak German, 'Tell the gentleman he's quite at liberty to go in. The room's empty.' But the officer nodded for us to go on.

'Here's another bedroom ... then the bathroom ... '

The soldiers whispered together. Then the rough-voiced man spoke again: 'Why you not at war? Why you not in uniform?' Father explained that he was a butcher, which meant he was exempt, being one of those who had to provide for the civilian population. The soldier grinned. 'You rich man, you eat good, yes?'

We went on, eventually stopping in front of the only door in the building which still worked. One of the soldiers shook the handle, but it refused to open. Grandma had for many years let this room to a tall, refined gentleman who was never at home. We had not seen him for months.

'Ask Granny if she's got the key!' ordered Father. I raced down to the cellar and returned shaking my head. 'We have let this room,' explained Father, 'I cannot open up.'

The butt of a rifle was substituted for a key. After a couple of hard knocks the door flew open and we went inside. One of the soldiers peered under the bed, and another rummaged through the chest of drawers, while a third one pulled up the carpet and wrenched open the cupboard. This revealed a Nazi uniform: a peaked cap, a coat complete with swastikas, breeches, riding boots... I thought, this is it! None of us had ever seen him dressed like this.

Suddenly the atmosphere changed, and an almost Siberian chill came over them. Eight pairs of eyes bore down on us, all burning with hatred. The rough-voiced man stepped forward, pressed the butt of his pistol into Father's stomach and hissed at him, 'You not little fascist swine! You very big fascist swine!' He was about to shoot him, and I tried to call out, but my voice failed me. I wanted to jump on the man, but stood rooted to the spot with fear. Then something quite unexpected happened: the lieutenant quickly pulled the peaked cap out of the cupboard and shoved it on Father's head. It came down over his ears. He looked idiotic, but it saved his life. Then I lost all control and burst into fits of laughter and it was some minutes before I could stop.

We had completed our tour of the premises. The officer, whose presence of mind had certainly saved Father's life, led his squad out of the front door. He then turned to my father and, to our astonishment, spoke to him in German: 'Why did you keep quiet about the girl in the cellar?' Father was so confused he could not reply. 'Is that your daughter?' the lieutenant went on. Father nodded. The lieutenant continued: 'We shall come back. But take note: we are men of honour.'

The officer's prediction proved correct: the Russian soldiers

returned next day and requisitioned the Lion Villa as their
officers' mess. They allowed our family to stay on in the house,
though they made my parents act as caretakers. Above the
entrance they hoisted a flag with a hammer and sickle. The
bomb-damaged lions they replaced with two guards, who
protected us from further harassment.

The Preys had to remain in the cellar. The officers ate and
enjoyed themselves in the ground-floor rooms, while the first
floor provided sleeping accommodation for cooks, drivers and
other soldiers. I quickly became friends with the soldiers. While
most Berliners went hungry and feared starvation, we ate our fill
thanks to these soldiers. The people of Berlin had already
suffered much hardship during the final years of the war. They
now found that the food rations were too little to live on, but too
much to die on. Most Berliners received ration card no.5. This
provided so-called starvation rations, which amounted to 9,000
grams (20 pounds) of bread, 600 grams (1 pound 5 ounces) of
meat and 210 grams (8 ounces) of fat per month. Ration card
no.1 was reserved for heavy workers and the privileged. It
entitled them to 18,000 grams (40 pounds) of bread, 3,000 grams
(6 pounds 10 ounces) of meat and 900 grams (2 pounds) of fat per
month, but sometimes these rations existed in theory only. All
the shops in the Soviet sector had been boarded up since the war,
and often provided herring or cheese in place of meat. Some
were luckier in having access to the black market. I should also
point out that Russia suffered equally badly from the effects of
war, and could not provide enough food for its own population
either.

Families gradually managed to get together again, and they
would pin up notices in shops, on fences and amongst the ruins.
Some offered items for exchange, such as 'genuine Persian rug
for half a dozen eggs'. Others requested information: 'We're
alive! Tell us where we can find you. Paul and Else!'

I cannot over-emphasise how incredibly lucky we were in our
family. Having the officers' mess in the Lion Villa meant that we
always had plenty to eat. More than that, I was invited to drink
vodka out of coffee cups with the soldiers, some of whom were
only two or three years older than myself. At sixteen I felt really

grown up now. The soldiers used to sing in the evenings, and I soon learnt to accompany them on my accordion. This was a beautiful instrument, with 120 chords and inlaid with mother of pearl. I had been given it for my tenth birthday, and had managed to keep it throughout the war. The officers and soldiers liked me to play or sing solos for them. My repertoire consisted mostly of popular songs, though for emergencies I did have one classical piece up my sleeve: the entry of the guests to the Wartburg from *Tannhäuser*—or rather my own version of it. I particularly liked to sing those beautiful Russian folk-songs. The soldiers became silent as they listened, often with tears in their eyes.

My schooldays are numbered

July 1945 saw the arrival of the Western Allied forces in Berlin. They took over the three western sectors of the city which had been allocated to them at Yalta. These became the American, the British and the French sectors respectively. My father and I went over to the western side of Berlin to see the event for ourselves. The Allied troops made a moving spectacle as they advanced into the city through the rubble of ruined buildings and took possession of West Berlin.

In the late summer of 1945, I attempted to resume my studies at the Grey Monastery. The school had reassembled in Berlin in temporary premises, as the old building in the Klosterstrasse had been destroyed.

It soon became clear that I had not made the necessary grade in Greek to take my *Abitur*. So in October 1945 I transferred to a *Realgymnasium* in Berlin-Weissensee (a technical school, which is somewhere between a grammar and a secondary modern with a scientific bias). I had four years' English to catch up, and as the school lay in the Soviet sector of Berlin, Russian had now become compulsory. I had considerable qualms about this from the outset, but I was willing to give it a try.

At the beginning of 1946 we had to leave the Lion Villa as the family was about to break up. Grandma moved in with an aunt of mine, while we ourselves moved into a small flat in Steffenstrasse, which was nearer the city centre. For a while, Father continued to work as a storekeeper for the Russians. He later tried some modest trading to help make ends meet. We were not exactly well off, but neither were we destitute.

To be honest, I no longer had the slightest interest in my schoolwork, being far more interested in music. I began by joining a small band which some boys had started at the school in Weissensee. This band flourished. One evening we played at a ball in a factory warehouse. There were thousands of people present, including both Germans and Russian soldiers with their families—a gesture of reconciliation. They asked me to sing for them; I kicked off with some Russian folk songs, and then went on to sing a few American hits which I had heard on the American Army wavelengths: *Give me five minutes more* and *Gonna take a sentimental journey.*

People were enchanted, and I realised for the first time that I must have inherited some special gift for singing. My success was a heady experience. I beamed at the audience as I made my bow, whereupon a Russian officer climbed up onto the makeshift stage and embraced me warmly. 'We will educate your voice!' he cried. 'The boy will become a great singer!'

Playing in the school band was not enough to satisfy me, so I teamed up with two other lads I had got to know. They were Alfred Hix who played double-bass, and Theodor Schnurbus who played guitar. We played in the evenings, emulating the style of *The Three Travellers*, a popular light-music trio of the time. We worked hard making rapid progress, and were soon able to offer our services to the landlord of a public house in Berlin-Lichtenberg called the *Rote Laterne* or 'Red Lantern'. He engaged us on the spot. On Saturdays we sometimes played the whole night through. Then on Sundays we began at four in the afternoon with a sort of *Kaffee-Musik* (or coffee-concert), and at six went on to play dance music. On Wednesdays I often appeared alone with my accordion.

Things sometimes went wrong at first, but the audiences were not too demanding and we often played requests for them. Most people wanted old chestnuts such as *La Paloma* or *Lili-Marlene*.

Operetta fans asked for waltzes from *The Merry Widow*, while British or American parties preferred *You Are My Sunshine* or a Boogie-Woogie. Of course we played Russian items too. I moved around with my companions from table to table, and was soon able to tell if a joke or a compliment was in order. I passed on any special requests to my friends, and collected all the tips. We had a special arrangement with the waiter: whenever a guest treated us to a vodka he brought us gin-glasses filled with tap-water; or instead of cognac he gave us tea. We drank to the health of our clients, who must have been amazed to find us sober after ten vodkas and five cognacs. We went halves with the waiter afterwards. Gradually we extended our repertoire and im- proved the standard of our performances. We also became more skilful at creating our own individual style.

We no longer considered ourselves beginners, and soon began to extend our activities to public houses all over the British and American sectors. We also played in an American sergeants' mess and in a British officers' club in Spandau. We were especially keen to play in places which paid us in goods such as coffee, butter or cigarettes. Such items were extremely valuable, and we either took them home or exchanged them for flour and eggs. It was no use selling them as the Mark was worthless at that time.

One late October evening in 1946, we were having a grand old time in the American officers' mess. They gave us a real ovation, but only gradually did we come to realise why they were so happy. It was eventually explained to us by an American lieutenant whom we had seen when we played there for the first time, only a week before. He had previously ignored us, and generally avoided speaking to Germans. But this time he told us, 'Berlin's won a great victory today.'

Why this sudden change in attitude? I hadn't been very interested in politics to date, being pre-occupied with school- work, band rehearsals and concert engagements. There had been an election in Berlin on the 20th October 1946, but I had not really appreciated its importance. East Berliners like my parents had mostly ignored the appeals of their Russian occupiers and the East Berlin newspapers which the Russians controlled. The Communist Party had, to all outward appearances, been dissolved. They had propagated worker solidarity and had called on people to vote for the SED (*Sozialistische Einheitspartei Deutschlands* or 'German Socialist Union'). Very few Berliners were deceived by this and Father commented, 'I'll vote LDP as usual.'

Here I must add one of Father's favourite jokes. A communist from East Berlin is talking to a West-Berliner. 'I suggest you vote SED,' he says. 'Things are on the up-and-up in the east.'

'I don't believe that,' says the West-Berliner. 'You can't even buy a pair of shoes where you live.'

'Oh,' he replies, 'we've got a whole new explanation for that.'

The result of Berlin's October election was a sobering lesson for the communist officials of East Berlin. The SED obtained a total of only 19.8 percent of the votes as against 48.7 percent for the Social Democrats (the SPD or *Sozialdemokratische Partei Deutschlands*). The newly-formed Christian Democrats (the CDU or *Christlich-Demokratische Union*), obtained 22.2 percent of the votes, while the Liberal Democrats (the LDP or *Liberal-Demokratische Partei*) achieved only 9.3 percent. So that night was a time of enormous jubilation.

My musical activities were certainly profitable, but they badly affected my schoolwork. I often came home early in the morning to find my father on his way to work. He would stop and look me in the eyes. Was it resentment or resignation? I have no idea. It was not quite the moment to give me a lecture. On the whole I believe he trusted me and was sure that I would make my own way in the end. And the goods I brought home with me were not to be sneezed at. Mother, alas, worried constantly about my future, because I would sit down exhausted at the table, dishevelled and unshaven, gawping at my plate and almost asleep. She had to get it off her chest. 'My God!' she would sigh. 'Look at those rings under your eyes! That stubble! What's going to become of you, lad?' Whereupon Father commented dryly, 'He'll make it yet.'

As I had feared, things went badly at the *Realgymnasium*. I failed to make the grade for *Abitur* in the Spring of 1947. But in the hope of still getting my *Abitur*, I wrote to *Gabbes Lehranstalt*, a private school in the Reichpietschufer near the Potsdamer Strasse. I also considered other possibilities. Mindful of my former 'film career', I decided to apply to drama college, the former Max Reinhardt College. For my audition I chose the first act from *The Maid of Orleans* by Schiller. I had learnt it off by heart, and for weeks my mother had to endure a battle commentary: 'We had raised six pennants and were about to attack Lorraine's forces. Our leader was Baudricour, the knight from Vaucouleurs.' I was welcomed by a gentleman whose name I did not register in my excitement. He led me up onto a podium, and after I had indicated my choice of text, said in a rather tired voice, 'Well then, knight, speak!' This I proceeded to do. When I came to the bit about Joan of Arc ('Let God and the maid be your leaders!'), he interrupted me. He explained that I had considerable talent but was still too young. Three minutes later I was back on the street. Naïvely, I made a similar application to the music *conservatoire*, where I auditioned with *Sah ein Knab ein Röslein stehn*. This too left me with a somewhat mixed impression.

It also showed up gaps in my general musical education. As I was primarily interested in playing, I had read very little about music. The only classical songs I knew were a few Caruso arias and the Schlusnus songs which Mother used to play. Her record collection had long since disappeared. I knew that Schubert had composed *Ständchen* and Brahms had composed the cradle song *Guten Abend, gute Nacht*. Wolf I only knew at second hand. Having sung in the Mozart Choir, I knew that Bach had written cantatas and Haydn had written masses. The State Opera had been burnt to the ground, but I had been to the Admiral's Palace to hear *The Mastersingers of Nuremberg*. That was the sum total of my musical education. At all events, the people at the conservatoire must have decided that I was not a complete failure as they gave me some very important advice. They knew of an up-and-coming young teacher who was about to finish college. He was, they thought, just the teacher for a beginner like me. His name was Harry Gottschalk. I did not hesitate for a moment, but took down his name and address and ran home delighted.

'Now you'll know how it's done,' said Mother when I gave her the news. I thought to myself, if I made anything out of all this I was going to do as well as Schlusnus. I immediately gave up the private school.

CHAPTER 7

My singing career begins

Studying music

My music teacher admitted that, like me, he had started out as a dance musician, so he clearly understood the reasons for my somewhat unorthodox career. Harry Gottschalk had been a student at the conservatoire before the war. He was then studying to become a pianist. Acting as an accompanist for young singers gave him ample opportunity to learn about many different teaching methods and vocal techniques. It was noted at the time that he was a gifted teacher and had a fine ear for the details of voice production. At this stage he had not the least intention of further developing these talents. He was almost established as an accompanist when he was drafted into the army. So his plans had to be put aside for the time being.

He went to Africa during the war and was captured by the Allies. As a prisoner of war he went first to America and then to England; he returned to Germany in 1947. He had badly injured one of his hands, so that a piano career was now out of the question. It then occurred to him how good he would be as a singing teacher, so he went back to the conservatoire, this time to study singing. The professors soon recognised Gottschalk's outstanding teaching abilities, and sent him private pupils while he was still at college. I was one of them. 'Have a go with Hermann Prey,' they suggested. 'He seems to have something about him. Bring him back for another audition in a year's time.'

I was earning a considerable amount as a light-musician. Moreover, Harry Gottschalk's fees were very modest. This meant that I could manage as many as four lessons a week. We always began lessons with twenty minutes of vocal exercises and then went on to the song repertoire. It is not every student who likes this method, and not every teacher would approve of it but for me it was ideal, and I progressed rapidly. Gottschalk was supposed to send me to audition for the conservatoire in the spring of 1948. However, I feared losing him as a teacher and tried to persuade him not to do so. Father did not exactly approve of this idea.

'Listen,' he said, 'you can't go on as you are at the moment. If you want to be a professional musician, you need to have the recognised qualifications.'

'Yes,' Mother added, 'you've always wanted to go to the conservatoire, haven't you?'

'But if I go to the conservatoire it means I'll have a different singing-teacher, and I already know I'm OK with Gottschalk.'

'But the man's still a student,' Father pointed out irritably. 'You won't get anywhere with him! You should go to a proper professor.'

'But even if he is a professor, that doesn't necessarily make him good at voice training,' I protested.

'But Hermi, you want to get your diploma. You want to sing on the stage.'

'Look Mum, it's not like it is for a doctor or a lawyer. You go to an opera manager and give an audition. If he likes you he'll take you on. Nobody cares two hoots about certificates or diplomas.'

This time Father lost his temper. 'It's either the conservatoire or nothing at all, is that clear? And that's my final word on the matter.'

So I applied a second time to the conservatoire and this time I got in. I was allocated to Professor Günther Baum's singing class. Any singer must take extreme care when choosing a teacher. Günther Baum was an outstanding oratorio singer, and could teach me some interesting things about deportment on stage. For example, he once said to me, 'When you go on stage, you must make the audience breathe with you from your very first breath.' I soon realised, however, that his voice training

methods were not suitable for me, which worried me, so I called
on Harry Gottschalk.

'The notes have gone all wrong around the break,' I
complained. 'E and F don't come as easily as they used to.
There's something not quite right there.'

'Let's hear you.'

I sang a few bars out of Mozart's *An Chloe*: '... *aber selig neben
dir*...'

'You're singing into your throat, lad,' said Harry.

'But that's dreadful. What shall I do about it?'

He shrugged his shoulders. 'Good advice comes expensive.
Don't you do the voice exercises any more?' I shook my head in
shame. 'Very little.'

'We can't hold that against you, but you'll have to start all
over again.'

'And what about Baum?'

'That's your own decision.'

'Could I come back to you again? Just to keep me on the right
track?'

'Yes, as far as I'm concerned.'

'But we must keep it to ourselves.'

'Nobody will find out from me.'

'When can we start?'

'Now! Straight away!'

I was overjoyed.

And so it came about that I had two teachers at the same time,
one of them official and one of them secret—though the whole
thing later exploded on me.

In the meantime I took full advantage of the many
educational opportunities which the conservatoire had to offer.
In this respect my parents had been right. One person who very
much influenced me was Jaro Prohaska, the famous heroic
baritone of the thirties and forties. He led the opera classes at the
conservatoire, and in this capacity guided my first steps on the
opera stage. On one occasion we were rehearsing Puccini's *Il
Tabarro*. I was singing the part of Marcel who, like Canio in
Pagliacci, jealously murders his wife's young lover. 'Now listen,
Prey. In this opera you should always enter the stage from the

audience's left. In this way you'll show the audience the right-hand side, the "heartless" side, of your chest; then they'll know you're the villain. They'll gain a negative impression of hostility and reserve. It's quite another matter if you're singing Figaro. Then you come in from the right, showing the audience the left-hand side of your chest, the side with the heart.' Many years later, when I was with my wife in Venice, we saw Verrocchio's formidable statue of Colleoni leading his forces into battle. The way he thrust his right shoulder forward reminded me of the words of Jaro Prohaska. The great Italian sculptors must have known about these secrets too.

It was vital for me to concentrate on aural training. I had so far paid little attention to this, even though Harry Gottschalk had often complained of poor intonation. The playing of too much light music had encouraged me to neglect ear-training. Singers should be able to recognise and eradicate poor intonation for themselves. If they persist in singing sharp or flat, they are not only a nuisance to conductors, fellow singers and members of the audience with sensitive hearing, they will also make life difficult for themselves. People will never stop telling them they are out of tune. It may be put down to faulty vocal technique (body-control, diaphragm or the like); if temporary, it may be attributed to mental or physical exhaustion; but usually it is due purely and simply to insufficient attention to the placing of notes and intervals. Accurate intonation is essential in passages containing difficult sequences of notes, such as chromatic passages, those containing the dreaded tritone (produced by a series of major thirds), augmented fourths and fifths, and ninths and tenths—not to mention the atonal leaps which are often required of singers in modern music.

Singers must also practise listening out for unusual modulations. Some songs may seem innocuous on the surface but contain some nasty surprises. A good example of this is Schumann's *Auf das Trinkglas eines verstorbenen Freundes* ('To a deceased friend's drinking-glass'), the sixth song of his Kerner cycle, in which the third and fifth verses move enharmonically through a series of veiled minor chords and dominant sevenths.

I had to work extremely hard to get my intonation under

control, and have never been free from the occasional lapse. Fritz Wunderlich once commented to me years later on the way to the dressing room, 'Your minor thirds are always a shade too flat. This is because you aim at them from below. You've got to aim from above!' This was an interesting observation, and I paid serious attention to it.

I studied singing at the Berlin Conservatoire with Adolf Stauch. As a teacher he was both excellent and hard to please. He is well-known in German musical circles as the co-editor of the recently republished opera guide known as the *Stranz-Stauchscher Grosser Opernführer* or 'Great Stranz-Stauch Opera Guide'. (I recommend the original German as a pronunciation exercise for students of German.) Adolf Stauch was well known in Berlin in the post-war years as accompanist to Margarethe Klose and Emmi Leisner, and as permanent accompanist to Karl Schmitt-Walter; he also frequently performed with Rudolf Schock.

Under Stauch's direction I studied as many as 300 songs, plus a large number of arias, duets and ensembles. He often presented us with as many as fifteen pieces to be brought up to performance standard within a week. This was because, in addition to teaching at the conservatoire, Stauch lectured on the development of opera and song at the *Volkshochschule* (College of Adult Education) in Berlin-Zehlendorf. It was our job to provide musical illustrations for these lectures, which attracted audiences of up to a thousand. We had to cover the whole of musical history: from the mediaeval *Minnelieder* to scenes from pastoral plays, arias from Monteverdi, Lully and Pergolesi; baroque songs by Adam Krieger and canzonets by Sebastian Knüpfer; music by Nicolo Piccini and Karl Ditters von Dittersdorf; not to mention all the great operas, from those of Handel and Gluck right through to Alban Berg and Alexander von Zemlinsky. It goes without saying that Schubert's Lieder were a central theme of Stauch's lectures, though the songs of Beethoven, Schumann, Brahms and Wolf were also important. This opened up new avenues for me. I had been thrown in at the deep end, so to speak, but within six months I had acquired a repertoire for a lifetime.

I no longer had any doubts about my career. The theatre was as attractive as ever, but as a singer I had found my ultimate fulfilment in the Lieder repertoire of the nineteenth century. It is thus no coincidence that even today I consider my song recitals as central to my work as an artist.

I made that decision thirty years ago. In those first exciting months, I was to be introduced for the first time to Schubert's *Erlkönig*, *Wanderer* and *Musensohn*, and to all those other marvellous songs in his first volume: also to Schumann's Eichendorff and Heine cycles, Brahms' *Mainacht* and Wolf's *Gesang Weylas*. I was moving into a new and magical realm. I sang with spontaneity, relying entirely upon my own poetic imagination. I have learnt a lot more since then, and years of involvement have greatly enhanced my understanding of the repertoire. Many songs I have sung hundreds and hundreds of times; and yet every recital is still a new experience for me—an adventure and a challenge.

Hard times for Berlin

The 20th June 1948 was the date of the West German currency reform, which considerably aggravated the tensions between East and West. When the reform was extended to include West Berlin, thus annexing it to the West German economy, this served to exacerbate the situation still further.

The music trio was by now extending its activities into Berlin's *demi-monde*, and on the night following the currency reform, we were playing at a night club at the western end of the Kurfürstendamm, in Halensee. I shall never forget that night. The audience was decidedly unconventional, for it included, quite apart from the usual quota of men and women of 'doubtful morals', a whole mob of genuine gangsters and racketeers. They wore black leather coats which for some strange reason they never took off. They drank champagne and whisky by the bottle, and became more and more generous towards us as the night wore on. A clean-shaven, rather greasy-haired individual came up and asked me, 'Can you play the *Badenweiler March*.?'

This had been Hitler's favourite march, so of course I still knew it—first C Major and then A Minor! As we played, I noticed a hand in my jacket-pocket. I afterwards found a new sixty-mark note in there, which at the time was an inconceivable fortune. Indeed, the situation was incomprehensible. For on that day no one should have had more than a maximum of forty new Deutschmarks, and this in exchange for old Reichsmarks on a one-to-one basis; this rule applied equally to both rich and poor. Where on earth could this crook have got so much money on the day after currency reform? And why was he willing to lay out such a sum for the *Führermarsch*?

The Russians reacted sharply to the currency reform, and on the 24th June 1948 cut off all transport routes between West Berlin and West Germany. This blockade was intended to prevent the Western Allies from setting up a West German government. However, the western powers did not allow this to influence them. By the next morning, General Clay had set in motion a massive air lift, which was to last a whole year, until the blockade was lifted. This 'air-bridge' provided Berlin with all its food requirements. The airport at Berlin-Tempelhof received a continuous stream of American aircraft, which soon came to be known as 'Rosinenbomber' or 'raisin-bombers'. After the blockade had at last been lifted, Berlin remained a divided city, with two councils, two mayors and two administrations.

Not only was Berlin divided, but the same was true of Germany as a whole. On the 23rd May 1949, the three western occupation zones were united into a single West German state, the German Federal Republic. East Germany was to follow suit only four months later, and on the 7th October 1949 was proclaimed the German Democratic Republic. Berlin suffered most from this division. Three years later the East Berlin authorities cut all telephone cables to West Berlin. The city's four sectors had, to all intents and purposes, been made into two military zones, one administered by the western powers and the other under Russian domination. Twelve more years were to pass, however, before a hundred-mile-long wall would tear the great city in two.

7.   In 1955 I appeared as Giglio in Honegger's operetta *Roi Pausole*. This was the performance which finally convinced Günther Rennert of my abilities in light baritone roles.

8. As Wolfgang von Eschenbach in the 1959 Hamburg production of *Tannhäuser*— my first great Wagner role.

9. As Papageno in Mozart's *The Magic Flute*, in 1970 in Munich—one of my favourite roles.

10. I have frequently played Figaro in Rossini's *The Barber of Seville*, including performances in Milan, New York and Berlin.

11. In 1980 at the *Nationaltheater*, Munich, in the title role in Carl Orff's modern version of *Orpheus*. The producer was Pierre Jean Valentin.

12.   Some roles have become almost a part of me. Here, for example, is a *Barber* with a bit of body! A. Reinhardt created the stage-design for Ruth Berghaus' 1974 production.

The curtain rises

From 1948 to 1950 I was working practically round the clock. My secret lessons with Harry Gottschalk soon became the most important part of my daily life, although most of the day was spent at the conservatoire. My main activities there consisted of singing-lessons with Professor Baum and classes in opera, but I had plenty to do apart from this, such as aural training, music theory, music history, piano lessons, language tuition, and movement and dance classes. In the evenings I was often playing with the trio, which we had recently dubbed the 'Rhythm Trio'. We played all the hits of the day, singing them in three voice-parts. I soon got to know as many as a hundred American songs with the help of what were known as *hit-kits*: small song-books which gave the melody and the words, but which, instead of providing the accompaniment, gave the correct chord har-monisations underneath. For example, the symbol 'F7' indicated a dominant seventh chord based on F. I was quite good at improvising on the accordion or piano, and soon got the hang of these little books.

Like many of my friends, I often went down to the GYA or German Youth Activities Club, an organisation run by the American Army. I performed here as a soloist, and organised a youth choir with whom I also performed. Sadly my singing aspirations were not taken very seriously in GYA circles.

'What!' said one of the sergeants. 'Want to be a singer? You'll drown in the soup.' I asked him what exactly he meant by this. 'Well,' he explained, 'it's as if all you singers were swimming around in an enormous soup-dish. If you're lucky, you'll make it as far as the edge and scramble out onto the rim. However, if there's anybody quicker than you, he'll swim past, then step on your hand and biff you one. Then you're back in the soup. Understand?'

I later discovered that the sergeant also had ambitions as a singer.

I remember that in those early years I would do anything to avoid appearing emotional or sentimental. Whenever words like *innig* ('tender'), *lieblich* ('sweetly') or *Herzensgrund* ('the bottom of my heart') appeared in the text, I was immediately on my guard. My singing was deliberately unemotional, which was considered a sign of a cool, rather bland temperament. This was in the spirit of the times. The critics talked of 'an interpretation typical of the younger generation', and were right in this. The compositions of the nineteenth-century were the product of a past which we were reluctant to acknowledge. Many had to overcome psychological barriers before they could even consider this music, while at the same time they bemoaned the lack of a substitute.

Many people had been so horrified at what their fathers' generation had done, that they had come to reject all that their forebears had stood for, while welcoming with open arms anything they knew to have been rejected in the past. I was not one of these and, on the contrary, I was fascinated with romanticism, the Lieder composers of the nineteenth century had become my greatest love. Deep down inside, I wanted to put my whole heart into these songs, but feared that this would conflict with the spirit of the age.

After all, I was not living in an ivory tower, but in a world where many of my young contemporaries had suffered much more than myself. If I had ignored the general trend, I could not have expected them to accept me.

For all my enthusiasm, I still had moments of doubt about my career. I sometimes felt that I had no chance of succeeding and would be best advised to give up. In short, there were moments of crisis: such as in 1948, when I heard Dietrich Fischer-Dieskau, only four years my senior, at the Titania Palace in Berlin. Herta Klust was his accompanist in Schubert's *Winterreise* and their performance impressed me enormously. As I left the concert hall, I wondered if there was any point in continuing as someone else had already achieved the ideal for which I was striving. I can now see that Fischer-Dieskau was setting new standards, without which I would never have achieved so much myself.

I later kept out of the way of this great contemporary of mine, which is understandable. I wanted to avoid his influence turning me into a mere carbon-copy of Fischer-Dieskau. Mutual friends have since told me that it might have been even more unpleasant for him, knowing that I was competing against him.

Time has naturally resolved these tensions. We have since shared the stage in both Salzburg and Munich, and I have many happy memories of working with this great singer.

In 1950 I treated myself to a diary into which I entered details of rehearsals, concerts and other engagements. I have continued to do so ever since. When a whole year had passed, I proudly noted down a 'balance' of twenty-one classical appearances, this punctuated with three exclamation marks. I have no intention of producing a boring list of appearances, but it may be of interest to note that in July 1950 I had my first professional concert engagement. This was with Erich Steffen, founder of the Berlin Mozart Choir. He had at last been released from Russian detention, and was making a comeback as leader of a new Mozart choir. The concert was in Grunewald Castle, and I sang baritone in Paul Höffer's *Woodland Serenade* based on a text by Peter Abraham Schultz. Steffen conducted a small orchestra. I also performed concerts in private houses, old people's homes, and a prison, and sang for the first time in Berlin's St Cecilia's Hall. Like any young and ambitious singer, I was gaining as much experience as I could.

My standard repertoire already included the ever-popular Loewe ballads, *Tom der Reimer* ('Tom the rhymer') and *Die Uhr* ('The clock'), and well-known popular Lieder such as Wolf's *Fussreise* ('Journey on foot') and Brahms' *Vergebliches Ständchen* ('Futile serenade'); also show-pieces such as Valentin's prayer from Faust and Wolfram's *Lied an den Abendstern* ('Song to the Evening Star') from *Tannhäuser*. All of which had by now become second nature to me. René's aria from the third act of Verdi's *Masked Ball* was also to take on a special significance for me later. Folk songs were never scorned, and items such as the *Volga Boat Song* and *Dunkelrote Rosen* ('Dark-red roses') were always welcome.

Decisions

As a Berliner, I was now able to acquaint myself with the Berlin public. 'Oh, this Berlin public!' said Theodor Fontane with a sigh. 'Everybody else goes to the theatre to enjoy himself. Only the Berliner goes there in order *not* to enjoy himself. His one joy in life is that of *not* enjoying himself. As he sits there in the stalls, he does not smile in grateful anticipation, but stares like a hunter about to stalk some poor rabbit.'

My colleague, Erika Köth, also speaks of the 'highly critical manner' in which the Berlin public greets an opera or a concert. 'But,' she continues, 'once you succeed their appreciation remains both lasting and sincere. The artist who can convince the Berlin public has really made it to the top.'

In the autumn of 1950 I made an important decision which had to be explained to Freddy and Theo, my fellow players in the 'Rhythm Trio'. 'I'm afraid I can't go on playing with you any longer, I've decided to concentrate on becoming a classical musician. If I carry on playing dance-music, sooner or later it's going to affect my career.' This was a blow for both of them as we had played together for most of the evenings since 1946, during turbulent times of political and economic change. We had been through so much together, indeed we had grown up together. I owed much to those four years, but I had made up my mind.

Giving up the band meant a considerable drop in my income. To fill this gap, I appeared in a number of popular concerts, school balls and similar events and could have made a career for myself in light entertainment. After winning first prize in a pop-contest at the *Rheinterrassen*, several opportunities were open to me to enter the pop-world. But I was firmly resolved on a career as an opera and concert singer. Popular music had to be sacrificed for the sake of the classical. Frankly, I have never been totally committed to either one or the other, and I know there are people who would criticise me for this. We are too often pigeon-holed by the public, who may love, indeed adore, my interpretations of *Winterreise, Dichterliebe* or Brahms' *Four Serious Songs*, but frown on a record of Prey singing popular songs. 'Does he have to?' they say.

Frau Goppel, wife of the former Bavarian premier, once heard one of my popular television shows, singing numbers from musicals. She commented, 'Must you tarnish that beautiful voice of yours with such rubbish?' Even when I stand on a concert platform, I still think of myself primarily as an entertainer and refuse to be labelled, whether as Papageno, as a Schubert recitalist or as a singer of popular songs. I will not be squeezed into a stereotype. I want to be free simply to sing and give pleasure to my audiences, and my only criterion is that I should do it well.

It should not be forgotten that the division between classical and popular music is a relatively recent phenomenon, belonging to this century alone. Mixed concerts were the rule in the nineteenth century, and the two forms existed happily together. A concert might, for instance, begin with an orchestral overture by Weber, followed by some violin solos by Sarasate. A baritone soloist might sing a couple of Schubert songs, followed perhaps by an aria from Lortzing. The orchestra might then conclude the first half with a polka. The second half might begin with Rimsky-Korsakov's *Flight of the Bumble-bee* on the violin; the baritone might then sing a few popular ballads; and finally, the orchestra might conclude the concert with Beethoven's 8th Symphony. Recitalists would always endeavour to produce a well-balanced combination of both popular and serious music in their concert programmes. Stars like Emilio de Gogorza and Mattia Battistini were revered as much for their Mozart and Verdi as for their Tosti and Toselli, or for their Spanish and Italian folk songs.

I suspect that this rift between classical and pop only really became general with the spread of jazz after the First World War. Jazz incorporated new dance forms which, unlike the waltz and mazurka, could not be easily assimilated into the classical repertoire: dances like the Charleston, the Foxtrot and the Lambeth Walk, all of which my parents had had in their record collection.

Pop and classical have gone their separate ways since then. Caruso was praised highly for his stunning performances of popular songs, whereas Richard Tauber was pilloried for the same thing only a quarter of a century later. This is most unjust. Any form of music which finds an audience has a right to be heard, so long as it is good. Hence I am not a classical singer, neither am I a popular singer: I combine the two.

CHAPTER 8

Bärbel

Seventy-five Deutschmarks

Early in 1951 we left our tiny flat in the Steffenstrasse. My parents had decided to move to West Berlin, so we found a flat in the Theodorstrasse, near the Franckepark in Berlin-Tempelhof, which was in the American sector of the city. Father was rebuilding his business, thanks partly to the encouragement of some of his old customers. 'Start again, Hermann, and we'll come and buy our meat from you.' And they did. The first years were very hard, three times a week, Father had to get up at eleven o'clock at night to be ready for the freezer-vans, which arrived with the meat at one in the morning. At fifty years of age, he had to do all the work himself, as he could not yet afford an assistant. This involved emptying the vans, carrying hundred-weight sacks into the market-hall and hanging up the meat. He could certainly have done with my assistance, particularly since Mother could no longer help him. Having suffered a stroke in the summer of 1950, she was bedridden from time to time. This meant that my sister had to look after her as well as doing all the housework.

As a result of her illness, Mother was never able to come to any of my recitals and only once heard me sing in public. This was in the Titania Palace, where I sang in the *Matthew Passion* with the Schola Cantorum of Berlin under Mathieu Lange. The concert was also attended by the Lord Mayor of Berlin, Ernst Reuter. Apart from this, Mother only heard me on the radio. My diary for 1951 included forty concert engagements, and also my debut with RIAS Berlin, the radio station for the American sector.

One of my first broadcasts included songs by my friend Helmut Kotschenreuther, and my family was able to listen to it. Frankly, I would have preferred to sing some Schubert songs, knowing that my family would not like Kotschenreuther's dissonances very much. When the time came, I turned on the wireless and began fiddling with the knobs, but our set was not exactly modern, as Father had bought it cheap from some acquaintance of his. At the vital moment it seemed in imminent danger of stopping altogether. I lost my temper and nearly threw the thing at the wall. Then Father came in and sat down, pressing his lips tightly together, in the way he had always done in the past when I handed him a school report. This expression was meant to say, 'Let's see what this lad can do.'

At last it was time. After the news, which we had heard before, there was first a piano piece, and then followed an announcement which made my heart skip a beat. 'The singer is the baritone, Hermann Prey, and the accompanist is the composer himself.' I glanced across at Mother, who seemed very excited. Father's mouth relaxed, though otherwise he betrayed no emotion. Yet he could not deceive me: I could tell he was at least as excited as I was. The singing began, but he still did not move. I was sitting on the edge of my seat.

After the first song, he asked me, 'Was that you?'

'Yes, of course.'

'It sounds dreadful.' He listened to the rest without comment. I switched off the set and awaited his reaction.

'I didn't like the songs either,' said Mother. 'But you must admit, Hermann, the lad does sing beautifully.' Father cleared his throat.

'I didn't choose the songs,' I explained. 'They were selected for me by the programme staff.'

'Yes, but did they pay you for it?' asked Father.

'Of course,' I replied coolly, 'seventy-five marks.'

Father had just got up to leave, but he quickly sat down again. 'Seventy-five marks!' he cried as he looked at me in astonishment. The amount gradually dawned on him. 'They gave you seventy-five marks for twelve minutes of caterwauling! You must be joking!'

I savoured that moment. 'Yes, seventy-five marks, I swear it.'

Father still could not take it in. Twelve short minutes had earned me as much money as he would have earned after hours of hard physical labour. I fetched a bottle of wine from my room which I had bought especially for the occasion and hidden away. We drank to many more broadcasts from Hermann Prey, baritone.

We spoke of that afternoon years later, by which time Father had once again built up a prosperous business. 'That radio broadcast was a turning-point for me,' he said. 'It made me realise that you knew your way better than I did, and I must say I preferred it that way. My own profession can only go downwards from now on, the middle-man is disappearing and the large combines are taking over. They've got their own farms and their own livestock, and everything goes direct to the consumer. The food delivered is cheaper and fresher when it comes from a large distributor than when it's from Aunt Emma with her milk straight from the cow.'

'But *I* could have become the boss of a large combine,' I protested, 'sitting high up in a skyscraper in Chicago.'

'That's true,' he said. 'I can just see you now, sitting on the twenty-second floor, fingering your lapels and pressing all those red buttons.'

Love at second sight

Bärbel and I have now been married for twenty-six years. When I think of this, my mind goes back to that evening in August 1951 when I fell head-over-heels in love with her.

The 23rd of August 1951 was my mother's forty-sixth birthday. So I said to my father, 'I say, wouldn't it be nice if we all went to the summer ball at the Zoo? Now that Mum's feeling a bit better, it'll make a marvellous birthday celebration.' Father agreed, so we all went there together on Saturday, 25th August. It was the first and last ball I ever went to with my parents.

Berlin Zoo is a vast park in the middle of the city. We arrived that summer evening to find the ball in full swing. 'Go and enjoy yourself,' said Father. 'You don't need to stay at our table.' So I mingled with the crowd and soon met a number of friends. One of them called Mäxchen called out, 'Come and join us. They're a marvellous crowd over here. Let me introduce you . . . ' I was delighted. Mäxchen led me over to his table and introduced me in turn to Dolores, Erhard, Micki, Sabine and Bärbel. The moment I met Bärbel, something seemed to click . . .

I can see her now, slim and soft-limbed, with a long oval face and short, fairish hair. She was wearing a flowery red dress with short sleeves, and looked across at me placidly, if somewhat sceptically.

Bärbel is a typical Berliner. In Berlin the women really have feeling. They may not show it, but they have it all right. 'A woman from Berlin is the liveliest, jolliest, kindest, cleverest, noblest, wittiest, most faithful, most understanding, most delightful creature in the world. If you think this is exaggerating, remove five or six of these traits and there are still enough left.' Thus spoke Gerhart Hauptmann, Berlin's great playwright. Dieter Hildebrand, the Berlin journalist and critic, would take issue with this: 'If you want to describe a Berliner, then keep your description brief.' A woman from Berlin is, in Hildebrand's opinion, not inclined to self-analysis, but can best be described in words of one syllable: brisk, smart and cool.

Well, I don't know about this. I would say that she only appears cool on the surface. At any rate, of one thing I am certain: a Berliner cannot do better than marry a Berliner.

My parents hardly saw me again that evening. In fact I never left Bärbel's side. I would say that, on my side at least, it was a classic case of love at first sight, or at second sight as we later discovered. Bärbel was more reserved initially, she had already heard things about me, and not all of them good. It turned out that we had already danced together at a party eight months before, and Bärbel had to remind me of this. She cannot have made much impression on me at the time. 'Yes, I can remember the party,' I said. 'It was at Trauti's—and I was there with Hatschi.'

Before we parted at midnight, I said to her, 'I must see you

again as soon as possible. Tomorrow? Sunday evening perhaps?'
We met on Monday too, and on Tuesday. On Wednesday
Bärbel took me home and introduced me to her parents, Herr
and Frau Erich Pniok, but I fear I was not altogether welcome.
An aspiring musician would not have been their idea of a son-in-
law. To Herr Pniok I must have seemed rather too casual. I did
not realise then that Bärbel's parents were the kindest people
you could possibly imagine.

That evening was my first opportunity to learn something
about Bärbel's life. Her family had barely managed to survive
the war. Erich Pniok had been in the army, and the mother and
two daughters had, like my own mother, been evacuated to
Silesia. At the end of 1944 they had fled to Göttingen, where
they had somehow managed to get by. Her father had been
released from a prisoner-of-war camp, and they had returned to
their native Berlin, where Erich Pniok had begun to re-establish
his business, just as my father had done.

After I had left, Frau Pniok took her daughter aside and said,
'What do you want with him? He doesn't look the steady type to
me. You won't get too serious about him, will you?'

When Bärbel described this to me later, I asked, 'Well, what
do *you* think?' She hesitated for a moment, and then replied, 'I
think you're just right for me.' Which is a declaration of love, if
anything is.

The Mastersinger

The events of 1952 were to determine the course of my career for
some years to come. In mid-June I entered the Mastersinger
Competition in Nuremberg. This was followed on 30th August
by my stage debut in Wiesbaden, and my first trip to America in
November and December. But before that there were problems
to be overcome.

The directors of the conservatoire were not happy with the
number of engagements I had booked for 1952, which included
both concerts and radio broadcasts. There were forty in all in
the time leading up to my departure for Wiesbaden at the

beginning of August. It was the general view at the conservatoire that studies and career did not mix. One must either be a student or a professional. I was an exception to this rule, having not only a second string to my bow in the concert hall, but a third string in my lessons with Harry Gottschalk, of which the conservatoire knew absolutely nothing.

One morning in the spring of 1952, I arrived at nine o'clock for an opera class with Dr Stauch. The maestro had not turned up yet, so I went into his room to warm up. Suddenly, the door crashed open behind me. I turned round, expecting to see Dr Stauch; but it was my singing-teacher, Professor Baum, who was standing in the doorway. He must have heard me from the corridor, and not only had he recognised my voice, he had also noticed that my voice exercises followed a method quite unknown to him.

'I didn't teach you those exercises,' he declared. This I had to admit, and went on to tell him everything, not realising how dangerous this was. 'But that's quite unheard of!' he cried. 'Since when have you been taking lessons outside college?'

'The whole time,' I replied.

'You'll soon be hearing from me!' he said as he left.

I thought his attitude petty at the time, though today I can see it in a different light. It must have come as a dreadful shock to discover that one of his star pupils owed his success, not to his own teaching, as he had previously assumed, but to someone else. From his point of view, my action amounted to a vote of no confidence in him, and was both dishonest and insincere. On the other hand, no one could have expected me to sacrifice my voice for the sake of the conservatoire, whose own regulations had forced me into this subterfuge. However, a scandal was now brewing.

When Dr Stauch came in, he could immediately see there had been trouble. I told him what had happened. 'And you told Baum that to his face?' I nodded. Dr Stauch sat down at the keyboard and sighed. 'Mm, yes, you and Fräulein Klose— you're both from butchers' families.'

I was forced to leave the college. Although I did not suffer career-wise, having long since signed my contract with Wies-

baden, I should have preferred not to have departed under such
a cloud. Since then, the college has restored me to favour by
offering me a teaching post there.

In the meantime, I had been competing in the regional heats
of the Mastersinger Competition, which in those days lasted the
whole year. This contest was a brain-child of the American
Army's German youth organisation, of which I have already
spoken. The Americans' intention was to discover new singing
talent in Germany, and the project enjoyed the support of many
important dignitaries, both in America and in Europe. That
meant that the organisers could afford the most lavish publicity.
It was quite clearly a propaganda exercise, its intention being to
promote goodwill and to demonstrate the abilities of young
German singers. In 1952, as many as 3,000 young people were
entered for the competition, of whom 2,970 were eliminated in
the so-called regional heats. The thirty who remained went on
to the finals in Nuremberg. The Berlin jury included, amongst
others, Helmut Krebs, the tenor and most celebrated 'Evangelist' of his time; Dr Herbert Brauer, the distinguished baritone;
Ludwig Suthaus, the Wagner tenor; and Margarethe Klose, the
outstanding contralto who, like me, came from a family of
butchers.

The 23rd of May 1952 saw the following headline on the front
page of the *Berliner Beobachter*, organ of the American military
authorities: 'Hermann Prey victor here'. This news was also
carried by the West Berlin press. By the end of May, there
cannot have been a single musical reader in Berlin who had not
heard of Hermann Prey, the young man from Tempelhof. I
experienced the power of the press for the very first time. I shall
limit myself at this point to a quote from just one of the critics:
'Barely twenty-three and very thin and pale, Hermann Prey
stepped onto the stage.' Nowadays, those words fill me with a
feeling of nostalgia.

My success in the Berlin contest produced a flood of offers and
requests, only a quarter of which was I able to fulfil. I now sang
on the North-West German Radio as well as on RIAS. Of the
many concerts I gave, two stand out in my memory. One was
with Martin Mälzer, a wonderfully sensitive accompanist, at

the British Centre in Berlin, where the manager, Frau von Wedelstedt, had rather a soft spot for me. There was a music club at this centre for British culture, where they went to great lengths to encourage young musicians. The second concert was at the *Haus am Waldsee* with Adolf Stauch. He often accompanied me, and it was with him that I later sang *Winterreise* for the first time. At that time I preferred other composers such as Brahms and Wolf; Beethoven's *Adelaide* was also frequently to be found in my recital programmes, though I did not as yet feel up to performing the Beethoven cycle *An die ferne Geliebte* ('To the faraway beloved').

The concert at the *Haus am Waldsee* received the following review in the Berlin evening paper, the *Nachtdepesche*: 'It would appear that this young singer is attracting an increasing number of admirers. The hall was not nearly large enough to accommodate them all, and many had to be turned away.' It is also interesting to note what K.W. said about my voice in the prestigious *Neue Zeitung*: 'His voice rises effortlessly to a brilliant top G; it is strong in the middle and higher registers, but somewhat uncertain at the bottom of the range, where his *pianos* are a little fuzzy and his *mf*s are occasionally lacking in tone.' The *Neue Zeitung* was published by the Americans for a German readership. One of its editors was Erich Kästner, the well-known music critic, who concluded an article of his with some highly flattering observations: 'Not only does he possess a fine baritone voice, but his artistry reveals enormous musical potential; we have the highest expectations for the future of this young singer.'

I soon came to realise how subjective were the views of music critics. The *Neue Zeitung* described Dr Stauch as a 'decidedly unobtrusive accompanist', while according to the *Berliner Anzeiger*, he 'accompanied in his usual ruthless, unyielding manner'. A few days later, on 20th July 1952, I was one of the up-and-coming young artists to be presented at Berlin's Renaissance Theatre by an organisation known jokingly as the 'Emergency German Arts Association'. The following comment appeared next day in the Berlin newspaper *Montag*: 'Hermann Prey is a pupil of Jaro Prohaska of the Berlin State Opera. His seemingly faultless interpretation of songs by Brahms and Wolf reminded one of the unforgettable Heinrich Schlusnus, who passed away so sadly only a few weeks ago.'

My mother was by now lying seriously ill, and could not be present on this occasion. She was, however, even more pleased than I, to know that I was being compared to Schlusnus.

In mid-June I took part in the finals of the Mastersinger Competition and won. All the winners had previously been women, so it was all the more remarkable for a man to earn the title of Mastersinger. My picture appeared in all the German papers, with such headlines as 'Young baritone says it's like a dream', 'On his way up' and 'Portrait of an up-and-coming star'. An announcement even appeared in the *New York Times*: 'German wins trip to USA.'

My party-piece for the Mastersinger Competition was Renato's aria, *Eri tu*, from the third act of Verdi's *Ballo in Mascere*, which I sang in German. In contrast to Germont's aria from *La Traviata*, which had been chosen by one of the Berlin contestants, *Eri tu* allows the singer to show off every facet of his technique: there are passages requiring dramatic expressiveness and others which are sweet and lyrical; there are high and low passages with every nuance between loud and soft; and the aria requires both authority and creative power. Moreover, it is a marvellous piece of music, tailor-made for a baritone. By this time, I had developed a strong instinct for the musical and artistic potential of an aria or a song.

As winner of the competition, I found myself surrounded by important people, including General Thomas T. Handy, commander of the American forces in Europe, a host of American commissioners, the State Secretary of the Bavarian Ministry of Education, and the Lord Mayor of Nuremberg, Otto Bärnreuther. Someone read out a letter of congratulation from the Federal President, Theodor Heuss, after which I was handed an envelope containing 800 marks by Mrs Jouett Shouse from Washington, D.C., a prominent benefactress of the GYA. For me, one of the most important people present was Howard Mitchell, conductor of the Washington Symphony Orchestra. For, as had been announced in the *New York Times*, I was due to go on a tour of America, and this was to include a number of concerts conducted by Dr Mitchell.

I said to Bärbel, 'I am off to the Hesse State Opera now; from there I'm going on to America, and next year we'll get married.' But two more years were to pass before this could take place.

CHAPTER 9

Schubert's *Winterreise*

From the singer's point of view

The *Winterreise* song-cycle by Franz Schubert: it was in the early summer of 1952 that I first plucked up the courage to perform this work. It was later to become a real favourite of mine, over and above all others. I have never stopped singing it since, and I expect I shall sing it at my final concert.

Musically, these songs have a special significance for me. Although I have studied them deeply over the years, there are always new discoveries to be made, and associations which had formerly escaped me. I have sung them innumerable times, and yet I never seem to tire of them. On the contrary, I am often overwhelmed by the desire to sing them again. I cannot wait to 'restart the journey', wondering what new discoveries I shall make this time.

The songs in this *Winterreise* cycle mean so much to me that I should like to discuss them individually. Later on in the book, I shall go on to talk about the Beethoven cycle *An die ferne Geliebte* and Schubert's six Heine settings. Please note, however, that I am no musicologist; I am merely an interpreter of music. I have no intention of providing detailed musical analyses, but would rather share my own personal thoughts on these songs, and show how I approach them as a performer. When, as a singer, I am faced with such a difficult work, and one with such an extraordinary density of expression, my approach must be different from that of a theoretician, who is primarily concerned with the formal and structural aspects of the music. These theoretical considerations are certainly extremely useful to me, but in the end I have to rely on the original inspiration which brought about these musical forms.

How, as a singer, do I go about the task of studying and performing these songs? This is not easy to explain in words. I first need to gain an almost visual impression of the theme of the song, in order to capture its mood and to identify with it. This approach must of necessity be a subjective one, since I must rely, to some extent, on my own feelings and emotions.

Schubert composed two song-cycles, the first being *Die schöne Müllerin* ('The Miller's Daughter') in 1823, and the second the *Winterreise* ('Winter Journey') in 1827, at the age of thirty. Both were based on poems by Wilhelm Müller, the Dessau philologist. Superficially, both cycles seem to follow the same general theme: a wandering youth who is heartbroken over his thwarted love for a young woman. The wandering youth is an ever-popular theme in the nineteenth century, symbolising unrequited love or, as in Wagner's *Parsifal*, the longing for spiritual fulfilment. Beneath the alders where the miller's daughter lives, the snow has melted, producing a profusion of gushing springs, babbling streams and bright flowers. The lark's song fills the air, the water roars through the mill-wheels, and the wanderer sinks gently beneath the shelter of the alders to converse with the moon and the stars.

In the *Winterreise*, by contrast, the water is frozen to ice, and dogs come to growl at the wanderer; he seeks in vain for a resting-place, which not even the cemetery can provide. To the miller-boy, the brook is his friend and confidant. His bid for suicide takes the form of a cradle-song, the gentle harmonies lulling him to sleep, and bringing him eternal peace, as though there were nothing more beautiful or more desirable in life than to sink into this gentle, kindly brook and lie there for ever.

In the *Winterreise* even the angels are silent, and there are no lilies, for even the river is imprisoned beneath a hard, unfriendly sheet of ice. It rejects the wanderer, just like the Elbe in Wolfgang Borchert's post-war drama, *Draussen vor der Tür* ('The Outsider'). This play describes the cruel rejection of a returning soldier by his fellow-countrymen, and made a deep impression on me at the time. Instead of Borchert's wreaths of fog and clear, expectant sky, the *Winterreise* ends with nothing more than a strange old man, staggering barefoot across the ice, the stark fifths in the bass recalling the hollow drone of his hurdy-gurdy. Who is this organ grinder? Death, perhaps? I think not. For herein lies that one fearful aspect of *Winterreise* which most distinguishes it from *Müllerin*: the miller-boy can, indeed does, find peace; the hero of *Winterreise* can never find peace. *Winterreise* is a hymn to eternal despair and never-ending affliction, to futility and the total negation of hope.

Schubert's adaptation of *Die schöne Müllerin* remained faithful to the original text with only a few omissions. His lack of success with opera is often attributed to a poor dramatic sense, but with Lieder his instincts proved sound. He deleted three poems, thus tightening and speeding up the narrative. In particular, he omitted Müller's prologue and epilogue, which satirise the tragedy of love. Schubert wished to take the fate of the poor miller-boy seriously.

Schubert put his own personal stamp on *Winterreise* by changing the order of Müller's poems.

Number in Schubert's song-cycle	The order of Müller's poem-cycle	The order of Schubert's song-cycle
1	*Gute Nacht*	*Gute Nacht*
2	*Die Wetterfahne*	*Die Wetterfahne*
3	*Gefrorne Tränen*	*Gefrorne Tränen*
4	*Erstarrung*	*Erstarrung*
5	*Der Lindenbaum*	*Der Lindenbaum*
13	*Die Post*	*Wasserflut*
6	*Wasserflut*	*Auf dem Flusse*
7	*Auf dem Flusse*	*Rückblick*
8	*Rückblick*	*Irrlicht*
14	*Der greise Kopf*	*Rast*
15	*Die Krähe*	*Frühlingstraum*
16	*Letzte Hoffnung*	*Einsamkeit*
17	*Im Dorfe*	*Die Post*
18	*Der stürmische Morgen*	*Der greise Kopf*

Number in Schubert's song-cycle	The order of Müller's poem-cycle	The order of Schubert's song-cycle
19	*Täuschung*	*Die Krähe*
20	*Der Wegweiser*	*Letzte Hoffnung*
21	*Das Wirtshaus*	*Im Dorfe*
9	*Das Irrlicht*	*Der stürmische Morgen*
10	*Rast*	*Täuschung*
23	*Die Nebensonnen*	*Der Wegweiser*
11	*Frühlingstraum*	*Das Wirtshaus*
12	*Einsamkeit*	*Mut*
22	*Mut*	*Die Nebensonnen*
24	*Der Leiermann*	*Der Leirmann*

What these poems lack in external action, they make up for in emotional depth. They leave a lot to the reader's or the listener's imagination, because Müller's words do not give the complete picture; they merely provide the bare bones of a description, which is just enough to arouse the listener's emotions.

As the singer continualy stops and then resumes his lonely winter journey, we should not complain if the drama can only be experienced outside the music.

In the first song (*Gute Nacht*), we are introduced to a homeless wanderer, who is plagued by the memory of a broken love-affair. He is, as we later discover, a loner, which is certainly unusual at a time of great comradeship. Perhaps he is an intellectual, but he is certainly an outsider. We are told nothing about his background or profession. He wanders through the winter scenery, driven on by past memories to seek out the place where once he was happy and where his sweetheart lives. She has now given her hand to another, a rich man. In his fantasies, this fickle creature is transformed into a weather-vane (*Die Wetterfahne*). This reduces him to tears, which turn to ice in the bitter wind (*Gefrorne Tränen*). He wanders around in the snow like a man possessed (*Erstarrung*).

He remembers a linden tree he once knew (*Der Lindenbaum*), which symbolises unfulfilled dreams and the loss of security.

This releases yet another great flood of tears *(Wasserflut)*, enough to flow like a river as far as the house of his loved-one. Then the nightmare becomes reality: the wanderer kneels beside a frozen river *(Auf dem Flusse)*. He uses a stone to write the name of his loved-one in the ice. Then it occurs to him how like the river he is, frozen on the outside but a raging torrent within. He jumps up in confusion, and sees the towers of the town where his sweetheart lives. He must get away from here, no matter where it leads him *(Rückblick)*.

He is driven on by fierce winds along the bank of the river, through endless snows. His senses become confused, and he thinks he is following a will-o'-the-wisp *(Irrlicht)*; breathless, he arrives at a charcoal-burner's hut, where he finds shelter and lies down exhausted *(Rast)*.

At night he dreams of spring and of love *(Frühlingstraum)*, but the cock crows, destroying his dream. As he peers at the icy window-panes in the pale morning light, he imagines he can see in them the flowers of which he dreamed. It is the dawn of a bright winter day.

As he continues upon his lonely journey *(Einsamkeit)*, a post-horn announces the arrival of the mail-coach *(Die Post)*. Perhaps it is bringing a message from the town, but it rumbles past. He will be hearing no more from his sweetheart, now he can only long for death *(Der greise Kopf)*. A crow circles overhead *(Die Krähe)*. Can it be the same crow which followed him through the town? Will at least the crow remain faithful?

Late that evening, crushed and bereft of all hope *(Letzte Hoffnung)*, he reaches a village *(Im Dorfe)*. Only the guard-dogs are awake... if only they would drive him away. He has no more dreams left to dream, he merely continues his journey. Early next morning a storm breaks out *(Der stürmische Morgen)*. He greets the raging elements with joy, as the storm rages, the will-o'-the-wisp returns and flickers around him. However, he is not taken in by it this time, knowing it to be an illusion *(Täuschung)*. Death now seems the only way out *(Der Wegweiser)*. He pauses in front of an 'inn' *(Das Wirtshaus)* which is in fact a graveyard. He stops and asks for a place to stay, but he is turned away. There is no room for him there either.

He battles on through the blizzard, feeling as though a burden has been lifted *(Mut)*. Now that God is no longer there to welcome him, he is free to be his own god. He becomes deluded and begins to hallucinate. He is obsessed by the vision of three suns *(Die Nebensonnen)*, which stare down at him like a representation of the Holy Trinity. But he wants no more of the light. He seeks darkness, and finds in it a total void of meaninglessness and utter nothingness. This is represented by the organ-grinder *(Der Leiermann)*, to whom no one listens, and who plays on into eternity to a non-existent audience.

In the year of *Winterreise*, things were going very badly for Schubert. Firstly he was plagued by continual bad luck with his publishers, then worries about his failing health filled him with dreadful premonitions (he died in the November of the following year), and thirdly he had serious doubts regarding his future career. He was thirty by now, and was still without any secure means of income. He had at one stage hoped to become *Kapellmeister* at the court of the Emperor Franz I or, failing that, at the *Kärntnertor Theater*; but such hopes had been dashed. No wonder Schubert was often ill-tempered and inclined to melancholy. Once, when walking with Eduard von Bauernfeld, he is said to have remarked, 'What is to become of me? When I'm older, I'll have to beg for bread like Goethe's Harfner.'

This mood finds expression in his music: of the twenty-four songs in the *Winterreise* cycle, sixteen are in the more doleful minor key. The *Müllerin* cycle shows the opposite tendency, with fourteen songs in the major as against six in the minor.

As is often the case in song literature, Schubert's choice of key can cause problems; in *Winterreise* it can drive the singer to distraction. Schubert's original manuscripts show a preference for a tenor who can easily reach a top G sharp or A, but his publisher, Tobias Haslinger, was more interested in potential sales. At first he had strong doubts as to the merit of these songs, and only after some considerable haggling did he agree to give even a small advance to the by now ailing composer. Then, for purely practical reasons, he transposed some of the songs down. This means that some of the keys in the first edition do not correspond to those in the original manuscript.

Being a baritone, my voice is too low to sing more than seven of the twenty-four songs in their original keys, these being *Der Lindenbaum, Einsamkeit, Im Dorfe, Der stürmische Morgen, Täuschung, Das Wirtshaus* and *Mut*. All the others must be transposed down by anything up to a minor third. I am particularly reluctant to do this with *Frühlingstraum*. Eusebius Mandyczewski found evidence to suggest that Schubert had originally intended the song to be in G major, but that after having written only a few bars of the piano introduction, he had opted for the somewhat brighter key of A major. Alas, I am forced to sing the piece in G major. There is no other solution for a baritone, let alone for a bass, other than to make the music seem gloomier than even Schubert intended. A recitalist must always bear this in mind.

Those who wish, however, to sing the songs in their original keys must always remember that, in Schubert's time, instruments were tuned to a lower pitch than ours: an A would have sounded like an A flat today. I myself subscribe to the view held by most of my contemporaries that a singer should always choose the key to which his voice is best suited. He can only give of his best in a song when he feels comfortable singing it.

		Original key	My key
1	*Gute Nacht*	D minor	C minor
2	*Die Wetterfahne*	A minor	G minor
3	*Gefrorne Tränen*	F minor	D minor
4	*Erstarrung*	C minor	A minor
5	*Der Lindenbaum*	E major	E major
6	*Wasserflut*	E minor	D minor
7	*Auf dem Flusse*	E minor	D minor
8	*Rückblick*	G minor	F minor
9	*Irrlicht*	B minor	A minor
10	*Rast*	C minor	B minor
11	*Frühlingstraum*	A major	G major
12	*Einsamkeit*	B minor	B minor
13	*Die Post*	E flat major	C major
14	*Der greise Kopf*	C minor	B minor
15	*Die Krähe*	C minor	B minor

		Original key	My key
16	*Letzte Hoffnung*	E flat major	D major
17	*Im Dorfe*	D major	D major
18	*Der stürmische Morgen*	D minor	D minor
19	*Täuschung*	A major	A major
20	*Der Wegweiser*	G minor	F minor
21	*Das Wirtshaus*	F major	F major
22	*Mut*	G minor	G minor
23	*Die Nebensonnen*	A major	G major
24	*Der Leiermann*	A minor	G minor

Winterreise is also characterised by a noticeable lack of cheerful *tempi*. Admittedly, *Die Wetterfahne, Der stürmische Morgen* and *Mut* are intended to be performed 'fairly quickly', but even here, only the wind is hurried. The only real exception is the mail-coach in *Die Post*, which gallops along in the major key. All the other faster songs are, more typically, in the minor. Once, after a highly successful performance of *Winterreise* in Chicago, the concert organiser commented to me, 'Fabulous, Mr Prey. But next time, please, sing something more gay.'

The twenty-four songs

Gute Nacht

Fremd bin ich eingezogen,
Fremd zieh ich wieder aus,
Der Mai war mir gewogen,
Mit manchem Blumenstrauss.
Das Mädchen sprach von Liebe,
Die Mutter gar von Eh',
Nun ist die Welt so trübe,
Der Weg gehüllt in Schnee.

Ich kann zu meiner Reisen
Nicht wählen mit der Zeit,
Muss selbst den Weg mir weisen
In dieser Dunkelheit.

Good night

A stranger I arrived here,
A stranger I depart,
The month of May favoured me
With many a bouquet of flowers.
The girl talked of love,
Her mother even of marriage,
But now the world is dreary,
And the path is swathed in snow.

I cannot choose the time
For this long journey,
But must find my own way
Through this darkness.

Es zieht ein Mondenschatten	The moon casts a shadow,
Als mein Gefährte mit,	Which is my constant companion,
Und auf den weisen Matten	As I follow the deer-tracks
Such ich des Wildes Tritt.	Across the white countryside.
Was soll ich länger weilen,	Why should I stay any longer
Dass man mich trieb hinaus?	Until they drive me away?
Lass irre Hunde heulen	Let the straying dogs howl
Vor ihres Herren Haus!	In front of their master's house.
Die Liebe liebt das Wandern—	Love itself loves to wander
Gott hat sie so gemacht—	From one to another—
Von einem zu dem andern,	God made it that way—
Fein Liebchen, gute Nacht!	So good night, my beloved.
Will dich im Traum nicht stören,	I will not disturb your dreams,
Wär schad um deine Ruh,	Having no wish to spoil your rest;
Sollst meinen Tritt nicht hören,	You shall not hear my footsteps
Sacht, sacht die Türe zu!	As I close the door softly.
Schreib im Vorübergehen	On passing through the gate,
Ans Tor dir: gute Nacht,	I write the words 'good night',
Damit du mögest sehen,	So that you may see
An dich hab ich gedacht.	That I still thought of you.

The tempo of this opening song is given as *mässig* or *moderato*, which is the same as for the two songs *Rast* and *Der Wegweiser*, and sets the general pattern for the whole cycle. This tempo remains constant as the piano hammers out quavers in a continuous march rhythm.

Gute Nacht (piano introduction)

Rast (postlude)

Der Wegweiser (interlude)

The two-four rhythm of *Gute Nacht* forms the pulse of the whole
work; all the other tempi are arranged about it, sometimes
slower, sometimes faster. It is a quiet song, in which the singer
must be able to make clear distinctions between *mezzo piano*,
piano and *pianissimo*. It also contains some echo effects typical of
Schubert's songs. Note, for example, how this melody fragments

and reappears later in the piano score.

Die Wetterfahne

Der Wind spielt mit der Wetterfahne
Auf meines schönen Liebchens Haus.
Da dacht ich schon in meinem Wahne,
Sie pfiff den armen Flüchtling aus.

Er hätt es eher bemerken sollen,
Des Hauses aufgestecktes Schild,
So hätt er nimmer suchen wollen
Im Haus ein treues Frauenbild.

Der Wind spielt drinnen mit den Herzen,
Wie auf dem Dach, nur nicht so laut.
Was fragen sie nach meinen Schmerzen?
Ihr Kind ist eine reiche Braut.

The weather-vane

The wind plays with the weather-vane
On my dear sweetheart's house.
In my madness, it seemed to me
To mock the poor fugitive.

He should have noticed it before,
This sign attached to the house;
Then he would never have expected to find
A faithful woman within.

Inside the house, the wind plays with hearts,
Though less noisily than upon the roof.
What do they care for my grief?
Their child is now a wealthy bride.

This song begins with a unison figure on the piano, which introduces the second protagonist of *Winterreise*, namely the wind. The voice then joins the piano in unison, creating an impression of the dreary light of a winter's morning, with the weather-vane turning on the roof. The most noticeable feature of this song is its use of dynamics, the score being full of crescendos and sudden diminuendos, like gusts of wind. There is a marvellous moment in bars 34 to 36, where the wind-theme is enriched contrapuntally. It is as though the wind were playing a game with itself.

Gefrorne Tränen	Frozen tears
Gefrorne Tropfen fallen	Frozen drops of water
Von meinen Wangen ab:	Fall from my cheeks:
Ob es mir denn entagangen,	I must have been weeping
Dass ich geweinet hab?	Without my noticing it.
Ei Tränen, meine Tränen,	Tears, oh my tears!
Und seid ihr gar so lau,	Can you be so lukewarm
Das ihr erstarrt zu Eise	That you turn to ice
Wie kühler Morgentau?	Like the cool morning dew?
Und dringt doch aus der Quelle	And yet you spring from a
Der Brust so glühend heiss,	Heart so hot with passion
Als wolltet ihr zerschmelzen	That it could melt
Des ganzen Winters Eis!	All the ice of winter!

This song of icy tears begins with a series of soft staccato chords, which must be played in strict time. You can almost hear the tears falling.

The tears are gradually exhausted, but the march rhythms continue throughout the piece. *Gefrorne Tränen* is a two-part *Wanderlied* in disguised form, the first part depicting the frozen exterior, and the second the anguish within. The anguish breaks through twice, in the form of a rising crescendo, expressing powerlessness and despair. These *forte* passages can sound rather too operatic if they do not develop naturally from what has gone before.

Erstarrung	Frozen to ice
Ich such im Schnee vergebens *Nach ihrer Tritte Spur,* *Wo sie an meinem Arme* *Durchstrich die grüne Flur*	I search the snow in vain For her footprints, Where we walked arm in arm Across the green meadows.
Ich will den Boden Küssen *Durchdringen Eis und Schnee* *Mit meinen heissen Tränen,* *Bis ich die Erde seh.*	I want to kiss the ground, And pierce the ice and snow With my scalding tears, Till I see the earth beneath.
Wo find ich eine Blüte, *Wo find ich grünes Grass?* *Die Blumen sind erstorben,* *Der Rasen sieht so blass.*	Where can I find a flower? Where can I find green grass? The flowers have faded, And the turf looks so pale.
Soll denn kein Angedenken *Ich nehmen mit von hier?* *Wenn meine Schmerzen schweigen,* *Wer sagt mir dann von ihr?*	Has she given me no keepsake To take away with me? Who will speak to me of her When the pain has gone away?
Mein Herz ist wie erstorben, *Kalt starrt ihr Bild darin;* *Schmilzt je das Herz mir wieder* *Fliesst auch ihr Bild dahin.*	My heart seems to have died, Her image is frozen within; If ever my heart thaws, then Her image will melt away too.

In *Erstarrung*, the air is once again chilled by a cold wind. The bass-line of the piano picks out the young woman's footprints. The triplets in the right hand must be played in strict time, like the quavers in the first song of the cycle. Schubert had originally intended to use a different melody for this poem, one of many changes he made during the composition of *Winterreise*.

The music is permeated with intense passion. Voice and piano weave in and out of each other as they move inexorably forward. For forty-six bars, the music modulates through a number of minor keys in a typically Schubertian manner, then moves unexpectedly into the major. The contrast between major and minor is as much part of Schubert as light and shade is of Rembrandt. The voice moves into the major on the words *Wo find ich eine Blüte* ('Where can I find a flower?'), and the tone-colour should reflect this change.

Der Lindenbaum	The Linden-tree
Am Brunnen vor dem Tore,	At the well beside the gate
Da steht ein Lindenbaum;	There stands a linden-tree;
Ich träumt in seinem Schatten	Many a sweet dream
So manchen süssen Traum.	I dreamt beneath its shade.
Ich schnitt in seine Rinde	Many a word of love
So manches liebe Wort;	I carved in its bark;
Es zog in Freud und Leide	I have always felt drawn to it,
Zu ihm mich immer fort.	Both in joy and in sorrow.
Ich musst auch heute wandern	Today I had to walk past it,
Vorbei in teifer Nacht,	This time at dead of night,
Da hab ich noch im Dunkel	Yet in spite of the darkness
Die Augen zugemacht.	I closed my eyes.
Und seine Zweige rauschten,	And its branches rustled
Als riefen sie mir zu:	As if to say to me,
Komm her zu mir, Geselle,	'Come here to me, my friend,
Hier findst du deine Ruh!	For here you will find rest.'
Die kalten Winde bliesen	The cold winds blew
Mir grad ins Angesicht,	Straight into my face,
Der Hut flog mir vom Kopfe,	And my hat flew off my head,
Ich wendete mich nicht.·	But I did not turn round.
Nun bin ich manche Stunde	I am now many hours' journey
Entfernt von jenem Ort,	Away from that place,
Und immer hör ich's rauschen:	But still I can hear it rustle,
Du fändest Ruhe dort!	'There you would find rest.'

Der Lindenbaum was the first song of the cycle to be written in the major. It is a precursor of *Frühlingstraum*, and its peaceful, horn-like melody is not at all typical of the cycle.

This song has often been oversentimentalised, but for many people, whether rightly or wrongly, it has come to epitomise German Lieder as a whole. *Vox populi vox Dei.* I hardly need to sing a bar to produce the same reaction all over the world, be it in the far north, in Europe or on an island, be it in Canada, Wisconsin or Texas: a joyful sigh comes up from the audience: 'At last!'

The piano score is full of fine details: the gentle modulation from major to minor; the bold harmonies which presage the cold winds and then slip away chromatically; the delightful interplay of the various triplet figures as they merge into one another. These triplets obscure the hymn-like quality of the E-major theme and distort the fine-drawn contours of the linden tree by the peaceful well, putting a question-mark over the pastoral idyll. In my view, the whole piece is summed up in a single line of the text: 'Here you will find rest.' This is ambiguous: does it mean a short rest or eternal peace? Behind the rustling tree there lurks the grave, and behind its beauty lurks the spectre of death.

The formal structure of this piece is incredibly complex for a song which at first sight resembles a simple, unsophisticated folk tune. Its structure is based on a form of medieval *Minnesang*, known as the bar form, which is not to be confused with the usual meaning of bar. *Der Lindenbaum* is in fact an example of a bar form which contains smaller bar forms within it. Wilhelm Müller's poem was not long enough for this, so the final verse had to be repeated.

The small letters below refer to the equivalent lines in the music score that follows:

Am Brunnen vor dem Tore
Da steht ein Lindenbaum;
Ich träumt' in seinem Schatten
So manchen süßen Traum.

Ich schnitt in seine Rinde
so manches liebe Wort;
es zog in Freud und Leide
zu ihm mich immer fort.

Ich mußt auch heute wandern
vorbei in tiefer Nacht,
da hab ich noch im Dunkel
die Augen zugemacht.

Und seine Zweige rauschten,
als riefen sie mir zu:
komm her zu mir Geselle,
hier findst du deine Ruh'!

Die kalten Winde bliesen
mir grad ins Angesicht,
der Hut flog mir vom Kopfe,
ich wendete mich nicht.

Nun bin ich manche Stunde
entfernt von jenem Ort,
und immer hör ich's rauschen:
du fändest Ruhe dort!

Nun bin ich manche Stunde
entfernt von jenem Ort,
und immer hör ich's rauschen:
du fändest Ruhe dort!
du fändest Ruhe dort!

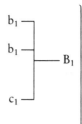
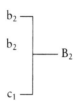

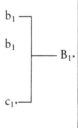

b_1 ⎤
b_1 ⎥— B_1
c_1 ⎦

b_2 ⎤
b_2 ⎥— B_2
c_1 ⎦

d_1 ⎤— C
d_2 ⎦

b_1 ⎤
b_1 ⎥— B_{1*}
c_{1*} ⎦

} REPRISENBAR

Der Lindenbaum.

1. Großstollen $b_1 + b_1 + c_1 = B_1$

b_1

Am Brunnen vor dem Thore, da steht ein Linden.baum; ich träumt' in seinem

b_1

Schatten so manchen süssen Traum, ich schnitt in sei.ne Rin.de so manches liebe

c_1

Wort, es zog in Freud' und Lei.de zu ihm mich immer fort.

2. Großstollen $b_2 + b_2 + c_1 = B_2$

b_2

Ich musst' auch heute wandern vorbei in tiefer Nacht, da

b_2

hab' ich noch im Dunkeln die Augen zugemacht. Und

c_1

seine Zweige rauschten, als riefen sie mir zu: komm' her zu mir, Ge

c_1 d_1

selle, hier find'st du deine Ruh. Die

Reprisenstollen $b_1 + b_1 + c_1{}^\cdot = B_1{}^\cdot$

Apart from a number of technical terms, the rest of the pages do not require translation. Here are the suggested translations for the technical terms involved:

REPRISENBAR—REPRISE BAR
Gross-stollen—Stollen
Grosser Abgesang—Abgesang
Reprisenstollen—Reprise

The main structure is in the form $B_1 + B_2 + C + B_1^*$ (=stollen+ stollen + abgesang + reprise).

—The first bar-form stanza (B_1) consists of $b_1 + b_1 + c_1$ (= stollen + stollen + abgesang).

—The second stanza (B_2) is in the form $b_2 + b_2 + c_1$.

—The abgesang (C) is in the form $d_1 + d_2$.

—The reprise (B_1^*) follows a slightly modified form of the first stanza: $b_1 + b_1 + c_1^*$.

The song should be performed in strict time, which means that the piano interludes must be played at the same speed as the voice sections. The same applies to the section in the minor.

The observant listener will be fascinated to note a subtle melodic resemblance to the medieval *Minnesang*, which tends further to reinforce the song's musical structure.

Wasserflut	Flood
Manche Trän' aus meinen Augen	Many a tear have I shed
Ist gefallen in den Schnee;	Into the snow;
Seine kalten Flocken saugen	The thirsty snowflakes
Durstig ein das heisse Weh.	Absorb my burning grief.
Wenn die Gräser sprossen wollen,	When the grass is about to grow,
Weht daher ein lauer Wind,	A warm wind blows,
Und das Eis zerspringt in Schollen,	The ice breaks apart,
Und der weiche Schnee zerrinnt.	And the soft snow melts away.
Schnee, du weisst von meinem Sehnen,	Snow, you know of my grief,
Sag, wohin doch geht dein Lauf?	But where are you going to?
Folge nach nur meinen Tränen,	If you follow my tears
Nimmt dich bald das Bächlein auf.	You will soon find the stream.

Wirst mit ihm die Stadt durchziehen,	It will carry you into the town,
Muntre Strassen ein und aus;	Through its lively streets;
Fühlst du meine Tränen glühen,	You will feel my hot tears
Da ist meiner Liebsten Haus.	As you pass the house where
	my loved-one lives.

Wasserflut is marked *langsam* ('slow'), but I prefer to sing it a little faster, as the piece has a tendency to drag. Although the harmonic progressions are relatively simple, the song has great emotional depth. The piano plays a kind of funeral march, while the voice swings wildly up and down, as though freed from earthly constraints.

Occasionally, one of the quaver-triplets in the voice-line coincides with the semi-quaver in the piano part, instead of forming a counter rhythm. This may be due to lax rhythm, but cannot always be avoided if the singer is to have free reign.

Auf dem Flusse	On the river
Der du so lustig rauschtest,	You clear rushing stream
Du heller, wilder Fluss,	That once ran so merrily—
Wie still bist du geworden,	How silent you have become!
Gibst keinen Scheidegruss!	You do not even bid farewell.
Mit harter, starrer Rinde	You have covered yourself
Hast du dich überdeckt,	With a hard, stiff crust,
Liegst kalt und unbeweglich	You lie cold and unyielding
Im Sande ausgestreckt.	Between long sandy banks.

In deine Decke grab ich	With a sharp stone
Mit einem spitzen Stein	I carve into your surface
Den Namen meiner Liebsten	The name of my sweetheart,
Und Stund und Tag hinein:	And the hour and the day:
Den Tag des ersten Grusses,	The day we first met,
Den Tag, an dem ich ging:	And the day I went away;
Um Nam' und Zahlen windet	A broken, twisted ring forms
Sich ein zerbrochner Ring.	About both name and figures.
Mein Herz, in diesem Bache	My heart, can you now see
Erkennst du nun dein Bild?	Your likeness in this stream?
Ob's unter seiner Rinde	Is there beneath its surface
Wohl auch so reissend schwillt?	A raging torrent just like this?

In contrast to the more passive introversion of *Wasserflut*, *Auf dem Flusse* is more typical of *Winterreise* as a whole, in the way the music again moves inexorably forward. The staccato chords in the piano introduction recall the 'frozen tears' motif in the earlier song of that name. So I take the quavers in *Auf dem Flusse* at the same speed as the crochets in *Gefrorne Tränen*. The song contains several rather abrupt modulations: from D minor to C sharp minor (as transposed in the baritone version) in bars 9, 18 and 45; then from D minor, via F major, to E minor in bars 54—58; finally from D minor to F minor in bar 64. They are nowadays considered typical of Schubert, particularly of his later works, but would have incurred the displeasure of more conservative listeners at the time. Schubert himself introduced an alternative G sharp on the second syllable of *Scheidegruss*, to make things easier for the singer. However, the alternative notes in the last two bars of the vocal line were a later editorial addition.

Here is yet another of my performer's secrets: take the greatest care to vary the tone-colour between the first two lines of the fourth stanza (bars 30—34). *Der Tag des ersten Grusses* ('The day we first met') is in the brighter key of D major, while *Der Tag, an dem ich ging* ('The day I went away') is in the darker key of D minor.

Leonard Hokanson is a wonderful colleague with considerable experience on the concert platform, but he is always annoyed by the expression 'piano *accompanist*'. I fully appreciate his feelings on this matter. It may be fitting in old Italian arias, and possibly even in Mozart, to speak of the keyboard-player as merely accompanying the singer. However, in Beethoven's *An die ferne Geliebte*, and in Schubert and Wolf, this can no longer be said to be the case. *Auf dem Flusse* is a prime example of this, and should put an end to the myth. The whole performance of this rather heavy-weight song will stand or fall by how well the pianist can master the bridge passage between the first and second parts. Everything depends on one apparently insignificant detail: the measurement of one and a half beats' silence, which must be of exactly the right length if the bridge passage is not to founder. It must fit precisely into the structure of the song: a task which lies solely with the pianist upon whose musical sense everything depends.

The bars immediately following the pause are equally significant. The performers' roles are reversed, the pianist taking over the main theme in the left hand while the singer accompanies him. The thematic development of the piece is very much enriched by this dialogue.

Rückblick

Es brennt mir unter beiden Sohlen,
Tret ich auch schon auf Eis und Schnee,
Ich möcht nicht wieder Atem holen,
Bis ich nicht mehr die Türme seh.

Hab mich an jeden Stein gestossen,
So eilt ich zu der Stadt hinaus;
Die Krähen warfen Bäll' und Schlossen
Auf meinen Hut von jedem Haus.

Wie anders hast du mich empfangen,
Du Stadt der Unbeständigkeit!
An deinen blanken Fenstern sangen
Die Lerch und Nachtigall im Streit.

Die runden Lindenbäume blühten,
Die klaren Rinnen rauschten hell,
Und ach, zwei Mädchenaugen glühten!
Da war's geschehen um dich, Gesell!

Kömmt mir der Tag in die Gedanken,
Möcht ich noch einmal rückwärts sehn,
Möcht ich zurücke wieder wanken,
Vor ihrem Hause stille stehen.

A backward glance

The soles of my feet seem to burn,
Though I am walking on ice and snow;
I cannot breathe again
Till the towers are out of sight.

I tripped on every stone
In my hurry to leave the town;
From every roof, the crows threw
Snow and hailstones on my hat.

How different was your welcome,
You fickle-minded town!
In front of your shiny windows,
Lark and nightingale vied in song.

The bushy lime-trees blossomed,
The merry streams ran clear,
Oh how brightly the girl's eyes shone!
But then you lost everything, my friend.

When I think of that day,
I wish I could look back,
I wish I could stagger back
And stand there in front of her house.

The dominant mood of *Rückblick* is one of anger. It thus

resembles *Der Jäger* ('The huntsman') in *Die schöne Müllerin.* Although it is not marked legato, the notes should not sound too disjointed. It is particularly important to avoid stressing too many syllables (*Es brennt mir unter beiden Sohlen*), as the vocal line forms a single phrase from *Es* to *Schnee.* It is interesting to note the contrast between the minor section, where the voice runs through the phrase so fiercely that the listener cannot tell where the bar-lines are,

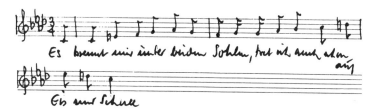

and the more reflective major section, where the melodic line is more obviously in three-four time.

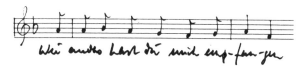

I take the tempo from the beginning of this major section: *Wie anders hast du mich empfangen.* In spite of the many fast notes in the piano part, I am careful not to hurry.

                          Irrlicht

    In die tiefsten Felsengründe
    Lockte mich ein Irrlicht hin:
    Wie ich einen Ausgang finde,
    Liegt nicht schwer mir in dem Sinn.

    Bin gewohnt das Irregehen,
    'S führt ja jeder Weg zum Ziel:
    Unsre Freuden, unsre Leiden,
    Alles eines Irrlichts Spiel!

Durch des Bergstrom's trockne Rinnen
Wind' ich ruhig mich hinab;
Jeder Strom wird's Meer gewinnen,
Alles Leiden auch sein Grab.

Will-o'-the-wisp

A will-o'-the-wisp lured me
Deep into the mountains;
I am not greatly worried
About finding a way out.

I am used to going astray;
Every way leads to my goal;
All our joys and our sorrows
Are a mere will-o'-the-wisp's game.

I calmly weave my way along
The dry bed of a mountain stream;
Every stream will reach the sea,
And every sorrow will pass.

This song requires perfect *mezza voce* technique. Later composers, such as Berlioz or Debussy, would have merely left the will-o'-the-wisp to waver and flicker. Schubert, however, begins by drawing the wanderer's steps as it leads him deep into the mountains.

In the voice-line the various dotted notes must be clearly differentiated, giving the exact value to both semi-quavers and demi-semi-quavers. The melody will otherwise become distorted.

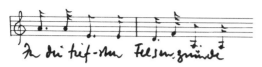

It is marvellous how the composer expands the will-o'-the-wisp motif.

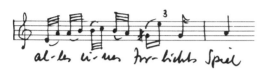

It begins as a mere ray of light, then is unexpectedly transformed into a gushing river on its way to the sea.

In bars 23 and 25, there is a marvellous example of a German consonant cluster. The words *Irrlichts Spiel* contain six consecutive consonants: 'CHTSSP'. Even more than that, the singer must somehow accommodate them over a bar-line following a demi-semi-quaver, which is a wonderful exercise in diction.

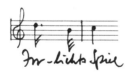

Rast

Nun merk ich erst wie müd ich bin,
Da ich zur Ruh mich lege;
Das Wandern hielt mich munter hin
Auf unwirtbarem Wege.

Die Füsse frugen nicht nach Rast,
Es war zu kalt zum Stehen;

Der Rücken fühlte keine Last,
Der Sturm half fort mich wehen.

In eines Köhlers engem Haus
Hab Obdach ich gefunden;
Doch meine Glieder ruhn nicht aus,
So brennen ihre Wunden.

Auch du, mein Herz, in Kampf und Sturm
So wild und so verwegen,
Fühlst in der Still' erst deinen Wurm
Mit heissem Stich sich regen!

Rest

Only when I lie down to rest
Do I realise how tired I am;
The walking kept me going
Along this desolate path.

My feet did not want to rest,
And it was too cold to stand still;
My back felt no burden,
And the storm drove me on.

I have found shelter
In a charcoal-burner's hut;
But my limbs cannot rest
With the stinging of their wounds.

My heart, you are so wild and bold
In battle and storm;
Only now in the silence can you feel your serpent
Stir with its venomous fangs!

Rast contains at least one motif from the previous song.

For me it is a song full of reminiscences. Even the crochet

rhythms in the piano introduction are to me a reminder of the previous day. The speed is again moderato, and the walking rhythm is one which permeates the whole work. The beginning of *Rast* is like the echo of a heavy day's walking, as the wanderer lies down exhausted in the charcoal-burner's house, and broods upon his experiences.

This also anticipates another walking motif in *Frühlingstraum*, the song which immediately follows.

Frühlingstraum

Ich träumte von bunten Blumen,
So wie sie wohl blühen im Mai;
Ich träumte von grünen Wiesen,
Von lustigem Vogelgeschrei.

Und als die Hähne krähten,
Da ward mein Auge wach;
Da war es kalt und finster,
Es schrieen die Raben vom Dach.

Doch an den Fensterscheiben,
Wer malte die Blätter da?
Ihr lach wohl uber den Träumer,
Der Blumen im Winter sah?

Ich träumte von Lieb um Liebe,
Von einer schönen Maid,
Von Herzen und von Küssen,
Von Wonne und Seligkeit.

Und als die Hähne krähten,
Da ward mein Herze wach;
Nun sitz ich hier alleine
Und denke dem Traume nach.

Die Augen schliess ich wieder,
Noch schlägt das Herz so warm.
Wann grünt ihr Blätter am Fenster?
Wann halt ich mein Liebchen im arm?

Dream of spring

I dreamt of bright flowers
As they blossom in May;
I dreamt of green meadows
And of merry bird-song.

But when the cocks crowed,
Then my eyes were opened;
It was cold and dark,
And the ravens cried from the rooftops.

But who had painted those leaves
On the window-panes?
Do you laugh at the dreamer
Who saw flowers in winter?

I dreamt of love again,
Of a beautiful girl,
Of hugging and kissing,
And of joy and happiness.

But when the cocks crowed,
Then my heart awoke;
Now I sit here alone,
Thinking about my dream.

Again I close my eyes;
My heart still beats so fast.

When will the leaves on the window grow green?
When shall I embrace my sweetheart again?

Every song in this cycle begins with a piano introduction, as do practically all Schubert's songs. It is as though the piano were laying out a carpet, upon which the drama is to be enacted. There cannot be an introduction more delightful than these four opening bars of *Frühlingstraum*. This dance-like tune in six-eight time is charming in its simplicity, and might almost have been written for a chamber work. The broken chords, first in the left hand and then in the right, add a suggestion of the broken-hearted love which underlies the song.

From the point of view of interpretation, *Frühlingstraum* is one of the most difficult songs in the whole cycle. Schubert requires the singer to reflect three completely contrasting moods in direct proximity to one another. The first stanza must be sung in a gentle, caressing voice, which suddenly dissolves into a dramatic recitative, rising to a climax in the space of six bars. The next change is equally abrupt: in the section about the leaves on the icy window-pane, the voice must sound disembodied and unearthly. The transition from the second to the third stanza is thus extremely difficult to achieve. Having just reached a fortissimo to give a ghastly impression of squawking ravens, the singer must immediately turn in on himself, quickly reducing both volume and tone to produce a deathly pianissimo. At this point, less experienced singers often find that their voices literally stick in their throats.

Einsamkeit	Loneliness
Wie eine trübe Wolke	As a dark cloud moves
Durch heitre Lüfte geht,	Across clear blue skies,
Wenn in der Tanne Wipfel	When a feeble breath of air
Ein mattes Lüftchen weht:	Goes through the fir-tops,
So zieh ich meine Strasse	So I go on my way,
Dahin mit trägem Fuss,	With dragging steps,
Durch helles, frohes Leben	Through a happy, joyful world,
Einsam und ohne Gruss.	Lonely and rejected.

Ach, dass die Luft so ruhig!   Alas, that the air should be so calm!
Ach, dass die Welt so licht!   And the world so bright!
Als noch die Stürme tobten,   I was never so wretched as now,
War ich so elend nicht.   Even while the storms were still
                                    raging.

Schubert's original manuscript was slightly different from the later printed version. On the word *Wolke* in the very first line, Schubert originally wrote a top D.

(Original key: D minor)

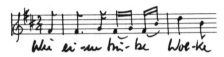

He eventually changed this to a C sharp, which very much accentuates the terrible feeling of loneliness.

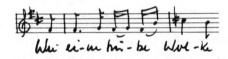

The song contains a wealth of fine modulations within a very short space of time. Note the harmonic changes he makes when repeating the last stanza: this is the first time he uses the dominant chord of F sharp [see (a) in the first example], while the repeat is on the tonic chord of B [(b) in example 2].

1.

2.

Note also how the tremolo in the repeat [(c) in example 2] is pitched a whole tone lower, making the 'bright world' seem more distant than ever.

Die Post

Von der Strasse her ein Posthorn klingt.
Was hat es, dass es so hoch aufspringt, mein Herz?

Die Post bringt keinen Brief für dich.
Was drängst du dich so wunderlich, mein Herz?

Nun ja, die Post kommt aus der Stadt,
Wo ich ein liebes Liebchen hatt', mein Herz!

Willst wohl einmal hinüber sehn
Und fragen, wie es dort mag gehn, mein Herz?

The post

From the road the sound of a posthorn is heard.
Why do you leap so wildly, my heart?

The post is bringing no letter for you.
Why do you patter so strangely, my heart?

Of course! The post comes from the town
Where I once had a sweetheart so dear, my heart!

Do you just want to look over
And ask how things are in the town, my heart?

Schubert wrote the first twelve songs of *Winterreise* in March
1827. *Die Post* begins the second half of the cycle, which was
composed in the November of the same year. *Die Post* is the only
song in the cycle to be infused with any real optimism. A mail-
coach rolls by: the listener must decide for himself whether it is
in the distance or on the same road as the wanderer himself. The
music is full of the vigour of the horses, and the *joie de vivre* of the
postilion as his horn echoes through the countryside, so that
even the wanderer is filled with fresh hope. Once the sound has
died away and the coach is out of sight, the cheerful image
dissolves into nothing. Only the wanderer's footsteps are left as a
faint reminder of the galloping horse.

It is marvellous how the horn motif is transformed into the
clatter of hoofs, while the voice-line imitates the horn with its
arpeggio figures to support the narrative. As the wanderer
questions his heart, the piece moves into the minor and often

tends to get a little slower. Such a change of tempo is not justified in my opinion. The music presses continually forward like the wanderer's heartbeat. Note how the bass-line rises as it returns to the major.

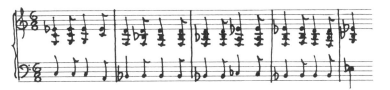

The second stanza shows a general harmonic progression from the minor to the major.

There is a particularly difficult moment where the voice moves up to a top F (a top A flat in the tenor version) in the middle of the 'e' of *Herz*. There are two possible pitfalls here. It is easy to distort the vowel, making it sound rather like 'hurts'. And you must avoid a certain nasty habit, which I like to call the 'H-risk factor'. It consists of an almost inaudible 'H', which is interpolated to make the high note easier and more controlled. It is both ineffective and annoying to the listener.

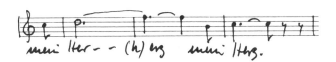

A singer often does not realise he is doing this until some understanding friend points it out to him.

Der greise Kopf

Der Reif hat einen weissen Schein mir übers Haar gestreuet;
Da glaubt ich schon ein Greis zu sein und hab mich sehr gefreuet.
Doch bald ist er hinweg getaut, hab wieder schwarze Haare,
Dass mir's vor meiner Jugend graut—wie weit noch bis zur Bahre!
Vom Abendrot zum Morgenlicht ward mancher Kopf zum Greise.
Wer glaubt's? Und meiner ward es nicht auf dieser ganzen Reise!

The hoary head

The frost has spread a white sheen across my hair;
I thought I must have grown old and was very pleased.
But soon it melted away, and my hair turned black again.
How I shudder to realise how young I am—how far it is to the grave!
Many a head has turned white between sunset and dawn.
Who can believe it? Mine has stayed the same throughout this journey!

This song is in many ways similar to *Irrlicht*. The opening bars of
their respective voice-parts show many rhythmic similarities.
However, in *Irrlicht* the melody moves down and then up, while
in *Der greise Kopf* it does quite the opposite, surging upwards in a
wide sweep and then returning. Schubert limits himself to the
most elementary tools of his trade. He eschews beauty, apart
from one exception, by concentrating on economy and brittle-
ness of sound, and creates an impression of cold unfriendliness
by means of continually plunging melodic lines. Sometimes the
piano merely accompanies the recitative, while at other times it
repeats the voice-line as if to emphasise what the wanderer is
saying.

   This song seems to throw out shadows into the future. On the
line *wie weit noch bis zum Bahre!* ('how far it is to the grave!') we
can almost imagine the reddish tip of Wotan's spear as it peeps
over the horizon. The song is full of cold charm, harsh intervals
and intense chromaticism, which to some extent reminds us of
Wolf. Schubert avoids even the faintest suggestion of warmth.
Only when the wanderer thinks he is growing old does he feel
any joy. We can discern a small crack in the ice, where longing
and desire creep through.

Robert Schumann must have unconsciously been thinking of this phrase when he once copied it almost note for note.

(Original in G major)

This is from his *Dichterliebe—Wenn ich in deine Augen seh* ('When I look into your eyes').

Die Krähe	The crow
Eine Krähe war mit mir	A crow had followed me
Aus der Stadt gezogen,	Out of the town,
Ist bis heute für und für	And would not stop flying
Um mein Haupt geflogen.	Around my head until today.
Krähe, wunderliches Tier,	Crow, you strange creature!
Willst mich nicht verlassen?	Will you not leave me?
Meinst wohl bald als Beute hier	Or will you soon want
Meinen Leib zu fassen?	To take my body as prey?
Nun, es wird nicht weit mehr gehn	Well, I shall not be
An dem Wanderstabe.	Travelling very much farther.
Krähe, lass mich endlich sehn	Crow, at last you can show me
Treue bis zum Grabe!	Faithfulness unto death!

Concert managers always prefer songs which in their view are easy to listen to. This could not be said of either *Der greise Kopf*, nor of *Letzte Hoffnung*, the song which follows this one. However, with *Die Krähe* it is quite another matter. Even the tune in the piano introduction, with its suggestion of a circling crow, is easily assimilated and impossible to forget. It might almost be said to be ready to take home. I sing this song legato, with plenty of light and air, and just a touch of irony. Although a lot happens in the song, I try to avoid being over-dramatic, and take care not to overlook the broken chords in the descant of the piano. These notes sound rather like wingbeats, and show a considerable resemblance to late Beethoven.

Letzte Hoffnung	Last hope
Hie und da ist an den Bäumen	Here and there on the trees
Manches bunte Blatt zu sehn,	A coloured leaf can be seen;
Und ich bleibe vor den Bäumen	I often stand in thought
Oftmals in Gedanken stehen.	In front of the trees.
Schaue nach dem einen Blatte,	I look at the one remaining leaf
Hänge meine Hoffnung dran;	And hang all my hope on it;
Spielt der Wind mit meinem Blatte,	If the wind plays with my leaf
Zittr' ich, was ich zittern kann.	I tremble all over.
Ach, und fällt das Blatt zu Boden,	And if the leaf falls to the ground
Fällt mit ihm die Hoffnung ab,	My hope falls with it;
Fall ich selber mit zu Boden,	I fall to the ground myself,
Wein auf meiner Hoffnung Grab.	And weep on the grave of my hope.

Letzte Hoffnung is surprisingly avant-garde, and a long way from the early romantic, or even from Biedermeier. Harmonies are often only hinted at, do not always belong to a particular key and are sometimes of uncertain duration. Thus it is not easy for the concert-goer to get used to this song. The vocal line is completely independent of the piano—another Wolf-like feature. The singer seems not to pay the slightest attention to what the pianist is doing, and goes on his own sweet way, freely improvising and apparently ignoring the dissonances which arise.

Every bar has some surprise in store. It is amazing how Schubert combines the various contrasting elements and fuses them into a perfect whole: the first part sounds like an improvisation; the second part gives a vivid impression of the wanderer's trembling, which is interrupted by a sudden dramatic climax, leading eventually to a soft and melancholy concluding passage. Together with *Die Stadt* and *Der Doppelgänger* from the *Schwanengesang, Letzte Hoffnung* is one of Schubert's most modern-sounding compositions.

Im Dorfe

Es bellen die Hunde, es rasseln die Ketten;
Es schlafen die Menschen in ihren Betten,
Träumen sich manches, was sie nicht haben,
Tun sich im Guten und Argen erlaben;
Und morgen früh ist alles zerflossen.
Je nun, sie haben ihr Teil genossen,
Und hoffen, was sie noch übrig liessen,
Doch wieder zu finden auf ihren Kissen.

Bellt mich nur fort, ihr wachen Hunde,
Lasst mich nicht ruhn in der Schlummerstunde!
Ich bin zu Ende mit allen Träumen,
Was will ich unter den Schläfern säumen?

In the village

The dogs are barking and rattling their chains;
The people are asleep in their beds,
Dreaming of what they do not possess,
Refreshing themselves in good and bad ways;
And by morning all of it has slipped away.
Ah well, they have enjoyed their share of life,
And hope to find in their dreams
All the things they still want to have.

Just bark and drive me away, you watchful dogs!
Give me no rest at this time of sleep!
For I have finished with dreams for good,
So why should I linger amongst those who are sleeping?

I was once rehearsing *Winterreise* in a private house in

Leverkusen with a boxer dog lying nearby. Unobserved, he dozed on gently through the squawking ravens and the loud bass-notes on the piano, without so much as cocking an ear or opening his mouth, until we came to *Im Dorfe*. Then, as I began quietly to sing about the dogs on their chains, he opened one eye and peered at me questioningly, and went back to sleep again. Later, as I came to the line *Bellt mich nur fort, ihr wachen Hunde* ('Just bark and drive me away, you watchful dogs'), the eye quickly opened again. I was very amused by this, and I can never sing these lines without thinking of that dog.

The piano gives a gentle growling noise, which is basically no more than a collection of simple chords which accompany the voice. The voice part is equally subtle, being no more conspicuous than the villagers asleep in their beds.

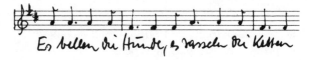

This motif is almost identical to that of the posthorn.

But in this song it suggests monotony, habit and indifference. On the second line, the voice suddenly leaps a sixth, and then a seventh, from its well-worn track. The effect is shattering. Now sleep has become threatening, and oblivion is dangerous, even criminal. Note the short crescendos.

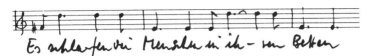

The middle section is ironic and at times almost spiteful in tone: *Je nun, sie haben ihr Teil genossen...* The words *Je nun, je nun* ('Ah well) remind us of the fraught silences of *Einsamkeit*.

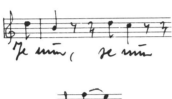

(compare the first example on pages 124/125.)

Der stürmische Morgen	The stormy morning
Wie hat der Sturm zerrissen	How the storm has torn
Des Himmels graues Kleid!	The heaven's cloak in two!
Die Wolkenfetzen flattern	The ragged clouds flutter
Umher in mattem Streit.	About in a feeble battle.
Und rote Feuerflammen	And red flames
Ziehn zwischen ihnen hin:	Leap around amongst them;
Das nenn ich einen Morgen	I call this a morning
So recht nach meinem Sinn!	After my own heart!
Mein Herz sieht an dem Himmel	My heart can see its likeness
Gemalt sein eignes Bild—	Painted in the sky—
Es ist nichts als der Winter,	It is nothing but winter,
Der Winter kalt und wild!	Cold, savage winter!

This song is to be sung loudly, but not with the healthy vigour of Brahms' *Der Schmied* ('The blacksmith'). It does not drive the wanderer forward, if anything it holds him back, as he bitterly bemoans his fate. The mood is one of anger and resentment, which comes especially to the fore in the words *Das nenn ich einen*

Morgen nach meinem Sinn ('I call this a morning after my own heart').

The song is barely forty-five seconds long—no more than a couple of angry brush-marks on a canvas. The rhythmic structure is primitive, though not in the derogatory sense. Melody takes second place, as a single rhythm is repeated five times with ever more punishing insistence:

The song goes past like a gust of wind, though it should not be sung *too* fast.

Täuschung

Ein Licht tanzt freundlich vor mir her,
Ich folg ihm nach die Kreuz und Quer;
Ich folg ihm gern und seh's ihm an,
Dass es verlockt den Wandersmann.
Ach! Wer wie ich so elend ist,
Gibt gern sich hin der bunten List,
Die hinter Eis und Nacht und Graus
Ihm weist ein helles, warmes Haus
Und eine liebe Seele drin—
Nur Täuschung ist für mich Gewinn!

Delusion

A friendly light dances before me,
And I follow its zig-zag course;
I am glad to follow it, and to note
That it is luring me away from my path.
Oh! Anyone as wretched as I
Would gladly give in to this trick of light;
For beyond the ice, and the darkness and dread,
It shows him a bright, warm house,
And a dear sweet soul within—
But my only gain would be a delusion.

In contrast to the previous song, the beginning of *Täuschung* sounds like a *moment musical*. Melody rules again, while the piano merely provides the harmonic basis, occasionally adding some counterpoint, a small comment of its own, or an echo. The whole song follows a gentle six-eight siciliano rhythm.

The song is thus closely allied to *Das Fischermädchen* from Schubert's *Schwanengesang* cycle.

There is a marvellous unity between the words and the music, as though they had both been cast in the same mould. They could almost have been written simultaneously. Schubert must have written the song on the inspiration of the moment. A particularly stunning feature is the lead into the reprise: *ihm weist en helles, warmes Haus*. The melody moves faultlessly into the reprise in a way which seems totally natural.

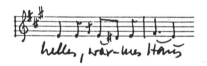

The melody at this point creates some interesting phrasing problems. From a structural point of view, it would appear most logical to end the phrase after the word *Graus*. This would, however, divide the reprise from what has gone before, thus spoiling the flow of the music.

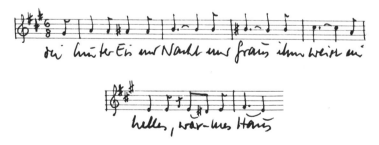

Following my own instincts, I prefer to phrase this differently, by finishing the previous phrase on the word *Nacht*, and linking the B sharp on *Graus* to the B sharp and C sharp of *ihm weist* by means of a small decrescendo.

The effect can be really delightful: the voice glides gently into the reprise, while the left hand of the piano resumes its bell-like staccato. Irwin Gage, who has accompanied me in many concerts, once told me that I myself had taught him the importance of all the small, insignificant features in the creation of a profound and thrilling performance. Perhaps he was thinking of just such a place as this.

The later songs in *Winterreise* are increasingly characterised by tautness and concentration, with persistent rhythmic patterns, as has already been demonstrated in *Der stürmische Morgen*. It is as though all external considerations had been rubbed away like tinsel, forcing the wanderer to look down into the depths of his soul.

Der Wegweiser	The signpost
Was vermeid ich denn die Wege,	Why do I avoid the roads
Wo die andern Wandrer gehn,	Which other travellers use,
Suche mir versteckte Stege	And seek out hidden paths
Durch verschneite Felsenhöhn?	Through snowbound fastnesses?
Habe ja doch nichts begangen,	I have committed no crime,
Dass ich Menschen sollte scheun,	So why should I avoid people?
Welch ein törichtes Verlangen	What is this foolish craving
Treibt mich in die Wüstenei'n?	Which drives me out into the
	wilderness?
Weiser stehen auf den Strassen,	There are signposts on the roads,
Weisen auf die Städte zu,	Which point towards the towns,
Und ich wandre sondermassen	And I wander ever onwards,
Ohne Ruh und suche Ruh.	Unresting, yet seeking rest.
Einen Weiser seh ich stehen	I see a signpost standing
Unverrückt vor meinem Blick;	Immovably before me;
Eine Strasse muss ich gehen,	I must travel a road
Die noch keiner ging zurück.	By which no one has ever returned.

The basic rhythm of *Der Wegweiser*

recalls a melodic figure from *Gute Nacht*.

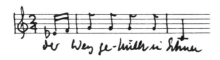

These hammered quavers are characteristic of so many of the songs in the cycle. At the point where the wanderer declares his innocence (*Habe ja doch nichts begangen*...), Schubert moves suddenly into the major, to extraordinary effect. The interpreter's main task is to use such musical devices as effectively as possible to bring the music home to the listener. For example, the singer must emphasise the contrasts by varying the tone-colour, accentuating all rhythmic features, and carefully regulating the dynamics. I employ all three techniques in the example which follows. On the words *verschneite Felsenhöhn* ('snowbound fastnesses'), I darken the tone-colour, accentuate the dotted rhythms and swell the volume at the same time. After the pause I create a contrast by singing in a bright legato, keeping the volume at a steady piano.

darkly

brightly

This could be shown in a diagram, thus:

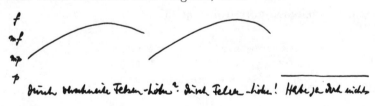

The *abgesang* begins on the words *Einen Weiser seh ich stehen ünverruckt vor meinem Blick*. These ten bars consist of a rhythmic figure which rises step-wise in thirds, with a gradual crescendo from pianissimo to forte followed by a sudden diminuendo. This could be described technically as a massive *messa di voce*.

These examples show how important voice-technique is to the performance of a song. Technique is one of the singer's tools, and must be under his control before he can venture to interpret Lieder. It is, however, not enough on its own. Only when the singer has made the song into an expression of himself, when its meaning is made manifest through him, can the song become a whole entity. Technique is then no longer a secondary element, but an integral part of the whole. The last stanza of *Der Wegweiser* is a particularly stringent test of the singer's art, especially the final whispered bars.

There are only seven notes, but what difficult notes they are! The singer must ensure that the tempo remains constant throughout these bars, as the *ritardando* has already been written into the music.

The final pianissimo should be sung in a toneless, disembodied voice, and is similar in this respect to the end of *Erlkönig: In seinen Armen das Kind... war tot* ('In his arms the child... was dead').

Das Wirtshaus	The inn
Auf einen Totenacker	My journey has now led me
Hat mich mein Weg gebracht.	To a cemetery.
Allhier will ich einkehren,	I thought to myself,
Hab ich bei mir gedacht.	I will stay the night here.

Ihr grünen Totenkränze	Those green wreaths
Könnt wohl die Zeichen sein,	Could well be the inn-signs
Die müde Wandrer laden	That invite weary travellers
Ins kühle Wirtshaus ein.	To come into the cool inn.
Sind denn in diesem Hause	But are the rooms all taken
Die Kammern all besetzt?	In this inn?
Bin matt zum Niedersinken,	I am so weary I must lie down,
Bin tödlich schwer verletzt.	And I am mortally wounded.
O unbarmherz'ge Schenke,	You cruel inn!
Doch weisest du mich ab?	Do you still turn me away?
Nun weiter dann, nur weiter,	Then onward, ever onward,
Mein treuer Wanderstab!	My trusty staff!

If the piano introduction of *Das Wirtshaus* is transposed into B flat major, it sounds exactly like a passage from Schubert's posthumous piano sonata in B flat major. There is a sudden jump from the dominant chord of the relative minor to the dominant of the original key, thus leading into the beginning of the voice-line.

It is as though Schubert were saying to us, 'I could in fact make a sonata out of this theme, but I won't, because I want to write a song.' In the midst of all the appalling tragedy, we can glimpse the humorous side of Schubert's character.

The chief rhythmic element of *Das Wirtshaus* also reminds us of an earlier song.

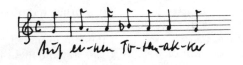

Rast

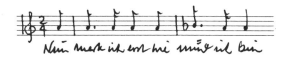

The song remains piano or pianissimo throughout, apart from one or two brief crescendos which return immediately to piano. The song must therefore be sung quietly and straightforwardly like a chorale. Thrasybulos G. Georgiades, a leading expert on Schubert's music, notes that this song has several formal and melodic affinities with the *Kyrie* from the Gregorian Requiem. Schubert may well have been thinking of his early experiences as a choirboy when he wrote *Das Wirtshaus*.

Mut	Courage
Fleigt der Schnee mir ins Gesicht,	If the snow blows in my face
Schüttl' ich ihn herunter.	I shake it off.
Wenn mein Herz im Busen spricht,	If my heart cries from my bosom
Sing ich hell und munter;	I sing brightly and merrily;
Höre nicht, was es mir sagt,	I have no ears to hear
Habe keine Ohren,	What it is telling me,
Fühle nicht, was es mir klagt,	And I ignore its complaints,
Klagen ist fur Toren.	For only fools complain.
Lustig in die Welt hinein	So gaily on into the world,
Gegen Wind und Wetter!	Braving wind and weather!
Will kein Gott auf Erden sein,	If there is no God on earth
Sind wir selber Götter!	We must be our own gods!

This lively song is full of repressed energy, and the first part must be sung quietly. Much has been said regarding its position towards the end of the cycle. Its boisterous tone forms a marked contrast, both to *Der Wegweiser* and *Das Wirtshaus* which precede it, and to *Die Nebensonnen* and *Der Leiermann* which follow. It might, for example, be considered more appropriate to insert it between *Die Post* and *Einsamkeit*. I personally think not. *Einsamkeit* speaks of a bright and peaceful world, whereas *Mut* speaks of snow being blown into the wanderer's face. Should it perhaps go between *Die Krähe* and *Letzte Hoffnung*? That would certainly be a possibility, but Schubert did not want that.

I have kept the song where it is, attempting to fit it meaningfully into the dramatic structure of the cycle. The wanderer raises his spirits for the very last time, like a coal which shifts in the fire before disintegrating into ashes. The music exudes all the spite and rebellion of an 'angry young man'. The mood is one of 'you can all take me as you find me', and is typical of late Schubert. Compare the middle section of his E Flat Major Impromptu (Opus 90), which was written in the same year as *Winterreise*.

Die Nebensonnen

Drei Sonnen sah ich am Himmel stehn,
Hab lang und fest sie angesehen;
Und sie auch standen da so stier,
Als wollten sie nicht weg von mir.
Ach, meine Sonnen seid ihr nicht!
Schaut andern doch ins Angesicht!
Ja, neulich hatt' ich auch wohl drei,
Nun sind hinab die besten zwei.
Ging nur die dritt' erst hinterdrein!
Im Dunkeln wird mir wohler sein.

The phantom suns

I could see three suns in the sky,
And stared at them for some time;
But they stuck there so rigidly
That it seemed they would not leave me.
You are not *my* suns!
Go and look into other people's faces!
A moment ago there were three of them;
Now the best two have gone down.
If only the third would follow them!
I shall feel better in the dark.

Die Nebensonnen seems almost irridescent in comparison to the incisiveness of the previous song. There could be no greater contrast than this sudden drop in volume and pitch. The melody is dominated by the same obsessive rhythmic motif which runs through the whole cycle:

This ostinato is repeated no less than twenty-nine times in the space of thirty-two bars, while the wanderer's thoughts move round in small circles within a range of a minor sixth. He is only a shadow of his former self.

And what is the meaning of these two phantom suns which stare fixedly at him and will not leave him alone? Can they be explained rationally? Or is he being persecuted by the eyes of his beloved, like a pair of blue eyes in Mahler's youthful work, *Lieder eines fahrenden Gesellen* ('Songs of a Wayfarer')? And what about the third sun, which he so much wants to leave him in darkness? Müller's words could have a whole variety of meanings, and yet the more deeply one analyses them, the further one seems to be from finding any real meaning. The whole cycle is full of mysteries, and I think this is how Müller and Schubert intended it. So I avoid any rational explanations, and prefer to rely on my own feelings and intuitions.

Der Leiermann	The organ-grinder
Drüben hinterm Dorfe	Out there beyond the village
Steht ein Leiermann,	Stands an organ-grinder,
Und mit starren Fingern	Grinding away as best he can
Dreht er, was er kann.	With frozen fingers.
Barfuss auf dem Eise	Barefoot, he staggers
Wankt er hin und her,	To and fro across the ice,
Und sein kleiner Teller	And his little plate
Bleibt ihm immer leer.	Remains for ever empty.
Keiner mag ihn hören,	No one wants to hear him,
Keiner sieht ihn an,	Or even to look at him,
Und die Hunde knurren	And the dogs growl
Um den alten Mann.	Around the old man.

Und er lässt es gehen	But he lets them all do
Alles, wie es will,	Just as they like,
Dreht, und seine Leier	And keeps turning the handle
Steht ihm nimmer still.	So that the organ never stops.
Wunderlicher Alter,	You strange old man!
Soll ich mit dir gehn?	Shall I go with you?
Willst du meinen Liedern	Will you grind your organ
Deine Leier drehen?	To my songs?

The appearance of the organ-grinder is no less puzzling than the strange suns. Our hero has so far only spoken to dogs, birds, rivers and inns, and it is not until eight bars before the end of the cycle that he utters a single word to any human being. When he does so, it is in the strangest manner imaginable, musically or vocally speaking. Indeed, it is a most peculiar piece of music altogether.

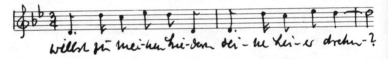

The barrel-organ repeats its little tune after every eleventh syllable with the persistent regularity of a pendulum. It seems as though it will never stop. The final tonic chord seems totally out of place, as though it were deliberately interrupting this never-ending tune. Underneath all this, the left hand of the piano keeps up its unending drone of bare fifths. The air is full of decay, for the wanderer has now entered the world of phantoms.

The poet of Winterreise

Let us now consider the man who inspired Schubert to create such apocalyptic music. Wilhelm Müller was born in Dessau on 7th October 1794, two years after Schubert, and died on 30th September 1827, the year in which *Winterreise* was composed. Both came from relatively poor backgrounds, Müller being the one surviving son of a master tailor, and Schubert the twelfth

child of a Viennese teacher. Both lost their mothers at a fairly
young age, Müller at twelve and Schubert at fifteen. Schubert's
father remained poor, though Müller's father went on to marry
a rich widow.

Both of them entered the same profession, that of school-
master. Schubert did this in order to avoid being called up, as
teachers were in short supply in Austria and therefore exempt
from military service. Müller became a teacher because there
was no other way for a philologist to earn a living. The parallels
end at this point.

Having such a rich stepmother meant that Müller was able to
go to college, and he matriculated at Berlin University in 1812.
He wanted to study philology, and even had a personal
reference from Schleiermacher himself. Only a year later,
however, he volunteered for the Prussian army, and took part in
two of the battles of the Napoleonic Wars: those of Bautzen and
Nollendorf-Kulm. Admittedly, he hardly ever fought on the
front line, preferring to remain in the relative safety of battle-
command. In 1815, when Prussia attacked Napoleon a second
time, he decided to stay in Berlin, where he resumed his studies
in the same year. He concentrated mainly on Middle-High-
German texts, and was particularly inspired by the German
Minnesang. But at this stage he had no intention of writing verse,
let alone that it should be set to music by that greatest of all
Lieder composers. In fact he never knew of the connection, as
the two men never actually met.

Following the example of Grimm, he devoted himself to
linguistic research, which was thought to reflect his keen
patriotism. At the same time, he joined with a number of young
friends from university and army days in forming an association
of poets. The group also included Wilhelm Hensel, who was
later to marry Felix Mendelssohn's sister, Fanny von Mendelssohn. Wilhelm Müller became secretary of the association.
Literary circles were very much in vogue in Berlin at this time,
all with a strong bias against the French and towards German
unity. Müller quickly found his way into these circles, where he
got to know Freiherr de la Motte Fouqué, author of *Undine*, parts
of which Schubert also set to music. He became a friend of

Gustav Schwab, translator of *Sagen des klassischen Altertums* ('Tales from the Ancient Classics'). Moreover, he found what he had most need of: a generous benefactor.

Müller's first claim to fame was his translation of Marlowe's *Doctor Faustus* in 1818, for which Achim von Arnim wrote the preface. At the age of twenty-five, he was sent by the Berlin Academy on a scientific expedition to Greece and Egypt. He went with Baron Sack, and was supposed to report back on works of art, collect inscriptions and acquire treasures for the government. However, he managed to talk the Baron into making a detour via Italy, where he went his own separate way. He found a noble benefactor to support him and spent his time in Rome, Naples, Perugia and Florence. He managed to get to know a number of important people, not the least of whom was Friedrich Rückert, with whom he went on a number of mountain hikes.

Rückert in fact owed his life to Müller, as was later described by his son, Friedrich Max Müller:

'In 1845 I learnt Persian from Rückert, who told me of how my father had once saved his life. They had been hiking together, and arrived at a rather run-down hostelry which was plagued with vermin. The following day they tried to rid themselves of these pests by jumping into a nearby lake. It was deeper than they had expected, and Rückert could not swim. He had very nearly drowned by the time my father got him to the shore. Rückert told me that after that he had written his first epic poem, and had called it *Die Lausiade* ("The Louse-iad").'

On his return to Germany, Müller continued to enthuse about freedom movements and German unity. These ideals were purely theoretical, and did not exactly correspond to those of the reigning monarch, Kaiser Friedrich III of Prussia. There were rumours to the effect that these poets' clubs might appear on the surface to be dedicated to the promotion of literature, but were in actual fact committed to subversion and the eventual downfall of the government. We shall never know for sure whether or not Müller belonged to such an organisation. He did come under official suspicion, but managed to protect himself sufficiently to evade the spate of arrests which ensued.

13.   Günther Rennert has presided over the most important developments of my career. Here
we are singing a duet from Gluck's opera *Orpheus and Eurydice* for his 1967 Munich production.

14. Claudio Abbado became a star overnight, following his Salzburg debut in 1968.

15. Joseph Keilberth was a great conductor of singers.

16. Karl Richter died tragically early in 1980. I have given many concerts with his world-famous choir, including this one in the beautiful church at Diessen am Ammersee.

17.   Karl Böhm was one of the greatest conductors of our time. Formerly conductor of the Dresden Opera, he went on to conduct the Vienna Opera. Here we are rehearsing *Cosí fan tutte* for the 1974 Salzburg production.

18.   With Leonard Bernstein. I am not telling him off. It is merely a lively discussion during a performance of Mahler's 8th Symphony in Vienna in 1975.

19.   Mozart's *Magic Flute* at the New York Met in 1967, with Marc Chagall as stage designer—my greatest American triumph. Pilar Lorengar is standing beside me.

20.   A Schuh/Sawallisch production of *The Magic Flute* in 1967. This was one of many to be directed by O. F. Schuh (left) and conducted by W. Sawallisch (right).

21. A concert conducted by H. -W. Henze (right) in the early sixties, in which I sang works by Carl Orff (left) and Henze's *Neapolitan Songs*.

22. Herbert von Karajan's highly-acclaimed performance of Haydn's *Creation* at the 1969 Salzburg Easter Festival, in which I sang with Gundula Janowitz.

24. I did some wonderful concerts with Gerald Moore, one of the most experienced of all accompanists.

25. This performance of *Winterreise* with Martin Mälzer in 1955 established my reputation as a Lieder singer.

26. Geoffrey Parsons is rightly considered to be Gerald Moore's successor.

23. I am always stimulated by an enthusiastic audience.

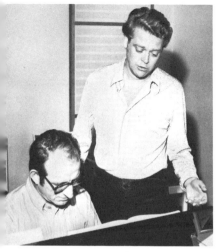

27. My first recording of *Winterreise* with Karl Engel.

30. I never had any problems with Friedrich Gulda, even when rehearsal time was limited.

28. Alexis Weissenberg and I got on marvellously from the outset.

31. Alfred Brendel and I shared a passion for Schubert.

29. I love to perform with Günther Weissenborn, who has also taught me a great deal.

32. Leonard Hokanson has been my chief accompanist for many years.

33.   Fritz Wunderlich was more than just a colleague, he was my best friend. He sang opposite me in the role of Lenski in the Hartmann production of *Eugène Onegin*.

34.   My friendship with Fritz lasted from 1959 until his sudden death in 1966. Whenever we sang together, we signed autographs together too.

In 1819 he returned to his native city of Dessau, where he taught Latin and Greek at a recently-founded *Gymnasium*. He also obtained a part-time post as assistant at the Ducal Library. Following a quarrel with the headmaster of the school, he became curator of the library, and soon after that was made a Privy Councillor, which meant that he could now be presented at court. He had good reason to be thankful to his benefactor, Duke Leopold Friedrich of Anhalt-Dessau, who was always ready to oblige him with the most generous gifts. In the meantime he married the daughter of a government official from Basedow, who soon bore him two children. He had an elegant apartment at the Ducal Library, which was a centre for all that was best in the arts and sciences.

His profession still left him plenty of time to produce a large and varied output of poetry and prose. *Die schöne Müllerin* was published in 1821, and was followed by *Winterreise* in 1823 and 1824. He called the cycle 'Poems from the posthumous writings of a travelling hornplayer'. The title bore little relevance to the subject-matter, though it may have added a certain element of parody. One is tempted to surmise that the 'hornplayer' was a secret pseudonym of his.

The first volume of his collection of 'Greek Songs', *Lieder der Griechen*, appeared in 1821, to be followed by four more volumes in the course of the next three years. In these poems, Müller broached the subject of the Greeks and their struggles for freedom from Turkish oppression. These verses were full of the maltreatment of the Greek people by the Turks. They aroused in the Germans, who had up to then remained indifferent to such matters, a strong sympathy for the sufferings of this poor, oppressed nation. It was followed in 1825 by an essay on Lord Byron, another notoriously idealistic poet, whose sympathy for the Greeks was well known. However, Müller's 'Ode to a Spanish revolutionary' failed to get passed by the censors.

In addition to this, he wrote a number of plays and novellas and a vast collection of lyric poetry. He also published a complete anthology of seventeenth-century German verse, which eventually went into ten volumes. Thanks to this, and to a number of literary and scientific contributions to various erudite magazines, he soon built up a considerable reputation as an expert in literary matters. His circle of personal friends and correspondants embraced all the leading German romantics, including Ludwig Tieck and Carl Maria von Weber, to whom he dedicated the *Winterreise* cycle, and for whom he planned an opera libretto. This later formed the basis of his much sought-after triumph, *Ludwig Uhland*.

In the late summer of 1827, he visited Justinus Kerner in Weinsberg, and was involved in a number of very strange events. Kerner was at the time researching into magnetism and what is now known as parapsychology. He invited Müller, who was by no means unversed in such matters, to take part in a seance led by the famous medium of Prevorst.

This medium was credited with healing powers, which was remarkable for a woman who had been suffering for more than a year from some mysterious illness. I myself have a considerable affinity with 'faith-healing', so I can appreciate the keen interest he showed.

We have no idea what happened to Wilhelm Müller in Weinsberg. But Gustav Schwab, who was the most reliable witness on the matter, recorded that Müller seemed extremely excited on his return from there. He had afterwards been to visit his friend Intimus, Baron of Simolin, and warned him that if he valued his life he must go straight to Weinsberg and introduce himself to the spirit world. He arrived back in Dessau on 27th September 1827. Only five days later, he complained of feeling tired and retired early to bed. By midnight he was dead, the doctor's diagnosis was 'heart-failure'.

There is no doubt that Müller was an academic of many and varied talents. What is more, he was passionately involved in the issues of his time and was not afraid to stand up for what he believed in, even to the extent of infuriating people. I admire him for this alone and no one can blame him for preferring the pen to the sword. He was clever, witty and kind, well versed in the social graces, and also honest and reliable. He must have made a deep impression on people, even at an early age. Otherwise he could not have included so many of his worthy and prestigious contemporaries amongst his circle of friends, champions and admirers. Such associations were to last a lifetime.

Whatever people may wish to believe, Müller's biography shows him to be nothing like the lonely hero of his two 'wanderer' cycles, who bemoans his lost love and wallows in remorse—far from it. As a much-acclaimed poet and literary critic, Müller must have led a rich and fulfilled life. Those who are tempted to identify the poet directly with the verses he wrote must always bear this in mind.

What most characterises the poems in *Die schöne Müllerin* and *Winterreise* is their simplicity of expression, the folk quality of the images they create and their intelligibility. Such qualities must certainly have impressed a man like Schubert. Müller's intentions had been to satirise romantic tragedy, but Schubert took the tragedy quite seriously, and through his music was able to lift it onto a different plane. The directness of Müller's words and narratives exactly suited Schubert's temperament. *Winterreise* speaks of frozen tears, but unlike those of Heinrich Heine, they do not produce flowers where they fall.

Everyone can identify with the images which Müller's wanderer creates, and with the feelings and longings which afflict him. Most of us have at some time or other walked with our loved-one through green meadows, have lain dreaming beneath some tree, have engraved a name somewhere, perhaps in a school-desk, or have seen our reflection in water, listened to the cry of ravens, stood musing by a cemetery, or have found some poor organ-grinder and put a coin on his plate. Müller's verses are naïve and regressive in tone, like Grimm's fairy-tales or Schikaneder's *Magic Flute*. Long-buried ideas come flooding back, take possession of us, and draw us back to our youth, our childhood and ultimately to our origins.

It could be suggested that this regression goes against the grain of today's more progressive attitude to art. The importance of the past must be denied or at least minimised, in the same way that our modern 'throw-away' society pushes its older members aside. Modern music becomes ever more contrived, avoiding anything that could possibly appear naïve, direct, comprehensible or even sincere.

The importance of the naïve should never be underestimated in the arts, especially in great works of music, where even the most naïve element can have an enormous effect on the work as a whole. Here is a secret which can confound the expert critic as effectively as Herr Beckmesser's rules in the presence of young Stolzing. I have experienced this time and time again with *Winterreise*, which can move an audience like no other work I have sung on stage. There is often a whole minute's silence before the final applause, and many people leave the concert-hall with tears in their eyes. But when I ask myself if we owe all of this to Schubert, the answer is a definite 'no'.

CHAPTER 10

Ambassadorial duties

Apprenticeship in Wiesbaden

The early fifties were a difficult time for my family. Mother was seriously ill, and Father was having enormous problems rebuilding his business. My sister, Anne, had the double burden of nursing Mother and doing all the housework. I escaped all this. My success as a musician meant that I had to leave home, though I could not help feeling guilty about my poor sister, who could hardly call her life her own, with all the worries of looking after Mother.

I moved to Wiesbaden on 1st August 1952, and immediately reported for duty at the Hesse State Theatre. The excitement of Nuremberg was now to be replaced by honest hard work. It would be ridiculous to assume that after my victories in Berlin and Nuremberg I should arrive at Wiesbaden in a blaze of glory and walk straight into the position of principal baritone. As far as they were concerned I had had no operatic experience whatsoever previous to my audition in February. There were quite a number of young singers in the company, but I was certainly the greenest of them all.

My contract at Wiesbaden lasted until 16th March 1953. I was to appear as many as eighty times during the intervening seven-and-a-half months. My first appearance was not as second prisoner in *Fidelio*, as some people have claimed, but as Moruccio, a miller-boy in the service of Sebastiano in Eugen d'Albert's opera *Tiefland*. This performance took place in Bad Salzschirf while the company was on tour. More than half of my colleagues were playing servants of Sebastiano too. One of them, a certain Fritz Stotzem, who was singing the part of Nando the shepherd, decided that I was far too full of myself and needed taking down a peg or two. To do this he was able to take full advantage of my inexperience.

An opera house is more to me than a place where operas are performed, and the stage door is not just any old door, it is the entrance to a temple. This idea is not as strange as it might seem. As far as the performers are concerned, the auditorium is a sacred chamber and the stage is hallowed ground. Before going on stage, we doff our hats in the time-honoured theatrical tradition. I still feel the same about it, even now. The reverence I felt for the theatre at Wiesbaden must have been all too obvious. The first thing happened while we were all changing in the dressing-room: Stotzem suddenly leaped stark naked onto one of the tables, did a twirl and called out to me, 'Well? How do you like me?' I could not believe my eyes. That such a thing should be allowed in the sacred temple of an opera house! I was shocked to the core, just as Stotzem had intended.

There were more ordeals to come, but I was quite unaware of this as I went on stage. In the first act of *Tiefland*, Sebastiano, an apparently virtuous man, secretly sells off his maid. Then Moruccio falls foul of him by giving him away in front of the parish elders. Beside himself with rage, Sebastiano cries, 'Away with you! I'll chase you out of this mill like a dog!'

'Me?' replies the cheeky young Moruccio. 'I'd like to see you do it!'

'Get out!' roars Sebastiano.

Karl Kronenberg, who was playing Sebastiano, was then supposed to attack me. He did this with unusual vigour, hurling me across the stage so that I landed in a corner of the wings. I was supposed to reply with the words, 'Before I go I must tell you the truth!' This time, however, the truth was never heard, neither was my first big solo, much to the delight of the colleagues who had gathered backstage.

The miller-boy in *Tiefland* was followed by the second prisoner in *Fidelio*, and Kromow, the Pontevedrian Ambassador in Lehár's *Merry Widow*. I then sang a somewhat larger role as Schaunard in *La Bohème*. 'Prey's acting must be brought under control', said the local paper, the *Wiesbadener Tageblatt*. Then came Dandini, the second choirboy and the fifth of the ghosts of dead musicians in Pfitzner's *Palestrina*. I also sang Rittmeister von Henrici in Millöcker's *Bettelstudent*, the educated gentleman in Rolf Liebermann's *Leonore 40/45*, the gypsy in Verdi's *Il Trovatore*, Achilles in Offenbach's *La Belle Hélène*, and finally the Magistrate of Richmond in Flotow's *Martha* and one or two minor roles in edited works from the thirteenth century.

I also appeared in *Turandot* in the role of Chancellor Ping, which was a severe test of my musical abilities. The star of this performance was the visiting tenor, Helge Roswaenge in the role of Prince Calaf. It was the first time I had ever been in such close proximity to a world-famous singer. I was amazed at the beauty of his high tenor voice. His performance of the aria,*Nessun dorma*, 'Let no one sleep', was breath-takingly beautiful, and as he finished on a shattering high B, I gawped in amazement and missed my entry: 'You should lower your eyes instead of gazing at the stars.' In spite of this, I was praised by the same critic who had found fault with my Schaunard: 'Hermann Prey's Ping is also worthy of mention. A marvellous achievement for such a young singer, his performance was both lively and refined.' So I must have made some progress.

Karl Elmendorff was to conduct *Lohengrin*, and I had to stand in as army herald. It was the first time I had worked under such an important conductor. Elmendorff was known in operatic circles as *Knochen-Karl* or 'Karl Bones', for reasons quite unknown to me. He had conducted operas in Wiesbaden as many as twenty years before, but had worked mostly in Bayreuth. He was, in the nicest sense of the word, an 'old hand' at opera. I was particularly impressed with his Wagner interpretations, especially in his skill with the orchestra. He stood out above all other singing-conductors in one particular feature: his clear and unambiguous beat. One simply could not go wrong. This was essential for me in *Lohengrin*, as I had to sing my role without a single orchestral rehearsal, just as I had done with Ping. This meant that I had only one rehearsal on stage, with a piano and no other singers. I simply had to imagine them all, and the orchestra too. Heinrich Köhler-Helffrich, who was directing the opera, would give cues from backstage: 'Here the Schelde flows by, and then Lohengrin arrives on horseback.' He drew me to the right-hand side of the stage. 'Here the king sits beneath the oak, you, Prey, must stand over there.' I was given a herald's staff, and instructed to strike the floor four times before each call as a mark of respect, soundly and smartly like a guard at the court of Friedrich Wilhelm, the old king of Prussia. In order to come in on cue, I had to begin striking at least four beats ahead of each entry. This was no easy task, as the herald's entries are extremely difficult, each one being preceded by a loud fanfare. I could not afford to bungle it as I had done in *Turandot*, so I was understandably nervous. 'Don't worry,' said Elmendorff. 'I'll give you all the cues.' It went off marvellously.

I would not have missed those months in Wiesbaden for anything. I gradually came to terms with stage routine, and learned how to respond to my fellow singers, how to act with them, and never to lose sight of the conductor while at the same time never looking at him directly. My colleagues were mostly singers of long standing, and some of them have since become great friends. We went out a lot together—I was still a bachelor at the time—and spent many a happy hour in the various Wiesbaden hostelries. One was called *Der beschissene Eimer* ('The filthy bucket', which was to put it mildly!).

Hospitality American style

On 15th November 1952 I was back in front of the cameras again. There is a picture entitled 'Europe farewell!', which shows me waving from the stairway of an American military plane. Underneath it are the words, 'Hermann Prey shortly before his departure on a four-week concert-tour of the States, which he won as victor in the 1952 young singers' competition.' I now faced a twenty-hour journey in a rickety old DC6 to the military air-base at Westover, Massachusetts, in the company of about fifty G.I.s, followed by a further eight hours by rail to Washington, D.C. I shall never forget my first impressions of America. Of course I noticed the sorts of things which might impress any European on his first trip to America. I had only recently left war-torn Berlin, let alone Germany, so I was naturally amazed at all the skyscrapers, the enormous factory complexes, the hundreds and hundreds of parked cars, the bright and informal clothes which people wore, and the way even little girls used lipstick and nail-varnish.

I was welcomed at Washington Station by Mrs Jouette Shouse, chairman of the General Lucius D. Clay Foundation of the GYA, whom I had met in Nuremberg. She was accompanied by representatives from the military authorities and the press. One reporter asked, 'Where are you staying, Mr Prey?'

I had meant to reply, 'I am the guest of Mrs Shouse,' but I got my English muddled up and said, 'I am the ghost of Mrs Shouse,' which produced roars of laughter.

If I remember rightly, Mrs Shouse had been one of the first American women to be awarded a doctorate. That must have been back in the twenties, for she was fifty-two when I first met her. She was married to a lawyer, who was one of the finest gentlemen I have ever met. As heiress of the Filene Store, one of the great Boston department stores, she was quite a rich woman. I also met her father, Mr Filene, whose health was already failing at the time. Mrs Shouse asked me to sing something to him. So I sang 'Five thousand valleys' from Lortzing's opera *Wildschütz*, accompanying myself on the accordion. 'It has been decreed from on high that I shall become world-famous.' This very much amused the old man.

Mrs Shouse showed me greater hospitality than I could possibly have imagined. Indeed, she took me so much to her heart that I have always called her my 'American mother'. When she discovered that I did not have enough warm clothes for the Washington winter, she immediately bought me a beautiful winter coat. She also gave me my first dinner-jacket. I still needed cuff-links for my shirt. 'Just wait a minute,' said Mrs Shouse. 'I think I can help you.' She went up to her room and came back with a pair of cuff-links. 'Do you like them?' she asked. I thought they were marvellous. 'They're a present from me,' she said, I still wear them today.

In about the second week I had the most dreadful toothache,

so Mrs Shouse took me to her dentist. He was a master-dentist, one of the very best in America and he discovered nine abscesses on roots in the upper jaw. Surgery was necessary to save the front teeth, and this he carried out with the greatest care. He used a method which is rarely employed these days: he excised the tops of the roots, not with a surgical blade, but with a fine chisel, in order to obtain the exact section required. The roots could then be drained off in an extremely simple operation. This method is considered the most accurate one, even today. 'Who operated on these roots?', dentists have asked me ever since, 'they're a real masterpiece.' In saving my teeth, Mrs Shouse had saved my career as well. Healthy teeth are essential for a singer. As you might have guessed, I never received a bill for the treatment. It was the most generous thing Mrs Shouse could ever have done for me, and I shall remain grateful to her for the rest of my life.

In the meantime I was fulfilling my duties as the GYA's 'singing ambassador', as the newspapers called me. To the public I was a sort of envoy from war-torn Germany, which was now to benefit from America's bounty. I had been chosen to dispel the old myth of millions of armed Huns, and to symbolise the peace-loving young people of modern Germany, with their passion for song. I moved across the parquet floors of the German Embassy as though it were the most natural thing in the world. Alas, my wardrobe was quite inadequate for all the many receptions. I had only one suit to wear apart from my dinner-jacket.

I appeared as guest star on Ed Sullivan's coast-to-coast television show, which was my first encounter with this new medium. They also went to great lengths to introduce me to the 'all-American way of life'. Together with Captain Henry Gettmann, my personal military escort, I was given a fifty-yard-line ticket' to the traditional 'army-Navy football game'. Faithful to my diplomatic duties, I pretended to enjoy it, but I could not make head or tail of the way they played around with the ball.

The several concerts in which I sang were a great success from an artistic point of view. They began with a number of private concerts in Washington, D.C., and other smaller towns, followed by a concert with the National Symphony Orchestra in Washington under Howard Mitchell, who, as an old acquaintance from Nuremberg, took me very much under his wing. Finally, I sang with the Philadelphia Symphony Orchestra under Eugene Ormandy. This concert took place in December and was therefore billed as a 'Christmas concert'. I sang orchestral songs by Hugo Wolf, including *Die Heiligen Drei Könige mit ihrem Stern* ('The Three Kings and the Star') on a poem by Goethe, and a number of arias. After I had finished the programme, Eugene Ormandy asked me to sing *Stille Nacht* as an encore. The orchestra played in four-part harmony from hymn books. As I stood there and sang this beautiful song, my voice rang out across the great hall of the Academy of Music, while the orchestra accompanied discreetly. As soon as I had finished the first verse, Ormandy turned and signed to the audience, whereupon they all joined in the carol in English: 'Silent night, holy night.' Three thousand people were singing, it seemed, for me alone. The sound of their voices engulfed me like a great tidal wave, threatening to carry me away with it. I was greatly moved and could not hold back my tears. I think it was the most moving moment I have ever experienced on stage.

When I left the United States on 14th December, I was surrounded by reporters for the last time. They fired lots of questions at me: 'What did you most like about America?'

'The wonderful hospitality.'

'Do you have any special wish as you leave America?'

'Yes, I'd like to sing at the Met one day.'

When I was at home for Christmas, I could have spent hours, or even days, telling Bärbel about all the concerts and receptions; and especially about my 'American mother', her kindness and generosity, and her wonderful house, where I had spent Thanksgiving Day, America's traditional harvest festival, which they celebrate in such style. The Thanksgiving meal is like an English Christmas dinner, with a turkey for the main course, something unknown to Germany at the time. 'It's a real dream of a bird,' I told Bärbel. That was true, and I shall never forget the smell of my first turkey. When I was at last able to introduce Bärbel to Mrs Shouse, it was a great occasion for all three of us. I have kept in contact with Mrs Shouse ever since then, and always go to see her when I am near Washington. She always comes to my concerts, and proudly tells her friends, 'Hermann made his career without a penny from me.'

The Sharpless affair

I returned to Wiesbaden, where on 26th December 1952 I was back on stage at the Hesse State Theatre in the role of the Pontevedrian Ambassador. I now moved in the high society of the *Merry Widow* just as I had done at the German Embassy in Washington only two weeks before. I had soon become readjusted to the more modest circumstances of Wiesbaden, and was feeling extremely happy with the cast. I had already learned the importance of every single member of the cast to the performance as a whole, just like the small pieces which make up a mosaic. Even the second prisoner or the fourth customs-officer must give of his best to enhance the overall effect. So it was not any underestimation of my abilities which caused the row over *Madama Butterfly*. I was bitterly disappointed when they announced the cast for the *première* on 4th March 1953. I had counted on getting the part of Sharpless, which I had sung in every rehearsal so far. I did what many actors and singers have done in the past and stormed up to the director's office. Heinrich Köhler-Helffrich was busy, so I had to wait all of half an hour before I was allowed to see him. He was sitting behind a desk piled high with papers. I had not been in this room since my first arrival in Wiesbaden.

'Come in, Mr Prey. I can just give you a few minutes. What's the trouble?'

'Director... I am extremely disappointed not to... '

'Disappointed? Well, we're all disappointed around here. Do you know how many there were in the audience at the last *Palestrina* performance? Two hundred and sixty-seven! You can see for yourself: 89 regulars and 103 other visitors. And the rest of the tickets? Given away! That's what I call a disappointment.' He looked me slowly up and down. 'Does the smoke annoy you?

I deliberately pollute the atmosphere so that singers won't stay too long, but do please sit down and tell me what you've got on your mind.'

'I've just seen the cast for *Butterfly* on the notice-board, and . . . Well, it's about Sharpless. You promised I'd be singing it in the *première*.

'My dear friend, if I told you that I must have been lying.'

'O.K. Not the *Butterfly première* in so many words. But surely we made certain arrangements.'

'And what were those arrangements, as you call them?'

'You said you were planning to give me a bigger role in a *première*.'

'But you did sing Schaunard in the new production of *La Bohème*.'

'That was last September, since then I've only been playing minor roles. This new production of *Butterfly* is the only one left for me in the second half of the season, so Sharpless is my last chance.'

'Look, Mr Prey, I've been watching you at rehearsal. I may have originally thought of casting you as Sharpless. But with Martin Kremer as Pinkerton . . . Why, he could be twice your age, and he's supposed to be younger than you . . . Well, I decided it would be better for you to stand down. You see, to come over well next to an experienced artist like Kremer, the consul must have a more reflective personality. Shall we say the part requires an element of diplomacy and finesse, which, I am sorry to say, you have so far shown no signs of achieving.'

'As far as diplomacy's concerned, I know all about that. You know I was in America last month . . . '

'As if I didn't know that! I was the one who gave you time off for it. We must come to a decision, Mr Prey. I hope you understand my point of view.'

'No I don't, sir.' I was close to tears. 'If . . . if I don't get the part of Sharpless and sing it in the *première* I can't believe in opera any longer! I don't even know if I'll sing any more opera at all!'

I stormed out. The upshot was that I got the part of Sharpless after all.

CHAPTER 11

My Career Gathers Speed

Beginnings in Hamburg

On 20th January 1953, between performances of *La Belle Hélène* and *Il Trovatore*, I went from Wiesbaden to Berlin to audition at the Electrola recording studios. It was an auspicious day for me, as I got to know Fritz Ganss, their chief classical producer, who has been one of my greatest champions ever since. He was very much taken with my performance, and proposed a number of future recordings. These included Christmas carols by Cornelius, Loewe ballads, well-known Schubert songs such as *Heindenröslein* and *Hark, hark the lark*, and many others. What was most unusual, however, was that he promised to introduce me to Michael Raucheisen.

Raucheisen was well known to me as Berlin's top accompanist and husband of the world-famous soprano, Maria Ivogün. Whenever a top singer gave a recital in Berlin, Raucheisen was always there at the piano. Such had been the case for twenty-five years, and I knew this was my best opportunity yet.

We met at the recording studios at the end of April and I was understandably nervous. Would he be impatient with me? Would he consider it rather beneath him to play with a beginner like me? Far from it! He was kindness itself, and we got on marvellously from the outset.

Loewe ballads have some of the most fiendish accompaniments, especially when the composer wishes to conjure up rough seas and autumn gales. Now it was either in *Lord Oluf* or in *Odin Riding On The Waves*, I can no longer remember which, but at any rate, I could tell that all was not well in the lower register of the piano; the recording manager did not say anything. A few more bars were to elapse before he interrupted us over the loudspeaker: 'Mr Prey, can you please start again from the bottom of page 77, *allegro risoluto*.' We obeyed, but the same wrong note could be heard again in the bass. I concentrated all my efforts, but in vain. The loudspeaker stopped us again: 'Mr Prey, would you be so kind as to let us try it again? Page 77, bottom line, *allegro risoluto*.' I cursed under my breath. What the hell was I doing wrong this time? When it happened yet a third time I asked, 'What's wrong with it?'

'Don't worry, Mr Prey, let's try it again. Page 77, bottom line, *allegro risoluto*.'

I was sitting next to the recording technician as he played it back for us. When we came to the *allegro risoluto* at the bottom of page 77, I whispered in his ear, 'Now tell me what was wrong here. You know perfectly well that I didn't make a mistake.'

'Yes,' he replied in a whisper, 'I know as well as you do that the professor played a wrong note, but we mustn't tell him or he'll walk out on us!'

In the same month I sang Christ in Bach's *St Matthew Passion* for the first time, with the Berlin Philharmonic and Schola Cantorum under Mathieu Lange. My dear mother was able to be present at this concert. Helmut Krebs was the Evangelist. The part of Christ is a difficult one, and he gave me some important advice on it, which I shall never forget. The *Nachtdepesche* called me 'a gentle and beautiful declaimer' while the *Tagesspiegel* called my singing 'incredibly mature'. The part of Christ is very short in comparison to that of the Evangelist, but is nonetheless equally demanding from a musical point of view. The few words which Jesus utters determine the whole tone of the work. My debut as Christ was by all accounts the most difficult ensemble part I had undertaken so far.

In 1953 I had a host of other minor engagements to fulfil. For example, the GYA had invited me to sing an extra item at the final concert of the 1953 singing contest in Nuremberg, in my capacity as the previous year's winner. This was on 17th June, exactly a month before my new contract with the Hamburg Opera was due to begin. From a musical point of view, the

Berlin Conservatoire was a kind of primary school for me, while Wiesbaden was my secondary school. Now I was off to university at the Hamburg Opera. My new teacher was to be Günther Rennert, who was manager of the Hamburg Opera from 1946 to 1956.

My work now included Dominik in *Arabella*, and parts I already knew, such as Moruccio in *Tiefland*, the army herald in *Lohengrin* and the second prisoner in *Fidelio*. Another new role was that of nightwatchman in *The Mastersingers of Nuremberg*. My engagement at Hamburg was in no sense a ticket to instant stardom. However, on 8th November 1953 I had my debut as Silvio in *Pagliacci* under Horst Stein, with its beautiful love-duet. This was real progress.

James Pease, the American baritone, had been due to sing this role under the auspices of the Hamburg Philharmonic Society. However, he fell ill only two days before the *première*. I was able to sing in his place, even though the dress rehearsal had already taken place the previous morning. The conductor was Leopold Ludwig. Immediately after this, I sang in my first Handel oratorio, as Manoah in *Samson*. The part of Delilah was sung by the youthful Leonie Rysenek, and it was the first of many occasions on which we shared the platform. I have kept one of the reviews, probably because it gave me a particularly good write-up. The date was 10th November 1953, and the newspaper was the *Hamburger Anzeiger*. 'Hermann Prey was the star of the evening in the quintet. His warm, pure voice gave full expression to the part of Manoah, and made him into a full and rounded character, thus forming the climax of part three. Only recently engaged by the State Opera, Prey shows enormous potential.' A good press like this gave me the courage to go on with my career. For in spite of my successes, I still had my 'downs' from time to time. Sometimes I could only see difficulties ahead. I still have such moments, even today.

My mother's illness was also a great worry to me. By now she was almost paralysed, and lay in bed with dreadful open wounds. Eventually my sister, who had sacrificed so much to look after her, became ill too. Bärbel wrote to me about it. 'I've recently become much closer to your mother,' she said. 'I was with her yesterday and changed her bandages for her, you don't need to worry at all. I'll go and see her every day. We talk a lot about you, and about *us*.'

Marriage

What would I ever have done without Bärbel? At that stage, alas, she was still living in Berlin, while I was hundreds of miles away, first in Wiesbaden and then in Hamburg. We could not then afford long telephone calls, so we relied on the post. It may seem incredible, but we wrote to each other every day, sometimes a few lines, sometimes a couple of pages, sometimes enough to fill a whole novel. If the expected letter did not arrive, I always feared the worst. By the end of 1953 I was able to start budgeting. In Wiesbaden I had only been earning 350 marks a month, which was never enough to live on. However, my three-year contract with Hamburg assured me of a salary of 500 marks per month in the first year, rising to 750 and 1000 marks in the second and third years respectively. On top of that, there were radio broadcasts, recordings and concert engagements, which added to my income. So by now I reckoned I could earn enough for two. Not that we could afford any luxuries—we would have to economise a lot—but what did that matter so long as we could be together? I managed to find a good, cheap unfurnished room with a kitchen and bathroom, in the Lucas-Cranach-Strasse in Othmarschen. We did not have any furniture at first, though Father gave us a corner divan as a wedding present. This opened up into two beds, and was just what we needed at the time.

On 12th February 1954 I was still working as second prisoner in *Fidelio*. The wedding took place at the registry office in Blankenese on the 13th February, on the anniversary of Wagner's death. My mother was far too ill to be present, and my sister had to stay and look after her. But my father came, together with Bärbel's mother and her Aunt Grete, who lived in Hamburg. After the wedding we had a celebratory meal at a hotel called the Othmarscher Hof, and then went back to the empty room. My mother-in-law Wally, Bärbel's aunt and my

father sat on the divan, while I sat cross-legged on the floor.
Bärbel had spread out a checked tablecloth over a suitcase, and
poured out the coffee. I could not stay very long, as I had a
concert engagement at that fine old masonic lodge, *An der
Moorweide.*

I arrived there punctually, and completed the programme of
six songs by Hugo Wolf. I was just about to go home when one of
the masons called me back. 'Do please stay,' he said. 'We should
love you to come to our feast.' I would have very much liked to
stay and eat with the masons. They were rather cool and polite,
as befitted such well-to-do merchants and their wives, but they
were also kind and friendly, and the prospect of a banquet was
very tempting. I thanked them for their invitation, explaining
why I had to go. My host beamed and warmly congratulated
me. He told his wife, who passed the news on, so that before very
long everybody knew. Up to then, the party had been rather
dull, but it suddenly became bright and cheerful. Everyone
shook my hand and congratulated me. Strangers clapped me on
the back and gave snippets of advice about marriage. The man
who had invited me to stay accompanied me to the door and
gave me an envelope. I thanked him again and as I left, I ripped
open the envelope. There were . . . But no, that was impossible!
There were 500 marks in the envelope! I could not believe my
eyes. This was a whole month's salary! Overjoyed, I dashed into
the nearest shop, bought five bottles of sparkling wine and
carried them home on the tram. We celebrated until nine
o'clock, when our guests decided to leave. Father thought the
happy couple should be left to their own devices, and said he
would show the two ladies around Hamburg. We later
discovered that he had taken them to the *Reeperbahn,* Hamburg's
famous brothel district, where they had spent the whole night
amusing themselves.

Bärbel and I continued our celebrations with the sparkling
wine, which was if anything far too effective. The wedding night
did not go exactly as Father had planned: certain things had to
be postponed!

Full sail

The first weeks of our marriage were overshadowed by my
mother's illness. I kept trying to fly over to Berlin between
engagements, but I never once managed to get away. Every
single night was booked. The blow came on 22nd March 1954,
only five weeks after the wedding. Mother died.

I shall never forget the last time I saw her. She had struggled
out onto the balcony to wave me off. I looked back before
turning into the Theodorstrasse. There she stood on the balcony
in a camel-hair jacket, waving feebly, her movements already
weakened by her illness. I stopped there for a moment. That
image is engraved on my memory.

Alas, I realised too late how much I had neglected her in
recent years. Now she was no longer there. For a long time I
simply could not take it in.

The hard work in Hamburg helped to occupy my mind. I
sometimes had a performance every night, and then there were
rehearsals and coaching sessions. Besides this, I was much in
demand at RIAS Berlin and at the North German Radio. In
May I flew to London to a recording session of Johann Strauss'
Gypsy Baron, which was my first big job for EMI. The conductor,
Otto Ackermann, was simply marvellous. I sang the part of
Count Homonay. The first song, 'Give me your hand, it must be
so,' had to be sung in its original key, which was rather high for
me.

I must have made a good impression, however, because as
soon as I had finished the Hamburg season at the end of June I
was asked to sing Harlekin in *Ariadne auf Naxos*. Recordings were
due to take place between the 9th and the 11th of July, with the
Philharmonia Orchestra under Herbert von Karajan. 'Well,' I
said to Bärbel, 'here goes! It's now or never.' She was
flabbergasted. 'Why on earth did they choose you?'

'It must have something to do with my old friend Fritz Ganss
from Electrola, the one who introduced me to Raucheisen. I
expect someone else turned it down, so he's asked me to do it
instead. I'm just the substitute. Look at the cast: Elisabeth
Schwarzkopf as Ariadne, Rita Streich as Zerbinetta, Irmgard

Seefried as the composer, Rudolf Schock as Bacchus, Karl
Dönch as the music-teacher... They're all world-class singers...
There's one big problem, though. I don't even know the part.'
   'Then you've got to learn it.'
   'In a week?'
   'You can manage it easily.'
   'You think so?'
   'Of course. You've got nothing else on.'
   'Well then, I'll give it a try.'
   The role of Harlekin turned out to be an extremely tricky one.
You had to count like a metronome. I shut myself away and
worked concentratedly for the whole week. Then I took a flight
to London. Herbert von Karajan had not yet arrived, and
Heinrich Schmidt from the Vienna State Opera had been
deputed to conduct the initial rehearsals. This he carried out
admirably.
   Everyone worked hard to please the maestro. Listening to the
play-backs was an extremely nerve-racking procedure. All the
soloists sat in a circle around the maestro while he commented
on our performance. As our voices came over the loudspeaker,
we would try to read his face as we awaited his reaction.
Sometimes he would just nod or grin, at other times he might
remark, 'Jolly good there, young man. What was your name
again?' I also watched Walter Legge, the chief recording
manager, and all the technical staff, as I tried to familiarise
myself with recording techniques. I never ceased to be amazed
at what they could achieve from their control desk.
   Back in Hamburg, I had plenty to tell Bärbel. 'It was rather
like the crematorium at Schmargendorf.' Bärbel looked puz-
zled, so I went on to explain. 'While I was studying at the
conservatoire, I occasionally sang for a funeral at Schmargendorf. The organist was a real old hand, a Berliner through and
through. He sat there in his grubby old waistcoat, striking the
keys and puffing so hard on his cigar that I began to worry about
my voice. I soon realised that the mourners always sobbed and
sniffed at the same points in the service. One day the organist
explained the reason why. "Look here, son," he whispered. "I
get ready with the swell just as we come to this chord. You see?

That diminished one. Now off we go, open the swell, there . . . "
He pressed the swell pedal, gently and with a lot of feeling.
Down below, the congregation began to wail. "What a beastly
thing to do!" I whispered back. He gave a satisfied grin, "That's
what *you* think!" he said, "they just lap it up." '

On 4th September 1954, the Hamburg Opera gave me my
first major role, which was that of Carlos in Verdi's *Force of
Destiny*. This was undoubtedly a milestone in my career. The
director had taken a considerable risk in promoting such a
young singer, but the press were delighted with the experiment,
and devoted whole articles to my debut. 'This singer has terrific
potential. We await future developments with great interest,'
wrote the critic in the *Hamburger Abendblatt* on 6th September
1954.

In October, I appeared again in *La Bohème*. This time I not
only sang the role of Schaunard, as I had done in Wiesbaden,
but more frequently appeared as his artistic friend, Marcello, in
the leading baritone role. This presented me with a new and
unexpected problem. There are scenes with four bohemians in
their garret, in which the conversation moves quickly from one
character to another. For a Marcello who has previously sung
Schaunard, it is all too easy to get the wires crossed and
inadvertently slip into the wrong part. Before you realise, you
are no longer singing Marcello, but are back in your old role,
singing Schaunard's lines. As I mentioned before, I alternated
these two roles in Hamburg, standing in for whichever singer
was unavailable, which certainly made the undertaking infinitely more exciting. I had similar problems later on in the
Marriage of Figaro when I was 'demoted' from master to servant.
The trickiest point was the beautiful finale of the second act,
where a one-time Almaviva can so easily slip from Figaro's bass
notes into the count's middle register.

1955 was in many ways a further milestone in my career. I
added two of the most important roles to my opera repertoire.
My debut as Figaro in Rossini's *Barber of Seville* was on 31st
October of that year. This was after many years of having to be
content with the part of his servant Fiorillo. Horst Günther
became ill and I was called in to replace him. I had fortunately

prepared the part beforehand, which had once again to be performed without a single orchestral rehearsal. I am particularly grateful to the musical director at Hamburg, Wilhelm Brückner-Rüggeberg, under whom I had already sung the Marquis of Posa in *Don Carlos*. He championed my cause more than anyone else in Hamburg, and gave me an enormous amount of teaching and encouragement. It was he who was chiefly responsible for my success in the *Barber*.

On 30th November I made my stage debut as Guglielmo in Mozart's *Così fan Tutte*. The tenor in the role of Ferrando was Rudolf Schock, who to my mind was *the* Mozart singer of the day. I have never heard anyone give a more beautiful rendering of *Un Aura Amorosa*.

I also did a large number of concerts. I sang my first Brahms *Requiem* in Aachen under Wolfgang Sawallisch. I gave Lieder recitals for the first time in England and Holland, performed *Die schöne Müllerin* for the first time, and sang *Winterreise* at the *Haus am Waldsee*, with Martin Mälzer on the piano. This performance was to set the seal on my career as a Lieder recitalist. 'A moving and inspiring performance,' said E.M. in the *Tagesspiegel* on 7th January of that year. 'Applause and ovation for a concert which will always be remembered,' had been the comment of H.Ko. in the *Neue Zeitung* on the previous day. The same critic had said in the *Kurier* on 5th January, 'He has plumbed the depths of Schubert's music like no other singer before him. Our previous speculations about this singer have now become certainties. He will soon be counted among the greatest of Germany's Lieder recitalists.' The concert was sold out, and finished with an ovation, the like of which I had never experienced before. I thought to myself, now I know I'm going to make it to the top.

I was soon to meet a number of top conductors. I have already mentioned Walter Sawallisch, under whom I made my debut, not only in the Brahms *Requiem*, but also in Mahler's *Lieder eines fahrenden Gesellen* ('Songs of a Wayfarer'). In the Brahms *Requiem* it was his first time too. Even though he knew every single note by heart, he insisted on performing with a score. He thus followed the tradition of Knappertbusch, whose comment on the many young conductors who performed without a score was,

'I *can* read music.' The same man is said to have remarked concerning a bad review, 'A cathedral stays a cathedral, even when a little dog pees on the wall.'

Sawallisch is a phenomenal sight-reader. He can transfer any orchestral score directly onto the keyboard. I once presented him with a collection of difficult and rarely-performed orchestral songs by Richard Strauss. He played at sight from the score, reproducing the parts of all the transposing instruments in the correct key.

Herbert von Karajan is similarly gifted as a pianist. Once, when he was trying to persuade me to sing Beckmesser, he played me all the relevant extracts from the opera on the piano, while at the same time singing all the vocal lines: Beckmesser, Zorn, Moser, Eisslinger, Nachtigall, Ortel, Foltz and Schwarz, David and Sachs, and even Eva. This he carried out at such speed that I could not turn the pages quickly enough for him. At the time, I did not have the courage to sing Beckmesser, thinking I was too young for the role. This I now regret.

In February 1956, I sang in the Brahms *Requiem* under Otto Klemperer in Cologne. As you will know, the third movement begins with a baritone solo: *Herr, lehre doch mich, dass ein Ende mit mir haben muss* ('Lord, let me know my end'). Klemperer turned and glowered down at me from the conductor's stand. 'You're a prophet, Mr Prey! Be prophetic,' he commanded in that tight, croaky voice of his. There are so many anecdotes about Otto Klemperer that in this respect he can only be compared to Sir Thomas Beecham. I heard a rather nice Klemperer story from Rudolf Gamsjäger, the then president of the Vienna Music Society. In the early sixties, Gamsjäger had pulled off a real *coup* by managing to persuade both Bruno Walter and Otto Klemperer to conduct the opening concerts of the Vienna Festival. Walter was to conduct the Philharmonic in the morning, while Otto Kemperer conducted the Symphonic in the evening. Klemperer was present at one of Walter's rehearsals, and told Gamsjäger the next day, 'I met Walter in the lift this morning. I said to him, "Mr Walter, I must say this, you conduct just like you did thirty years ago."' He gave a cynical laugh. 'And he took it as a compliment.'

It was a great loss to me when Joseph Keilberth died in July 1968. Of all conductors, he was the one I knew best. We had been close friends, ever since our first meeting in Hamburg, and especially after working together in Gluck's *Iphigenia in Tauris* in Vienna in June 1956. Keilberth was the kind of conductor I very much miss these days. He had the patience to lead the singer by the hand and work him gently into a new role, especially if it was somewhat outside the singer's usual domain. The role of Mandryka in *Arabella* is a good example in my case. I could have tackled this part with Keilberth, even though it borders on the heroic, because he would have been careful as always to reduce the volume of the orchestra to suit a singer like myself. He would have rested the voice gently on the accompaniment. With Keilberth, there was never the slightest danger of overtaxing the voice. For example, he paid the strictest attention to every forte piano in the wind, which means he played it exactly as the composer himself intended. It is difficult to play quietly and at the same time to preserve the tension in the music. Walter Legge, who died in 1979, and was married to Elisabeth Schwarzkopf, was famous for decades throughout the world as a producer at EMI and one of the greatest musical brains of the century. He said to me shortly before his death, 'Crudeness is here to stay in the theatre.' I am afraid he is right.

Heinz Tietjen is another man who must be mentioned. He was a conductor as well, though I myself came to know him as director of the Hamburg Opera. He arrived in Hamburg in 1954, and took over from Rennert in 1956. He remained as director until the arrival of Rolf Liebermann in 1959. Tietjen (1881—1967) was undoubtedly one of the most important figures in the German musical world of the first half of this century. He began successfully in Trier, moving on to become director in Saarbrücken and Breslau. Then, in 1925, he took over the directorship of the Berlin Opera. Thanks also to the help of top conductors such as Bruno Walter, Otto Klemperer and Erich Kleiber, this company enjoyed enormous success during his time there. He was general manager of the Prussian State Theatre from 1927 to 1945, a difficult office during a time of great upheaval, which cost him dearly in the years immediately following the war. However, in 1948 he returned to direct the Berlin Opera until 1954, when, as I said, he moved on to Hamburg. Tietjen was famous in the theatre world for his diplomacy, his tact and his organising abilities. His art consisted in appearing to be invisible, which provoked Alfred Polgar to ask, 'Was there ever a Tietjen?' As a young singer who owed much to his friendship and encouragement, I very much benefited from the pleasanter side of his nature. Indeed, he had hardly taken over as director when I was summoned to his office. He began, 'I happened to hear you singing on RIAS. You've really got something to give to the world. Now, how are things with you? I imagine you're very much in demand.' That was true, I agreed, I often had to turn down requests because I was appearing in some minor role in Hamburg the same night.

'Let's both have a look at your diary,' he suggested. 'May I have a look? What have you got on at the moment?'

'Eight recitals.'

'Hmmm... Duisburg? Is that one important?'

'Yes. It's my first *Schöne Müllerin*.'

'Good,' he replied, and released me for all eight recitals at a stroke. 'You know what, Mr Prey?' he went on. 'I'm going to release you from your present contract and engage you as a guest soloist from now on. Then you can give as many recitals as you like.'

I was flabbergasted. I had never dreamed of this. In the event, Heinz Tietjen had to find a substitute for all the roles I was doing, which was by no means easy. It was a terrific morale-booster to find somebody to champion my cause as a Lieder recitalist, and someone who really believed in me.

As from the middle of 1956 I was my own boss, and I plunged headlong into my work. My old diaries give a good idea of how busy I was. Apart from five or six weeks' annual holiday, I managed to squeeze in an average of ten or twelve appearances per month. The rest of the time was spent travelling and rehearsing. I shall only mention the more important events. In November 1956, I gave my first Lieder recital in New York, which included Beethoven's *An die ferne Geliebte* and Schubert's *Die schöne Müllerin*. At the end of the same month, I sang the same programme in Vienna. This was the beginning of a long and happy friendship with Austria, that most musical of countries, which was the home of Mozart, Beethoven, Schubert and Brahms. My Vienna Opera debut was in Rossini's *Barber of Seville* in 1957. It was in Munich in 1958 that I first sang the Count in *The Marriage of Figaro*, and the poet Olivier in Strauss's *Capriccio*. I also appeared in a television opera for the first time, as the toreador in *Carmen*, and appeared in my native city of Berlin as Rossini's Figaro, throwing shaving soap all over the stage. I first appeared in the Salzburg Festival in 1959, again in the role of barber, but this time in Strauss' *Die schweigsame Frau* ('The Silent Woman'). Only a few days after this, I appeared as Wolfram in *Tannhäuser* at the Munich Festival. I had sung this role in Hamburg the previous February, under the direction of Wieland Wagner. Here are some of the records which I made during this period: in 1958 a disc of Brahms' Lieder with Electrola, and a recording of Weber's *Freischütz* with Keilberth conducting; in 1959 Hugo Wolf's *Italienisches Liederbuch* with the great Erna Berger, and Günther Weissenborn on the piano; at the end of 1959 Bach Cantatas Nos. 56 and 82 with EMI, at St Thomas' Church, Leipzig, under their musical director, Kurt Thomas.

All this meant that I never once stopped travelling between 1956 and the end of 1959, apart from a few weeks' holiday or the odd bout of illness. My wife and I could not enjoy a decent home life together for years. She was always in Hamburg, while I was stuck in some hotel room, restaurant or aeroplane. It could not really be called a proper marriage, and sooner or later, the situation was bound to come to a head.

SOS from Cologne

It was while playing Don Giovanni in the early part of 1960 that I suddenly realised what a mess I had made of our lives. In February I sang the role for the first time, in a recording of highlights for Electrola, with Elisabeth Grümmer as Donna Anna, Hildegard Hillebrecht as Donna Elvira, Erika Köth as

Zerlina, Fritz Wunderlich as Don Ottavio and Karl Christian Kohn as Leporello. In March I gave my first stage performance of the Don in Cologne.

I was far from happy at the time. The stress of being continually away from home was beginning to take its toll, and I was rapidly approaching a crisis. I looked back on my life with Bärbel. While living with our parents in Berlin, we had seen each other every day. We had been separated for long periods while I was in Wiesbaden, and during the first months in Hamburg, but we had accepted this as a necessary sacrifice. Then in 1954, we had at last been able to set up home together. This happy state of affairs had lasted scarcely two-and-a-half years when my increasingly nomadic existence put an end to all that.

Our first child, Annette, was born in the middle of this hectic period. I can still see Bärbel's glowing face as she announced she was pregnant. She later remarked, 'Now the baby's here I can't imagine life without her.' We had argued at length as to whether we could justify having children in view of my career. Bärbel, who was more realistic, had said no, while I had said yes. My decision was not a mere whim. I not only wanted to become a father, I was convinced I could be a really good father. Alas, I greatly underestimated the wisdom of Bärbel's arguments. 'Look here,' she said, 'first you talk about singing all over the world and touring America and Japan. Then in the next breath you're dreaming of a happy family, gathered around the fire. The two things simply don't add up.'

Often I did not see my family for weeks on end. There was one occasion when I was about to go off on tour. Bärbel had already packed, and Annette was lying in bed. 'Sleep well till the morning,' said Bärbel to her. 'Sleep well,' I said. I wished I could have added 'till the morning,' but I was off to Vienna in two hours; and after Vienna it was Graz, then from Graz back to Vienna, then on to Ottobeuren, Berlin and Munich—when would it ever end? I lingered on in that darkened room. I said to Bärbel afterwards, 'You know, I don't think I can carry on like this much longer, being alone all the time.'

'Neither can I,' said Bärbel, 'but what else can we do? You

know I can't come with you. Who'll look after the baby? What do you suggest?' I had no answer to this.

It was March 1960, and I had just finished rehearsing *Don Giovanni*. I was sitting in my hotel room, brooding to myself and feeling desperately lonely. Something just snapped and I grabbed the telephone receiver and asked to be put through to Hamburg. 'Darling, I'm just going to pieces, I can't go on like this. I'm fed up with being alone. I can't stand it any more. If you don't come over here straight away, I'll... '

I know I was being very selfish, but I really loved my wife, and I wanted to save our marriage. Bärbel urgently summoned her parents, and her mother arrived the following day from Berlin. Then she dropped everything and took the next train for Cologne.

Since that time we have never been apart.

I cannot thank my parents-in-law enough for the way they jumped into the breach at that moment, and for the fact that they later accepted our invitation to move in with us to help look after the children. The family grew fast. Florian was born in 1959, and Franziska in 1961. Whenever we went away, Bärbel's parents were there. When we got back, they would always be packed and ready to leave. 'Do stay for a bit, please,' we insisted. Their reply was invariably, 'No, you must have the children to yourselves for the short time you're here,' which was incredibly kind of them. If one of the children asked, 'Grandad, can I do this?' or, 'Can I do that?' Grandad would reply 'Wait until your parents come home. It's not my decision to make.' This meant that we were always involved in what they were doing, even when we were thousands of miles away. Alas, the children have inevitably suffered from the long separations, as we have done too.

It is particularly difficult for any mother if she is always having to leave her children. In a marriage where one partner is more often than not away from home, there is a real danger that they will grow apart. Bärbel and I have at least had the chance to grow and develop together. She is involved in everything I do, and is always ready to talk to me. A recital can be very uplifting, but I often come down to earth with a bump afterwards. I need to have somebody to talk to, if only to get it all off my chest.

CHAPTER 12

Beethoven's *An die ferne Geliebte*

The textual difficulties

I have just spoken of the period when I suffered greatly from being separated from my wife. The pain of separation, and the associated feelings of loneliness and longing, have been marvellously reproduced in the music of Beethoven's song cycle, *An die ferne Geliebte* ('To the Far Away Beloved'). For this reason I was determined to add these songs to my repertoire as soon as I felt able to do so.

These days, no composer would ever think of choosing verses as sentimental as those of Aloy Jeitteles for setting to music. For a modern singer to master them requires considerable imaginative powers. It is thus easy to understand why many young singers of today have no idea what to make of them. However, I myself find Beethoven's music so incomparably beautiful that any other rendering of the same poet's work seems pale by comparison.

The *Ferne Geliebte*, as I call this work for short, is one of Beethoven's later compositions, and comes from a period when he was writing music of increasingly epic proportions. Another work from the same period (1815/16) was his piano sonata in A major, Opus 101, the first of his final group of sonatas; only two years later, he began work on the 9th Symphony. The *Ferne Geliebte* is of similarly epic proportions, and is thus in many ways unique in song literature. It is true that Schubert's *Schöne Müllerin* and *Winterreise* cycles were also conceived as epics. However, these two cycles are made up of sets of individual songs, whereas the six *Ferne Geliebte* songs were composed as a single, indivisible unit. There is no pause between any of them: they flow smoothly from one song to the next. If I decide to sing this cycle in a recital, it usually forms the major work in the programme.

The form of the cycle could most simply be described as 'A—B—C—D—E—A'. The final song returns to the original theme, thus encircling the songs in between. Each of the four middle songs depicts a different but related mood. Each takes the form of a short monologue, in which the main theme of the cycle, that of unrequited love, is expressed in a different way.

Even though the work is fairly long—it takes about thirteen or fourteen minutes to perform—it is noticeably lacking in external action, a factor which presents a number of inter- pretational problems. The theme is in stark contrast to that of Schubert's 'Wanderer' cycles, with their continual forward movement. In this cycle, the young man merely sits down on a hill and gazes into the countryside towards the place where his loved-one lives. The songs are all addressed to her, as an expression of his longing for her, and as an attempt to rid himself of the pain this causes him. As the first song implies, he considers his singing quite powerful enough on its own to pass through all intervening obstacles and to reach as far as his beloved.

The second song leads the singer into an idyllic landscape beyond the mountains, where gentle breezes blow and spring flowers bloom, and where pain is no more. It is like the country of his dreams. In the third song he asks nature to help him: the passing clouds, the birds, the stream. This reminds us of Schubert's *Liebesbotschaft* ('Message of Love') and the Müller songs. He even calls on the wind to help him, which in the fourth song is supposed to lift him up and carry him to his beloved. The fifth song is a hymn of praise to the spring, and its power to reunite lovers. However, he is denied the pleasure of such a reunion, and is abandoned to tears of despair. He concludes the cycle by dedicating these songs to his beloved. The intervening spaces will retreat before the beauty of the music, and they will be reunited once more.

Problems of tessitura

Beethoven's *An die ferne Geliebte* presents the singer with a number of *tessitura* problems, in that there are several passages which are unusually low. This cycle is quite unlike those of Schubert, in which the key of each song may be determined individually. In Beethoven the singer must choose a pitch for the cycle as a whole, because the work was composed as a single entity, as has already been explained. However, it is up to every singer to choose the pitch at which the *tessitura* is best suited to his own range and vocal capacity.

When considering problems of *tessitura*, the singer must take into account the individual make-up of his own vocal organs. This is to a large extent determined at birth, and is mostly inherited. The same is true of the other bodily characteristics which contribute towards the quality of the voice, such as the shape of the head, the height of the forehead and the way the gums are formed. The voice depends especially on the quality and elasticity of the vocal chords themselves. One of the most important tasks of any singing-teacher is to determine the position of his pupil's ideal middle register. Only then will the singer be able to develop the full range of the voice by working up and down from this middle point.

The most beautiful male sound is that of a tenor on a high C, where his vocal chords are held in the greatest tension, creating the sound which is most exciting to the listener. This is not just because the note is high. It owes more to the quality of the sound created, and the pleasure this induces in the listener's senses. We baritones have nothing comparable to offer the listener, a fate which I have learned to accept.

Gifted pupils very quickly sense where their middle register lies, and they are well advised never to forget this. There is a great temptation to overstretch the vocal chords by forcing the voice up to notes above its natural range. In opera, contraltos and mezzo-sopranos are often open to this temptation, especially when they are dissatisfied with the many rather 'negative' roles which are available to them, such as Azucena, Amneris and Delilah, Ortrud, Magdalena and Brangäne. They would rather be singing Fidelio and Isolde, but will ruin their voice if they do so. We should never forget that age-old motto, 'The cobbler should stick to his last.' Parts which are low can be just as dangerous, as they can encourage bad habits. The voice will tend to lose its sparkle, becoming dark and husky, and there is also a risk of losing the higher register. Mozart's Figaro is a character role after my own heart, but I had to take extreme care when I was first introduced to the part. From a vocal standpoint, I am far better suited to the part of the Count. Between 1958 and 1978 I have sung this latter role many times all over the world.

It is also important to take account of the size and timbre of the voice. For this reason, I usually limit my repertoire to lyric baritone roles. I think twice before even considering a heroic role such as Sachs, Wotan or Jochanaan, much as they attract me as character roles. On the other hand, I hope that, with care, I may still be able to sing *Winterreise* at the age of sixty-five or even seventy.

The body's elasticity decreases with age, and the vocal range is consequently reduced, particularly at the top end. I have so far suffered very little from this. At present, my most comfortable range lies between the F below middle C and the D just above it. Songs or parts whose average pitch lies below the G below middle C are too low for me, forcing my voice down, to the detriment of its quality, and with all the problems which this entails. For example, the Count's aria *Vedrò, mentr' io sospiro* from *The Marriage of Figaro* is not likely to cause any difficulties, while Beethoven's *An die ferne Geliebte* can prove somewhat problematic. In order to illustrate this point more clearly, I have counted up the number of occurrences of each note in these two examples. Untransposed and ignoring accidentals, the Count's aria contains (working up from the bottom space of the bass clef) three occurrences of A, none of B, nine of C sharp, 22 of D, 57 of E, 60 of F sharp, 66 of G, 70 of A, 33 of B, 34 (!) of C sharp, 35 (!) of D, none of top E, and just one of top F sharp at the end. The range thus extends from bottom A to top F sharp. The most frequent note is the A below middle C, closely followed by the G just below this. The strongest of my higher notes are also well represented: B (33), C sharp (34) and D (35). The graph opposite shows these statistics in visual form. The comfortable middle register of my voice is indicated by the shaded area. This shows just how well suited is the range of this aria to my own particular baritone voice.

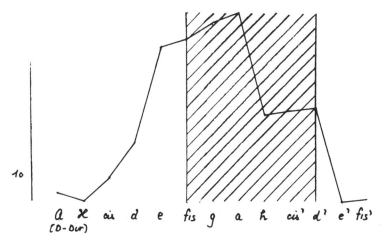

I should add, incidentally, that I take the greatest of care with my higher notes. This means that the voice is more relaxed on the bottom ones, so that I have no problem when singing a bottom A or G.

An die ferne Geliebte is quite a different cup of tea. The original version of this cycle requires a range of a tenth, from the E flat below middle C to the G above it. Untransposed and ignoring accidentals, the cycle contains (again working up from below) 22 occurrences of E flat, 51 of F, 145 of G, 148 of A flat, 193 of B flat, 174 of middle C, 126 of D, 93 of top E flat, 21 of top F and 13 of top G. These notes are represented by the broken line in the graph on the next page. At this pitch there are far too many high notes for a baritone, especially in the fifth song, where they must also be sung piano. Although the first two songs are well within the baritone range, the *tessitura* of the cycle as a whole is more suited to a tenor. A baritone must invariably transpose, the only question being how far.

Most of the commercial baritone editions give C major as the main key, transposing the cycle down by a minor third. This results in 22 occurrences of C, 51 of D, 145 of E, 148 of F, 193 of G, 174 of A, 126 of B, 93 of middle C, 21 of D and 13 of top E. This is shown by the continuous line on the diagram below. The range is concentrated on the G below middle C, above which the notes become rapidly less frequent. Thus very little use is made of my higher notes.

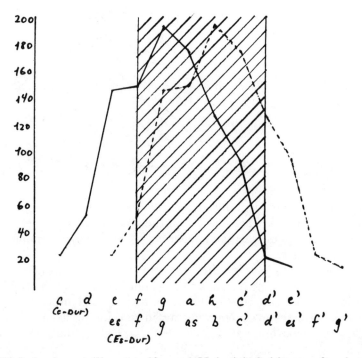

High baritones like myself—and Heinrich Schlusnus for that matter—are thus forced to choose a key lying somewhere between E flat and C major. This solution is far from ideal, but it is the best possible compromise. I prefer to sing in D flat major, as it allows me to sing in flat keys which are related to the original key of E flat major. It also offers a more comfortable *tessitura* than that of the C major version, which is the best precaution against voice-strain. The singer must always be able to sing the jubilant final song with plenty of gusto.

Beethoven's music

Song No. 1 (D flat major)

Auf dem Hügel sitz ich spähend	I sit on the hill, gazing
In das blaue Nebelland,	Into the misty blue land,
Nach den fernen Triften sehend,	Towards the distant meadows
Wo ich dich, Geliebte, fand.	Where I found you, my beloved.
Weit bin ich von dir geschieden,	Now I am a long way from you;
Trennend liegen Berg und Tal	Mountain and valley divide us
Zwischen uns und unserm Frieden,	From each other, from our peace,
Unserm Glück und unsrer Qual.	Our happiness and our sorrow.
Ach, den Blick kannst du nicht sehen,	Ah, you cannot see the passion
Der zu dir so glühend eilt,	Of the look I give you,
Und die Seufzer, sie verwehen	And my sighs are wafted away
In dem Raume, der uns teilt.	In the space that divides us.
Will denn nichts mehr zu dir dringen,	Will nothing reach you
Nichts der Liebe Bote sein?	Which might tell of my love?
Singen will ich, Lieder singen,	Then I will sing songs
Die dir klagen meine Pein!	To tell you of my suffering!
Denn vor Liedeslang entweichet	For the sound of song can put
Jeder Raum und jede Zeit,	To flight all space and time,
Und ein lieband Herz erreichet,	And a loving heart can attain
Was ein liebend Herz geweiht!	What a loving heart hallowed.

The first line ends with the words, ... *sitz ich spähend* ('I sit gazing'), not as I once sang as a student, ... *sitz ich stehend* ('I sit standing')! The narrator has sat down on the hill, and lingers there, while his thoughts range far and wide. So the first essential is to sing quietly. The song has a leisurely tone, which must be communicated to the listener.

It is difficult to determine the various **tempi** for the six songs.

There is no exact answer, and it is a matter of individual interpretation. The choice of tempi can be said to indicate the character of the narrator. If you see him as a sad and melancholy character, you should begin fairly slowly, following Beethoven's own indications. But take care! The song can so easily drag. Being more cheerful and sanguine by nature, I prefer a slightly faster tempo.

Beethoven was primarily an instrumental composer. He is said to have had enormous problems writing for the human voice, which is remarkable for such a great composer. The fact, however, cannot be denied, as the composer's own notebooks reveal. The melody is relatively simple, and is repeated five times in all. It apparently drove him to distraction.

(Orig. version in E flat major)
Fairly slow and expressive

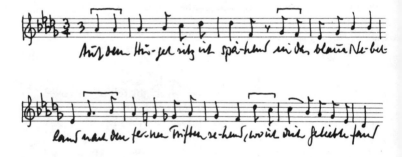

You should take care to observe every little detail, including the fine differentiation of the various up beats (the notes bracketed above): two crochets on the words *Auf dem* in the first bar; two quavers on *in das* in bar three; a dotted crochet and a quaver on *nach dem* in bar five, giving a syncopated effect; finally, two quavers again on *wo ich* in bar seven. Beethoven preserves these rhythms in the four repeats which follow, but varies the melody slightly by means of small ornamentations. For example, on the word *Lieder* in the fourth stanza, a simple repeat of the previous stanza would have gone like this:

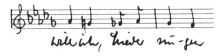

But the composer makes slight modifications, thus:

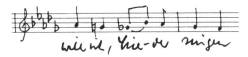

These ornaments should be performed with loving care.

The piano part is the most remarkable element of this song. While the voice-line remains essentially the same, the piano part becomes continually more involved, as befits the music of a true symphonist. It begins with just a few chords, like the accompaniment to a recitative. These are punctuated by a strange accent on the word *spähend*, not on the first syllable as one might expect, but on the second, which appears to heighten the element of chance. This syncopation is further developed in the next two stanzas, then dies down in the fourth verse, only to return even more breathlessly in the final verse. Just as the singer seems to reflect the narrator's feelings, so the piano depicts the stirrings of his heart. This song is a masterpiece of piano variation.

Song No. 2 (F major)

Wo die Berge so blau	Where the blue mountains
Aus dem nebligen Grau	Peer down through grey mists,
Schauen herein,	Where the sun sheds
Wo die Sonne verglüht,	Its last dying rays,
Wo die Wolke umzieht,	Where the cloud rolls away,
Möchte ich sein!	There I would be!
Dort im ruhigen Tal	Down in that quiet valley,
Schweigen Schmerzen und Qual.	Pain and anguish cease.
Wo im Gestein	Where silently among
Still die Primel dort sinnt,	The rocks the primrose muses,
Weht so leise der Wind,	And the wind blows so softly,
Möchte ich sein!	There I would be!

Hin zum sinnigen Wald   I am driven into the quiet forests
Drängt mich Liebesgewalt,   By the power of love
Innere Pein.   And the anguish within.
Ach, mich zög's nicht von hier, I would never leave here,
Könnt ich, Traute, bei dir   If I could be with you
Ewiglich sein!   For ever, my love.

The transition from the first song is typical of Beethoven. The F in the tonic chord of D flat major acts as a pivot note, leading the music into the mediant key of F major.

So far the narrator has only spoken of himself, and of his sighs and longings. Now he reaches for his lute and serenades his beloved for the first time. One might almost call it a song within a song.

Now I am transported by a new vision, that of blue mountains, glimpsed through grey mists, where the sun sheds its last dying rays, and valleys where the primrose muses among the rocks. The piano recreates the sound of horns, dying away softly beyond the horizon. I can almost smell the pungent forest air which I so love. I can imagine a luscious forest scene, like the Leitzachtal: fresh and green in the spring, in the summer it is shaded by birch groves; in the autumn it shimmers in the mist, and in the winter lies dormant beneath a layer of white snow.

A singer must always be a visionary, not in the sense of a prophet, but in the power of his imagination. Whatever would we do without fantasies? How could a singer ever recreate the despair of Schubert's wanderer? Or how could Gretchen's awful plight ever seem credible to the listener? For this to be possible, the singer must be able to put himself in the place of the person in the song.

This song has more low notes than any other in the cycle. If all six songs were as low as this one, I should leave it to a bass to sing. One of the most moving parts of the whole work is the second verse, where the piano picks out a simple pattern of thirds over a held bass, while the voice-line consists of an F repeated 36 times. By the simplest possible means, Beethoven is able to create an atmosphere of peace and inner tranquillity which is quite out of this world. Yes, with Beethoven we can be certain that in this valley pain and anguish cease. The contrast with the dissonances which follow makes the mental anguish of the third verse seem all the more striking. It is important to restrain the anguish somewhat, or the piece will sound melodramatic. The music is so expressive in itself that it does not require any further emphasis.

Song No. 3 (G flat major)

This song is announced by yet another change of scene. The tonality is shifted up a semitone. The singer must create new tone-colours to match the new tonalities in the piano part.

Leichte Segler in den Höhen
Und du Bächlein klein und schmal,
Könnt mein Liebchen ihr erspähen,
Grüsst sie mir viel tausendmal.

Seht, ihr Wolken, sie dann gehen
Sinnend in dem stillen Tal,
Lasst mein Bild vor ihr entstehen
In dem luft'gen Himmelssaal.

Wird sie an den Büschen stehen,
Die nun herbstlich falb und kahl,
Klagt ihr, wie mir ist geschehen,
Klagt ihr, Vöglein, meine Qual.

Stille Weste, bringt im Wehen
Hin zu meiner Herzenswahl
Meine Seufzer, die vergehen
Wie der Sonne letzter Strahl.

Flüstr ihr zu mein Liebesflehen,
Lass sie, Bächlein klein und schmal,
Treu in deinen Wogen sehen
Meine Tränen ohne Zahl.

You soft clouds that sail on high,
And you, narrow little brook,
If you catch sight of my beloved,
Give her a thousand greetings from me.

If you clouds then see her walking
Pensively through the quiet valley,
Then recreate my image before her
Across the airy firmament.

If she is standing by the bushes,
Now so pale and bare in the autumn,
Then tell her what has befallen me,
You birds, and tell of my anguish.

You gentle west winds, waft my sighs
Towards my heart's desire,
Sighs that disperse
Like the sun's dying ray.

Whisper to her my loving supplications,
You narrow little brook,
And in your ripples, show her
The true measure of my numberless tears.

Such verses may well be incomprehensible to the modern singer,
who has grown up to the loud cacophonies of disco music. If you
are secretly amused at the idea of longing and sighing, then you
should keep away from these songs.

Now it is the pianist's turn to take the lead. He should aim for
clarity and transparency of tone, while the singer gives a gentle
accompaniment. These bare notes in the voice-line are probably
the most unvocal passage in the whole cycle. They might almost

have been written for the violin, where a violinist would stroke
the strings softly with his bow. A singer must manage as best he
can, though a staccato should be avoided, as the melody will
then become disjointed. At the beginning of the third verse, the
music modulates into the minor for the first time. It would be
wrong to darken the tone-colour at this point, and a smooth
legato will give better expression to this autumn lament.

Song No. 4 (G flat major)

Diese Wolken in den Höhen,
Dieser Vöglein muntrer Zug
Werden dich, o Huldin, sehen.
Nehmt mich mit im leichten Flug!

Diese Weste werden spielen
Scherzend dir um Wang und Brust,
In den seidnen Locken wühlen.
Teilt ich mit euch diese Lust!

Hin zu dir von jenen Hügeln
Emsig dieses Bächlein eilt.
Wird ihr Bild sich in dir spiegeln,
Fliess zurück dann unverweilt.

These clouds on high and
This lively flock of birds
Will see you, my gracious one.
Waft me away with your gentle breezes!

These west winds will merrily play
Around your cheek and bosom,
And stir your silken tresses.
Oh that I could share in your pleasure!

This brook hurries eagerly
Towards you from those hills.
If her image is reflected in your waters,
Then flow back without delay.

There is a glorious modulation from the minor back to the

major. While the voice sustains the pivot note, the piano leads
the transition into a vividly descriptive passage, which suggests
the clouds passing by.

(Orig. version in A flat major)

Beethoven's directions are, 'Not too fast, pleasant and expressive.' Such detailed instructions suggest that the music meant a
lot to him. I love the syncopated rhythms, which seem to hurry
the clouds and the brook on their way.

As the clouds rise, so also does the *tessitura*. At last I am given a
top E flat to sing, and can move into the top register. This is a
good preparation for the final song, which is the only one in the
whole cycle to have a fairly high *tessitura*.

Song No. 5 (B flat major)

Es kehret der Maien, es blühet die Au.
Die Lüfte, sie wehen so milde, so lau.
Geschwätzig die Bäche nun rinnen.
Die Schwalbe, sie kehret zum wirtlichen Dach,
Sie baut sich so emsig ihr bräutlich Gemach,
Die Liebe soll wohnen da drinnen.

Sie bringt sich geschäftig von kreuz und von quer
Manch weicheres Stück zu dem Brautbett hierher,
Manch wärmendes Stück für die Kleinen.
Nun wohnen die Gatten beisammen so treu,
Was Winter geschieden, verband nun der Mai,
Was liebet, das weiss er zu einen.

Es kehret der Maien, es blühet die Au.
Die Lüfte, sie wehen so milde, so lau.
Nur ich kann nicht ziehen von hinnen.
Wenn alles, was liebet, der Frühling vereint,
Nur unserer Liebe kein Frühling erscheint,
Und Tränen sind all ihr Gewinnen.

May is returning, the meadow is in bloom;
The warm, mild breezes blow;
The brooks run chattering on.
The swallow returns to the welcoming roof,
And eagerly builds her bridal chamber,
Where love shall dwell within.

She dashes all over the place to bring
Many soft scraps for the bridal bed
And many warm scraps for her young.
Now the pair lives faithfully together;
What winter had parted, May has reunited,
Knowing how to bring lovers together again.

May is returning, the meadow is in bloom;
The warm, mild breezes blow;
Only I cannot depart from here.
Though spring unites all lovers,
Our love alone knows no spring,
And tears are its only gain.

The piano interlude between the fourth and the fifth songs is extremely important. An enormous amount is contained in these dozen or so bars. It begins with a syncopated rhythm which almost anticipates the *Hammerklavier* Sonata. Is this the beating of an impatient heart?

(Orig. version in C major)

We hear the calls of nightingale and cuckoo. Soon the melody winds gently, as though through a forest in spring, in a delightful fairy dance. The first phrase of the voice part is very difficult technically, as intonation is always tricky when high notes have to be sung quietly.

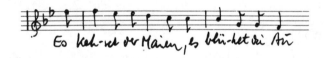

Beethoven has marked this song *vivace*, which means 'lively and brisk'. This time I take the composer at his word, while at the same time paying full attention to the ritardandi which bring the song to an adagio at the close. This song is full of variations in tempo, sforzandi, sudden piani, crescendi, accelerandi and ritardandi. It can sometimes happen in a concert that I vary the tempo more than usual, draw out a pause, or emphasise an *espressivo*. My accompanists know to expect this. Surprises like these are always great fun.

Song No. 6 (D flat major)

Nimm sie hin denn, diese Lieder,
Die ich dir, Geliebte, sang,
Singe sie dann abends wieder
Zu der Laute süssem Klang.

Wenn das Dämmrungsrot dann ziehet
Nach dem stillen blauen See,
Und sein letzter Strahl verglühet
Hinter jener Bergeshöh;

Und du singst, was ich gesungen,
Was mir aus der vollen Brust
Ohne Kunstgepräng erklungen,
Nur der Sehnsucht sich bewusst:

Dann vor diesen Liedern weichet,
Was geschieden uns so weit,
Und ein liebend Herz erreichet,
Was ein liebend herz geweiht.

Now take these songs
Which I sang to you, my love,
And sing them again in the evening
To the sweet sound of your lute.

When the red light of dusk creeps
Towards the calm blue lake,
And its last ray dies
Behind those high mountains;

If you sing the words I sang,
The unaffected sounds
Of an overflowing heart,
Only conscious of longing:

Then these songs will cross
The gulf that divided us;
And a loving heart can attain
What a loving heart hallowed.

As long as the pianist and I can achieve the right atmosphere
during the adagio transition from the previous song, the seven

bars of the piano interlude can be marvellously moving and effective.

(Orig. version in E flat major) Andante con moto, cantabile

'Now, my love, take these songs which I sang to you.' These words seem to sum up the whole object of my career as a recitalist.

The softly repeated F-major chords create an impression of the red glow of evening, while the gentle harmonies recall the mountain sunset of the second song. I colour my voice accordingly, in the hope that this association will not escape the listener.

Song No. 1 (Orig. version in E flat major)

Song No. 2 (Orig. version in G major)

The reprise and coda which follow are symphonic in nature, and indeed unique to the song literature. The voice melody of the first song now reappears on the piano towards the end of the work. This device is typical of Beethoven.

The theme is taken over by the voice, and is further developed into a triumphant finale. This is particularly appropriate in that the last two lines of the first and last songs are in fact identical. Returning to the opening melody is thus the most natural way of concluding the work.

CHAPTER 13

Eventful years

The good old Met

In December 1960 I was to fulfil a wish I had made eight years previously: I made my debut at the New York Metropolitan Opera. This was not at the new building at the Lincoln Center, which was not yet in existence, but at the legendary old Met on the corner of Broadway and 39th Street. The opera was *Tannhäuser*, with Hans Hopf in the title role, Leonie Rysanek as Elisabeth, Irene Dalis as Venus, and with Georg Solti who was conducting at the Met for the first time. The performance took place on a Saturday afternoon, and was as usual broadcast via radio throughout America. Never before had I been so awed by a theatre.

The greatest singers of the century had stood on that stage, among them Lilli Lehmann, Melba, Destinn, the de Reszke brothers, Ruffo and Caruso. Gustav Mahler, Arturo Toscanini, Bruno Walter, Fritz Busch and Sir Thomas Beecham had all conducted from that orchestra pit. Nothing had been bombed or destroyed here during the war, and nothing had been rebuilt. The 'Golden Horseshoe' rose up behind the stalls just as it had done for fifty years or more—row upon row of seats and boxes, reaching up to the gods, or the 'Family Circle' as it was called. To anybody sitting up there, so the stage manager told me, I was 'just about three inches high'.

Not only was the Golden Horseshoe as it had been for time immemorial, but the same was true of the dressing rooms, the electrical fittings and even, it was claimed, the scenery. In 1960, there were already rumours to the effect that the old theatre's days were numbered, but no one took any notice. The Met and the Carnegie Hall had for decades been the focus of all musical and cultural activities. They represented all that was best in music. The usual comment was 'What? Pull down the Met? Nobody would dare!' This soon proved to be mistaken.

While rehearsing *Tannhäuser*, I attended a rehearsal of *Don Giovanni*, in order to see Cesare Siepi, the most famous Don Giovanni of the day. It was a thrilling experience. 'Simply overwhelming!', I said to a chorus singer who was waiting to go on stage, a German *émigré* with thirty years' experience at the Met. 'Ya shoulda heard Pinza!' he replied. If it had been Ezio Pinza on stage, he would no doubt have said, 'Ya shoulda heard Scotti!', and with Scotti it would have been, 'Ya shoulda heard Maurel!' This is the sort of mentality which does not so much reject the good for what is better as reject the new for the sake of the old.

In 1960 I had sung Don Giovanni in German in Cologne and Hamburg. In 1962 I sang the role in Italian for the first time, at Aix-en-Provence. It was directed by a member of the *Comédie Française*, who wished the drama to take place in the salon and boudoir of a certain Madame Pompadour. I myself see Don Giovanni as a handsome man with a black beard, rather like the picture which Max Slevogt painted of a contemporary singer called D'Andrade. In Aix I was transformed into a degenerate gigolo of the rococo period, prancing up and down the stage, dressed in a red and orange striped tunic with matching breeches, and balancing a lorgnette between the fingertips of my right hand. It was torture. The whole idea was anathema to me, and I was extremely reluctant to follow the director's instructions.

Our conversation usually went like this: the director would say, 'Monsieur Prey, you muzz now come from ze left side.' I would glare at him. Frightened, he would dither, 'But eef you prefair, you can come from ze right side.'

On top of this, I had a lot of trouble with the Italian text. The part of Don Giovanni consists mostly of difficult recitative passages. Although I knew them back to front in German, I simply could not master them in Italian. I could foresee a disaster. The night before the *première*, my body began to react psychosomatically in a highly sophisticated fashion. I was suddenly attacked by a painful inflammation of the ear, and spent the night in agony. The next morning, my back suddenly went 'click' and I remained stuck in a bowed position with my first ever attack of lumbago. I simply could not get upright again, and staggered and groaned around my room until the excitement made me hoarse. It was a Saturday, and my wife had the greatest difficulty in getting hold of a doctor. She eventually found one who lived about seven miles away. He prescribed an injection, which in France is always carried out by a pharmacist. The injection was so clumsily executed that I developed a limp as well. You can imagine what Don Giovanni must have looked like that night, bent over like the Hunchback of Notre Dame, deaf in one ear, lame and hoarse, and what is more he didn't know his part. Add to that the absurd production and the idiotic direction, and you have the biggest nightmare of my whole career! Imagine my relief when we at last left the dry, parched countryside of Provence after twelve performances, including some as the Count in *Figaro*, and returned to the green fields of Central Europe. We fled immediately after the final performance, and at nine o'clock the next morning I had a cool dip in the waters of Lake Zürich, as if to rid myself of all disease.

I went on to sing at the Munich and Salzburg Festivals, where I sang Guglielmo for the third time in Rennert's production of *Così fan Tutte*, and was able to make a complete recovery. Elisabeth Schwarzkopf gave an unforgettable performance as Fiordiligi, with Christa Ludwig as Dorabella, Graziella Sciutti as Despina, Waldemar Kmentt as Ferrando, Karl Dönch as Alfonso and Karl Böhm conducting. Further engagements included a recital tour of Germany, followed by a tour of the eastern United States at the beginning of 1963. In December 1962 I recorded *Così fan Tutte* with Irmgard Seefried, Nan Merriman, Erika Köth, Ernst Häflinger and Dietrich Fischer-Dieskau under Eugen, Jochum. I also did a number of recordings for Electrola, including one of Schumann's *Dichterliebe*, *Kerner Lieder* and song cycle Opus 39, and one of ballads by Loewe, a much-neglected composer whose music I like very much. I might add here that Loewe left an enormous legacy of 150 ballads and about 250 songs.

On television I sang Silvio in *Pugliacci*, and Robert Storch, the court conductor, in Strauss' *Intermezzo*. In the autumn of 1963 I paid my first visit to the western United States, where I was due to sing the Rossini *Barber* at the War Memorial Opera House in San Francisco, together with my much-loved colleague Reri Grist and with Cesare Valletti. Fortunately I had plenty of time between rehearsals to get to know the environs of this most beautiful of American cities.

On the Golden Gate Bridge

I am one of the few people to have walked the whole length of San Francisco's Golden Gate Bridge. How do I know that? Because I was told this by the most reliable witness there could possibly be: Mr Armistice Happyweather Under-the-bridge Peabody, whose name is almost as long as the bridge itself. In those days pedestrians were still allowed along the wire footpath which runs the whole two miles from one end of the bridge to the other. I went for a walk there one afternoon following a *Barber* rehearsal. I stopped to admire its engineering and enjoy the view. I peered over the railings into the sea and down the funnels of passing ships. I was just about to move on again, when my way was barred by a thick-set man holding a bucket of paint. He examined me sceptically, though by no means unkindly, through a pair of rimless spectacles.

'Takin' the view in, mister?' he said.

'Yes—lovely!' I replied. 'I want to go from one end of the bridge to the other.'

'Oh yeah? So ya wanna cross the bridge.'

'Of course, why not?'

'That's dandy!' The painter took off his red cap, which looked like a cross between a factory and a baseball cap, and had 'Shell' written across it. He scratched his head and put the cap back on again. 'Lotsa folks them's comin' for other reasons...'

'I expect they come to look at the view.'

'Yep! They love the view. They all say them's comin' to see the view.'

I looked him up and down. What did he want from me? Perhaps he was not quite all there. I had been warned that there were rather a lot of strange people around here. But this was not the impression I had from this thick-set figure in clean overalls. He looked perfectly reasonable to me, and he was clean shaven.

'Live in Frisco?' he asked me.

'No, I'm from Germany.'

'Thought so. A mate of mine spoke just like you. Johann Kargerer. Ya know him?'

'No, I've not yet had the pleasure.'

'Got his name from folks like you. Yep! Armistice Happyweather Under-the-bridge Peabody. Armistice 'cause I was born on Armistice Day, 11th November 1918. Yep! Happyweather 'cause the sun was shinin' then on Armistice Day, and Under-the-bridge 'cause I was born under a bridge. By Eau Claire, Winconsin. But just call me Arm.'

A funny chap, I thought. 'And I'm Hermann Prey. From Munich. But just call me Herm.'

'Nice knowin' ya, Herm. But tell me, ya really goin' for a walk? Ya know, I've helped lotsa folks, by golly! Summer or winter, it's cold down there in the water.'

Then the penny dropped. 'Good God! You don't think I'm going to jump in the water, Arm?'

'Sure do, Herm! Just that. Most of 'em say them's come to see the view, but goin' for a walk, that's new. Yep! That's real new! First time anybody thoughta that.'

I could not help laughing. 'But I say, Arm. What in the world would make me jump in the water?'

'You know best. They all have reasons. I don't ask no questions. Ya well built, Herm. Barrel-chested. You a boxer or summat? Or maybe a wrestler? A hard job, by golly, I know. You'll drop quickly, believe me. Before ya half way down it's curtains for you. Like Jack Dempsey or Joe Louis's walked past. Ya won't hear the splash.'

'But I swear to you, Arm. I'm not thinking of jumping.'

'Have a smoke.'

'Thanks, Arm. As long as my wife isn't here.'

'Ah, ya gotta wife.'

'Yes, and three children.'

'They all gotta wife an' three kids. And they all laugh just like you when I talk to 'em. But as soon as I turn my back them's off. A hundred a year. Sometimes more.'

'What? More than a hundred?'

'The Gulf Stream eats 'em up like a hot dog for lunch. Yep!'

I'll never get past him this way, I thought. So I decided to change my tactics. 'I say, Arm. How do you know all this?'

'Work here. Me an' my twelve mates. Paint the Golden Gate. Get into my metal basket. Start where ya come from, and stop where ya say ya goin' to. Then I go back to the beginning. Nearly twenny years now. But not much longer.'

'Why? Will you jump into the water yourself?'

'Nope! I'm retirin'. Movin' back to southern California. There's lotsa retired folks there. In Frisco them's retired or them's fired. And sometimes they comes out onto the Golden Gate. All the dumpers and Chevvies go past, but none of 'em stops. They never see nothin'.'

'Look, Arm,' I said. 'You're wrong about me. I'm a singer. And singers like exercise and fresh air.'

'What! A singer?'

'Yes, an opera singer. I've come to Frisco to sing at the opera.'

'Fine! Sing me summat from *Oklahoma*.'

'I can't think of anything from *Oklahoma*. But I can sing you something from *South Pacific*. Do you know *South Pacific*?'

'Heard of it.'

'Well, there's a lovely song in it called *Some Enchanted Evening*.'

Arm loved it. He even tried to join in. 'Gosh, Herm. I really liked that! Whatta ya say ya called?'

'Hermann Prey.'

'No, I mean whatta ya do?'

'Opera.'

'Gee whizz! Opera. I must tell the mates. We never had that on the Golden Gate before. Opera! A queer job ya got, Herm! By golly! Ya quite a character! Ya take a walk on the Golden

Gate and ya sing opera! But gosh darn it! I like it. Y'oughta see if
they'll have ya on the TV.'

'I'll do that, Arm. I promise you. But I must hurry up now, or
I'll never get to the other end.'

'Nice meetin' ya, Herm.'

'The pleasure was mine, Arm.'

'Yep! You're a real character. Hihi! Opera, ya said?'

'Yep! O-P-E-R-A!'

'I'll never forget ya, Herm.'

'No, Arm. I'll never forget you either.'

Always on the move

Our two older children had come with us to America, while
little Franziska stayed with Bärbel's mother in Berlin. With the
help of Paul Pollazceck, an old school friend of my accompanist,
Paul Ulanowsky, we rented an elegant villa in Green Street for
480 dollars a month. An imposing building, it looked out on the
Golden Gate Bridge. It was old and grey, but sported an ornate
façade. Its fifteen rooms were large and tastefully furnished, and
Bärbel was greatly impressed with the kitchen. It was exciting to
find lemon-trees in the garden, for the first time in our lives we
could pick our own lemons. Annette was six at the time, and
went to a local school, even though she could not speak any
English. Bärbel took and fetched her every day. We could not
understand why she was getting so thin, until we eventually
discovered she was going without lunch. She told us she could
not stand the food, and did not know how to explain this to them
in English. However, she began to talk American slang after
only a week and after a fortnight she was already correcting my
un-American pronunciation. She sat next to Lynn Eisenhower,
grand-daughter of the former president, and they quickly
became friends.

After my performance in San Francisco, we travelled on
down the beautiful California coast to Los Angeles. I then went
on alone to Montreal, where my first task was to buy a winter
coat. It was still bathing weather in Los Angeles, but in

Montreal the thermometer stood at minus 20°C. A singer is always having to cope with climatic changes, which make heavy demands on the voice.

No one will ever forget the day President Kennedy was assassinated on 22nd November 1963. Two days later, I was in the Herkulessaal in Munich, performing *Winterreise*, with Karl Engel on the piano. The concert was to become a requiem to the late president. There was no applause as I left the stage, neither had I expected any. For all of us were still in a state of shock.

I had a similar experience after a performance of Mahler's *Kindertotenlieder*, beautifully interpreted by the incomparable Joseph Keilberth. The gentle cradle song was followed by total silence. Keilberth looked across at me and came down from the conductor's stand; he shook my hand and thanked the leader of the orchestra; then we left the stage together. Just as we reached the stage door, the audience broke into loud applause. The same thing once happened in Bayreuth after a performance of *Tannhäuser* with Wolfgang Windgassen in the title role. The curtain fell, but not a clap could be heard. Wieland Wagner asked for the safety curtain to be lowered and time stood still until it was half-way down. Then the ovation began; in all there were forty-four curtain-calls, which was quite an experience.

Silence can be more effective than loud applause. I am always amazed at the length of the pause which follows a particularly successful concert, before the first claps begin, almost hesitantly, for fear of spoiling the awed silence. This is almost inevitably true of *Winterreise* in particular. The length of pause has for me become an indicator of the quality of my performance. The longer the silence before the applause, the greater the impact I have made.

November 1963 saw the re-opening of the grand new National Theatre in Munich, exactly twenty years after it had been destroyed in the war. I appeared there shortly before Christmas in Handel's *Julius Caesar*, and later on during the Richard Strauss Festival, in *Ariadne auf Naxos* and *Intermezzo*, all of which were directed by Rudolf Hartmann. I have worked with him since 1958, and it has always been an amazing experience. Hartmann must undoubtedly be *the* great Strauss director of his time. Singers like myself owe much to his profound knowledge of the Strauss operas, and also of others, such as Mozart's *Magic Flute* and *Don Giovanni*, which he produced in the Cuvillié Theatre in 1966.

I did some recordings in February 1964, and then went on to Vienna to do *Intermezzo* and the Count in *The Marriage of Figaro*. From there I flew back to America to do eight more recitals with Paul Ulanowsky.

Paul Ulanowsky was one of the most interesting accompanists I ever had. He is full of Viennese wit, and had something to say on every occasion. 'Now listen, Paul,' I once said to him with great enthusiasm. 'I'd like to sing the top E just like this.'

'O.K.,' he said, 'let's do it that way.' Afterwards he asked with a twinkle in his eye, 'Do you feel better now?' He was always pulling my leg.

If I sang a song in A flat major, he might use the G-major or B-major version, but never the one in the right key. 'It's boring playing these songs in the key they're written in,' he explained. He always had to have something to transpose, if only to keep him on his toes. I remember one concert at the Ladies' Music Morning Club. We were supposed to be singing twelve Strauss songs in the second half, but when we arrived in Montreal, neither of us had the music, as each of us had thought that the other one had it. What should we do now? Change the programme? 'Wait a minute,' said Paul, and thought for a moment. 'Yes, I can do it.' He accompanied all twelve songs by heart from beginning to end. Apart from one or two improvised chords, he was note perfect.

By May I was back in Vienna to give two recitals with Alfred Brendel as part of the 1964 Vienna Festival. Alfred and I have never agreed, right up to the final rehearsal, but we have still produced some unforgettable performances.

A concert in Wiesbaden once included one of Wolf's *Eichendorff-Lieder* entitled *Heimweh* ('Homesickness'). The last line of this song runs *Grüss dich, Deutschland, aus Herzensgrund!* ('I greet thee, Germany, from the bottom of my heart'). Alfred did not approve of the conservatism of the Wiesbaden public. He said to me in the interval, 'Hermann, I'll give you fifty marks tonight if you sing *Grüss dich, Sarah, aus Herzensgrund!*'

I should love to perform with Alfred again, although I expect we would be arguing once more within the first four bars.

The Vienna Festival continued with Mahler's 8th Symphony under Josef Krips, in which I sang the baritone solo, and Rudolf Hartmann's production of *Capriccio*, with Lisa della Casa as the countess, Otto Wiener as La Roche, Fritz Wunderlich as the Italian tenor and Georges Prêtre conducting. I then went on to the National Theatre, Munich, where I sang in *Julius Caesar*, with Clare Watson as Cleopatra and Fritz Wunderlich as Sextus Pompeius. I was always on the move.

Another landmark in my career was my first appearance as Papageno, in Harry Buckwitz's production of *The Magic Flute* in July 1964. I came relatively late to this my most popular role. Fritz Wunderlich sang Tamino, with Erika Köth as Queen of the Night, and Anneliese Rothenberger as Pamina. The conductor was Fritz Rieger, director of the Munich Phil-harmonic.

At the end of the year I returned to the Met as the Count in *The Marriage of Figaro*, with Lisa della Casa as the Countess, Judith Raskin as Susanne, Teresa Stratas as Cherubino and the much-admired Cesare Siepi as Figaro, in the role which Pinza had sung there before him.

I must also mention 5th August 1965, the date of my Bayreuth debut, when I again sang Wolfram, my one and only Wagner role, with Leonie Rysanek as Elisabeth, Wolfgang Windgassen as Rompilger, Martti Talvela as the landgrave and André Cluytens conducting.

I shall never forget my first recital in Moscow on 24th October 1965. In earlier recitals in Leningrad and Tbilisi, I had sung a selection of songs by Schubert, Schumann, Wolf and Strauss, only to find that a mixed programme did not go down so well with Russian audiences. So in Moscow I had decided to sing *Winterreise* instead. I walked on stage and announced in my best Russian, 'Ladies and gentlemen, this evening I wish to sing *Winterreise.*' In the stunned silence which followed I feared the worst, only to receive a massive ovation. This was repeated at

the end of the performance, together with the statutory
Winterreise pause.

These were years of continuing success, but I remember them
best of all for the most important friendship of my life, that with
Fritz Wunderlich.

Amico Fritz

We first met in Salzburg in 1959, during rehearsals for Strauss'
Die Schweigsame Frau ('The Silent Woman'). Fritz sang the part
of the jovial young nephew of Admiral Henry Morosus, an old
man who will only marry a woman who is silent, but ends up
getting swindled like Don Pasquale. I was making my Salzburg
debut as the cunning barber. Fritz was born in Kusel in the
Palatinate in 1930, so we were about the same age. It was his
second time in Salzburg, while I was still a novice. In *The Silent
Woman*, the nephew and the barber are both involved in plotting
against the old man. We immediately took to one another as co-
conspirators, and our friendship took off from there. It was to
last seven years, up to Fritz's sudden death in 1966. They were
happy years of friendship and collaboration with a dear and
talented colleague, who within the space of a few years
established himself as one of the greatest singers of his time.

There was no other Tamino like him; he played Don Ottavio
with a virility which I often miss in other singers, and sang that
notoriously complicated aria of Belmonte's with incredible style
and confidence. We sang together in August Everding's first
Italian production of *La Traviata* in Munich in March 1965,
with Teresa Stratas and the young Brigitte Fassbaender. Fritz'
Alfredo was quite stunning, and I regret we made so few
recordings together. My favourite is a record of Lortzing's
Wildschütz made in May 1963, with the charming Anneliese
Rothenberger as Baroness Freimann and the irrepressible Fritz
as Baron Kronthal.

One almost had the feeling that he knew his days were
numbered. He lived such a busy life, enjoying every moment to
the full. Even today, when I meet up with friends or colleagues,

scarcely half an hour goes past without Fritz being mentioned.

Fritz loved to go hunting. I hate shooting animals, but Fritz once persuaded me to come with him when we were staying in Erding. He had quite a compelling way of getting other people to enjoy his hobbies. Fritz took three rifles of various calibres, and handed the fourth one to me. Off we went, walking on for several hours through the autumn forest, sometimes abreast and sometimes in single file.

Although some of my songs are often about spring, my favourite season is the autumn, when I love the pungent air, and the reds and browns and yellows. Fritz was in an excellent mood, although he would have been less pleased if he had known we were going to spend the whole day without seeing a single animal. At last we found the shooting post, climbed up into it and began waiting. We waited for hours on end, but nothing moved, not even a blade of grass.

'Take this pipe,' whispered Fritz. 'Play it a little at a time, like Papageno in Sarastro's dungeon. It'll attract the game.' I put the pipe in my mouth and began blowing. 'Not so quickly, you fool!' he hissed. 'Take your time. Like a kid calling for its mother.' So I slowed down, but to no effect. I was bored to death, and my backside had gone to sleep on the hard planks. Fritz suddenly tapped my shoulder and pointed at a large beech-tree. Something was actually moving, it was peering out from behind the trunk. I saw something jump out and disappear into the thicket. 'A wild cat, dammit!' said Fritz. Thank goodness he missed it, I thought to myself. Fritz packed up his arsenal. 'I'll put up some targets,' he said irritably. It was already half past three.

In spite of my aversion to hunting, I do have some experience with firearms. When we were evacuated to Landsberg an der Warthe in 1943, there had been compulsory shooting practice every week. So I was a perfectly good match for Fritz.

We climbed down from the post. 'Let's say about 120 metres,' suggested Fritz. He opened his bag and took out a roll of sticky-tape, a pocket knife and a target. The last thing to appear was a rapid-fire pistol. 'I bought it only a couple of days ago,' he said. 'Let's try it out. Can you hold it a minute?' I took the pistol and gripped it. My finger slid automatically to the trigger. 'Wait there,' he said. 'I'll just stick the target up.' At that moment there was a loud bang. The pistol had gone off.

I reeled as everything swam before my eyes—Fritz, the forest, the pistol in my hand.

> *'Mein Sohn, was birgst du so bang dein Gesicht?'*
> *'Siehst, Vater, du den Erlkönig nicht?*
> *Den Erlkönig mit Kron und Schweif?'*
> *'Mein Sohn, es ist ein Nebelstreif...,*
>
> 'My son, why do you so anxiously hide your face?'
> 'Father, do you not see the Erl-King?
> The Erl-King with his crown and train?'
> 'My son, it is only the mist.'

I had recently recorded this Goethe ballad on disc. For days now, I simply had not been able to get Schubert's tune out of my head. This happens to me from time to time, and it is quite dreadful. The notes go round and round in my head until I can stand it no longer.

'Shit!' said Fritz. In the meantime, I had come to my senses. 'Are you mad?' I cried. 'You give me a gun with the trigger cocked, and I nearly shoot you to kingdom come!'

'Just an oversight,' protested Fritz.

'An oversight, my foot! I call it crass stupidity!'

'But nothing happened.'

'Nothing happened? I very nearly shot your head off. That's what happened!'

I had to sit down and compose myself again, for I was trembling all over. I could picture myself crying over Fritz' body, like Eugène Onegin over his friend Lenski. My future career and happiness had hung by a thread, an inch to the left and that would have been it. What a scoop for the press!

I could see the headlines: 'Singer murdered in Erding Forest!' or 'Prey kills Wunderlich with pistol.'

I often think of this incident when I am dozing in the morning, or waiting before a concert in the silence of the green room. I have often had nightmares about it. Sometimes I see myself in the dock, with a jury made up of singers from the Bavarian State Opera. Hans Hotter is among them. He stands up and declares in his booming bass voice, 'No, m'lud, you are mistaken. It was not Prey. It was Brickshit Charlie.'

The mythical *Steinschiesser Karl* or 'Brickshit Charlie' was for months the biggest star backstage at the Munich Opera. His best proponents were Benno Kusche, Gottlob Frick, and Fritz of course, but especially Hans Hotter. We would spin some of the most dreadful yarns about somebody. But nobody was supposed to ask who it was, unless he did so by touching his left ear with his right index finger, as a sign that he was not to be fooled. For example, Benno might come into our dressing-room and say, 'Did you hear? The secretary tells me he went to the director and said to him, "Director, you know what you can do? I won't stand for it any longer. You keep promising me parts and then not giving me them. Please note that I wish to terminate our contract as from now."' If anyone asked who it was, the answer was 'Brickshit Charlie!' We kept up this game for months. As I said, Hans Hotter was the invincible champion.

It became my ultimate goal to pull Hans Hotter's leg. On one occasion, during rehearsals of *The Barber*, Figaro was seen to go into Hotter's dressing-room. Hans was sitting there in his black costume, having his long Don Basilio nose stuck on by his make-up man, Herr Rasche. 'Herr Rasche,' I said as if in passing, 'is it true that his wife cuts his hair for him?'

Don Basilio looked up? 'Who?' he asked.

'Brickshit Charlie' was Figaro's triumphant reply.

In another dream, I am being tried on stage at the New York Metropolitan Opera. I see a figure standing there. He is tall, thin and severe, and is dressed in the same gown as the Richmond Magistrate in *Martha*. It is Rudolf Bing. He holds the sticky-tape in one hand and Fritz Wunderlich's target in the other. 'Gentlemen,' he declares in his Austrian accent, 'not only was the victim, Mr Wunderlich, a connoisseur and collector of valuable guns, he was, if you please, a trained and experienced marksman. It is highly unlikely that he should have carried a loaded pistol around with him. That the accused should claim that not only was the pistol loaded, but that the trigger was cocked . . . ' The scene suddenly changes to Gounod's *Faust*, final act, prison scene. Mephisto appears. I realise to my horror that it is Dr Lieben from the Grey Monastery in Berlin. 'Guilty' is the song of the heavenly choirs. 'Now then, Porky!' says Mephisto. 'Which is it to be? Vanilla or chocolate?'

I was often tempted to play a schoolboy prank on Fritz. This once happened in Munich at the 1966 *première* of *The Magic Flute*. Fritz was in top form, and was soon to become world famous, having already signed a contract with the Met. There is a scene in the first act of the opera, in which the three ladies from the Queen of the Night give Tamino a picture of Pamina, whom he is to rescue from the clutches of Sarastro. He is supposed to fall in love with her. He is overwhelmed by her beauty. Gazing rapturously at her picture, he sings the aria, *Dies Bildnis ist bezaubernd schön* ('This picture is enchantingly beautiful').

I have no idea what got into me. On the day of the *première*, I went up to Frau Moser, the props manager, and asked for some sellotape. Over the top of Pamina's picture I stuck a photograph of my own face in a horrid grimace. I was standing backstage as the opera began. The overture had finished and the snake was beginning to move. I was suddenly afraid. This aria is vital for Tamino. If something went wrong and Tamino were to laugh at my picture, it might stop the aria and create a scandal. In desperation I looked for the three ladies, and caught them just as they were about to go on stage. 'The picture! Which of you's got the picture?'

'For goodness' sake, Hermann, leave us alone! We're about to go on stage!'

'I must have the picture!' One of the ladies gave it to me. I ripped out my photo and gave it back to her. What a relief! On that night of all nights, Fritz fluffed the top A flat at the end of the aria, for the first time ever. If I had not taken my picture out, I would no doubt have been blamed for this mishap.

I can never sing Papageno without thinking of Fritz. It was so exciting to set out with him for Sarastro's castle. Our voices were beautifully matched. We even thought of 'selling our services' as a duo for operas such as *Così fan Tutte*, *Don Giovanni*, *The Magic Flute*, *The Barber of Seville*, *La Traviata* and *Eugène Onegin*.

35.   As Gabriel von Eisenstein in the 1977 Covent Garden production of Johann Strauss'
Fledermaus, with Kiri Te Kanawa as my wife Rosalinde.

36.   In the 1960 Salzburg production of
Cosí fan Tutte, with Elisabeth Schwarzkopf
as Fiordiligi.

37.   In the same Rennert production, with
Christa Ludwig as Dorabella.

38. My first appearance as the poet Olivier in Richard Strauss' *Capriccio*, in the Prinzregenten Theatre, Munich, in 1959. Lisa Della Casa sang the part of the countess.

39. With Erika Köth in *The Barber of Seville* in 1959—my Vienna debut.

40. My Berlin opera debut as the Barber in 1958, with Rita Streich as Rosina.

41. In 1976 we filmed *The Marriage of Figaro* in London. Mirella Freni sang the part of Susanna in this fanciful production by the French director Jean Pierre Ponnelle.

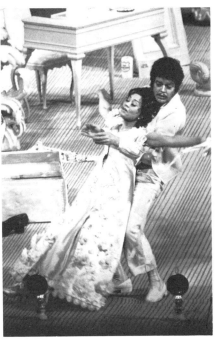

43. Reri Grist played my temperamental wife in *The Barber* in Munich in 1974.

42. The 1975 television production of Carl Orff's *Carmina Burana*, with Lucia Popp.

44. My television show entitled *Schaut her, ich bin's* ('Look, it's me') included a number of opera excerpts. This is a scene from Tchaikovsky's opera *Eugène Onegin*, with Sena Jurinac.

45. The 1966 Munich production of *The Magic Flute*, with Anneliese Rothenberger as Pamina. This was the last time I sang with Fritz Wunderlich.

Fritz had had a difficult childhood. He always wanted to show me his birthplace in Kusel, which lay in the Palatinate hills between Trier and Kaiserslautern. 'You must see where I was born,' he told me. One day he eventually took me there. He led me into a tiny miner's cottage and up a small stepladder; this was where he had slept as a boy. There was no plaster on the walls, and the furniture consisted of two wooden beds and a table, with a hand-basin and a jug. 'I had nothing but a mangy old tom-cat,' he said. 'Now you know why I sometimes crack up.' We went out to an apple tree. What was so interesting about an apple tree, I asked? 'They killed the cat and I buried it here.'

The week up to Fritz' death was one of the strangest of my life. At the beginning of September, we had recorded highlights from *Madame Butterfly* with Pilar Lorengar, and we had made a Christmas record with Fritz Neumeyer and his band. Immediately after that, I was due to begin a tour of eleven South American cities on behalf of the Goethe Institute. We intended to stop off en route to do a recital at the German Embassy in Dakar. For some reason I felt unwell. Something was not right, and I kept thinking we ought to cancel the tour. 'Something dreadful's going to happen,' I said to Bärbel, 'let's call the whole thing off.' But in spite of this we went.

In Paris, the connection for Dakar was four hours late, owing to a jet failure. We decided to go into town, rather than wait around in Orly for four hours. We got into a special Air France bus. I made myself comfortable and had a look at the map. The bus then cornered too fast, so that six pounds of camera equipment fell from the luggage rack onto my head. 'There, what did I tell you?' I shouted. 'That's a nice start!'

We arrived back punctually to Orly. Then someone rammed a luggage cart into my heel. The pain was so excruciating that I nearly passed out. 'I'm not going!' I declared. 'I refuse to get on that plane.'

'But Hermi,' said Bäbel soothingly, 'think of your contract with the Goethe Institute, and all the work they've put into this tour. Anyway, you always wanted to go to South America.'

We flew on, but thanks to further jet failure we landed not in

Dakar, but in Las Palmas, at two in the morning. We sat in the airport lounge until five. 'Hermi,' said Bärbel, 'Can you do me one big favour?'

'And what would that be?'

'Stop telling me that we shouldn't have flown.'

We eventually got to a hotel. Exhausted, we went straight to bed, only to be woken by the most appalling din. Tourists might be willing to put up with such 'minor' inconveniences, but a singer on tour sees them in quite a different light. I stormed across to the window. It was a pneumatic drill, they were building a promenade directly in front of our hotel. 'We must call the tour off,' I cried. 'We'd be mad to go on.' Bärbel did her best to pacify me. 'We'll both get killed!' I insisted.

'Oh shut up!'

'I'm telling you, Bärbel. In three days' time they'll find a life-raft drifting across the Atlantic, 961 miles from the nearest shore. And who'll be in it? You and me. And I'll have the pleasure of whispering in your ear, "Bärbel dear, what did I tell you?"'

It was evening before we flew on to Dakar, where it was sweltering. I started to have dizzy spells, something I had never had before. I called a doctor on the embassy's recommendation, hoping that he would advise against the tour and give me a certificate. Far from it, he told me not to worry, prescribed some pills and that was that. 'He must have been a medical officer in the Foreign Legion,' I said to Bärbel, who was none too well either, having developed phlebitis in Las Palmas. I was getting more and more nervous. Our dear friend Karl Engels tried to encourage me as he accompanied me at the embassy that night, though he was not in the best of form himself.

As I went on stage that evening, I noticed a man in the front row self-consciously smoking an enormous cigar. You could have cut the atmosphere with a knife. For the first time in my life, I took off my dinner-jacket during the performance. Then something strange happened before the interval. In the middle of Schubert's *Willkommen und Abschied* ('Welcome and adieu'), the stage seemed to heave beneath my feet like a ship in a gale. I was having yet another dizzy spell, and I clung to the piano. I had a rest as soon as the song was over, and battled through the rest of the concert as best I could. 'That's it! Finished!' I said when it was over. 'Goethe may fall from his pedestal in Weimar, but *I'm* off home!' By 10th September we were back in Germany. Bärbel went back to Munich, where she received treatment for her phlebitis. I went north to the North-Sea island of Amrum, where we had bought a lovely holiday cottage a few years previously. The thatched roof needed repairing. I was more worked up than ever, so I tried to relieve the tension by climbing up on the roof and helping the thatcher. I was sitting up there when our neighbour, Jonny Lorenzen, called me to the telephone. It was Bärbel. 'Hermi, something awful has happened. Fritz is dead.'

I refused to take it in. 'What? Who are you talking about?'

'Fritz is dead.'

'Fritz? Fritz who?'

'You know... ,' Bärbel stammered. 'Fritz... *our* Fritz.' He had been spending the weekend at a friend's house in the forest. He had been called to the telephone and had fallen downstairs. It happened a week before his thirty-seventh birthday.

Was it a premonition that had been nagging at me all the time? I felt a sudden release of tension inside me, and in spite of the shock I could breathe freely again.

Grillparzer had the following words engraved on Schubert's tombstone: 'Death has buried not only a priceless treasure, but even greater hopes.' These words might have been even more relevant in the case of Fritz.

Our last recording together was published only a month later under the title *Eine Weihnachtsmusik* ('A Christmas concert'). I wrote on the record sleeve, 'My friend Fritz is dead. This fact seems to me to become more incomprehensible every day. In recent years our work together had bound us ever closer, both as fellow artists and as friends. We had so many amusing adventures and interesting conversations. He could talk all night about music and about the problems of life. The hours I spent with him on stage and in the recording studios were the happiest of my career. We never needed to discuss tone-colour or phrasing—we simply felt the music together. We would often spend hours playing piano duets or walking through the forest together.

'Fritz understood so much about singing. I have learned an enormous amount from him. He had a natural gift for music which was quite insurpassable, and yet he was only at the beginning of a quite amazing career. Imagine what he might have achieved in the future. The last time we were together, he said to me, "The best years are yet to come. A singer must reach forty before he reaches his peak." Alas, he had no idea that he had already reached his peak.

'We were going to take the world by storm. We were to become the Castor and Pollux of song. But fate would have it otherwise. I must remain as the lonely and abandoned twin. I mourn the loss of a friend and brother singer, whom no one can ever replace.'

CHAPTER 14

Mozart's *Magic Flute* with Marc Chagall

The Met sets new standards

The 16th September 1966 was the date of the opening of the new Metropolitan Opera at the Lincoln Center, the most impressive and most cosmopolitan cultural centre in the world. The new Met's first productions included Richard Strauss' *Die Frau ohne Schatten* ('The woman without a shadow'), Verdi's *La Traviata*, and, in February 1967, Mozart's *Magic Flute*, with costume and stage-design by the eighty-year-old Russian painter, Marc Chagall. Josef Krips was conducting in New York for the first time, with Lucia Popp as the Queen of the Night, Nicolai Gedda as Tamino, Pilar Lorengar as Palma and Jerome Hines as Sarastro. It was to be my first Papageno in America. The opera was to be performed in the original German, which was something quite new to the Met. On account of the large amount of spoken dialogue, the Met had for decades preferred the English version.

I was very pleased with the new theatre, and took the first opportunity to have a good look at it. Dressed in jeans, I stood on the stage at the first rehearsal, and stared in amazement at the massive auditorium. The curtain had been raised to reveal a vast edifice, which glistened with gold-leaf decorations. A comparison may give some idea of its size. The National Theatre, Munich, can seat just over two thousand people, while the Met is almost twice that size, having a seating capacity of 3,800. The circles and gallery formed four broad semi-circular rows above the stalls. The décor was quite indescribable, and gave the impression that the architect had wanted to create something modern, but had been thwarted by a rather conservative committee.

'Well, how do you like it?' asked Mrs Shouse, my American mother. She had come specially to New York to be with us, and to see me play Papageno. 'It reminds me of the old Met,' I replied, 'what with its size, and all the gold leaf and red cushions—rather kitsch. But the acoustics must be fantastic.' This comment proved to be right.

The opera fans of New York did take some interest in my Papageno, but the real star of the forthcoming production was Marc Chagall, who had created the costumes and stage-design. The whole of the art world of Europe and America had their eyes fixed on this one event.

The Magic Flute was not, as people imagined, Chagall's first venture into opera. After all, Chagall's teacher and champion, Léon Bakst, who had taken the twenty-one-year-old painter under his wing in 1908, had been a stage-designer himself. As early as 1945, Chagall had created the scenery for a production of Stravinsky's ballet *Firebird* at the old Met. You can imagine how the subject must have appealed to him. Chagall had always loved to paint fiery red birds, as many of his paintings show.

In 1958 he designed the scenery for Ravel's ballet *Daphnis and Chloë* at the Paris Opera. He began his work on *The Magic Flute* in 1965, for which he created thirteen vast drops of 70 by 40 feet, not to mention twenty-six smaller drops and 121 individual costumes—an incredible achievement for a man of nearly eighty.

Chagall loved to create fantasies. His stage-designs can still be seen at the Met today. They are chiefly made up of various Chagall motifs, which seem almost to dance to Mozart's music. They include a multitude of faces and objects, women's heads and torsos, and people in birds' costumes playing fiddles. During the overture, the drop seemed to be covered with these bright red motifs, only one of which was directly connected with the opera itself, namely that of Papageno. Of all the figures in Mozart's opera, Papageno was Chagall's favourite. The most fantasy-like figure in the opera, Papageno corresponded most closely to Chagall's ideas, and thus inspired him more than any other.

Papageno as I see him

Chagall's interpretation of Papageno came very close to my own, and this is not merely due to the fact that I too see him as a figure of fantasy. I have heard it said that my Papageno is very much in the tradition of my illustrious forebears, Gerhard Hüsch and Heinrich Rehkemper. Like me, they were neither of them Viennese, which is a sore point. Mozart's librettist, the versatile Emanuel Schikaneder, who had created the role of Papageno for himself, was Viennese, and since then the part has always been considered the prerogative of Viennese singers. I can admittedly give a more or less convincing imitation of a Viennese accent, but I cannot hope to emulate Erich Kunz, to whom the dialect comes quite naturally.

Many people look on Papageno as a kind of Punch or Harlequin in feathers. But I do not. Like Chagall, I see the bird-catcher as a creature of fantasy, like Puck or Peter Pan. Papageno cannot weave spells himself, but he comes from the world of fairies. He tells us about his origins in the first act. Like much of the dialogue, this part is usually omitted. Papageno tells Tamino about his mother: 'I never actually knew her, but I have often been told that my mother once served the star-spangled queen in this castle. I have no idea whether she is alive, or what has become of her.' So Papageno comes from the realm of the Queen of the Night, just like the other three ladies. I therefore play him as a light-footed, ethereal creature, with much wisdom in the rather naïve comments which he makes. Chagall and I saw very much eye to eye on this point. Once, after a performance of *Winterreise* in the *Musée Chagall* in Nice, Chagall took me to one side and said in a delightful mixture of Russian, French and German, 'Monsieur Prrey, Mozaaarrr and Beethovaine arr genius. But Schubairrr is a miracle!'

I have often disagreed with conductors about the tempi in this opera, even with Herbert von Karajan. They always want to keep to certain fixed tempi. They take the music of Papageno far too quickly in several places, and are thus in danger of making the opera into an imitation of *Pagliacci*. For this reason, Mozart often writes andante rather than allegretto. A good example of this is Papageno's opening song, *Der Vogelfänger bin ich ja* ('I am the bird-catcher'), which sets the tone for the whole opera. If Papageno comes hopping onto the stage like a clown, the audience will look on him as a figure of fun for the rest of the performance, which is exactly what I want to avoid. The same applies to the scene in the second act in which Papageno is handed a beaker of wine. He drinks it up, but becomes neither playful nor drunk. He is merely lifted onto another plane. We hear a glockenspiel playing quietly in the distance, while Papageno sings, as if in a dream, *Ein Mädchen oder Weibchen wünscht Papageno sich* ('Papageno would like a young girl or a little wife'). Here, as before, Mozart expressly wrote andante, and not allegretto.

On this occasion the conductor was Josef Krips, who is in my opinion one of the greatest interpreters of *The Magic Flute*. We were in full agreement as to the nature of my role. In New York I sang *Ein Mädchen oder Weibchen* very quietly, like a simple song and it received the biggest ovation I have ever had in my life. 'You see, Prey,' said Rennert afterwards, 'they've never heard it sung like that before. It's a genuine European import.'

The music is also marked andante at the point where Papageno decides to end it all. I stand beneath a tree and meditate upon whether to hang myself: *Nun wohlan, es bleibt dabei . . .* ('Now it is time, I shall keep to my decision because there is nothing to stop me, so goodnight, you cruel world!'). These bars are in G minor, the key which is always used in *The Magic Flute* to indicate sadness and despair. It is the same key as that of Pamina's aria, *Ach, ich fühl's, es ist verschwunden* ('Alas, I know it has vanished'), which is also marked andante. Papageno's farewell should be sung at the same speed as this aria, which incidentally is often taken too slowly. If Papageno's farewell is sung too fast, it sounds far too much like play-acting, which is not the intention. Papageno is not being funny, he genuinely wants to die. His monologue under the tree is rather like his own version of *Winterreise*.

A painter creates opera

Operas on fabulous themes lend themselves to a lot of fantasy. I remember one young Austrian director, who went on at great length about the social and political implications of *The Magic Flute*. This young man sees the Queen of the Night as a kind of coloratura Claire Zachanassian, ancestral mother of capitalism. The three ladies represent the world money market in the guise of the three great world currencies, the Dollar, the Deutschmark and the Japanese Yen. In his production they are dressed accordingly: the Dollar reminds one of Mae West, and the Deutschmark is a kind of Blue Angel, while the Yen appears in the latest Suzuki outfit. The snake which attacks Prince Tamino is covered in machine code, and is supposed to represent the scourge of the computer in this age of capitalist exploitation. Its head is in the shape of a coca cola bottle, which leaves us in no doubt as to its origins. The director must have had a sleepless night, trying to work out why Schikaneder got the three ladies to kill the snake. But here too he has managed to come up with an answer, for the snake is only *apparently* dead. It is another of the Queen of the Night's ploys to make the worker Tamino unaware of the exploitation around him, and of his role as a representative of the pure revolutionary idea. My role as Papageno would be to symbolise the more earthly aspects of the revolutionary idea. In order to gain further insights, Tamino takes me to see his Daddy, high priest Sarastro, with his politburo. There Pamina is waiting for us. Once lost, she has now returned to the fold, and must now defend herself against the counter-revolutionary tactics of Monostatos and his slaves.

The director in New York was that experienced man of the theatre, Günther Rennert. He patiently and calmly went about the task of co-ordinating the various disparate elements and seeking compromises where Chagall's imagination went too far. His vast creations were marvellously colourful and inventive, but they brought about a number of problems. 'Can anybody see me at all?' I asked Rennert. 'It feels as though the scenery were swallowing us up.' Rennert assured me that the problem would be solved by skilful lighting. But Chagall objected, saying that he wanted every single detail of his decorations to be fully lit. For every square inch of those drops contained something of his own experience. I began to feel like one of Chagall's motifs—the twenty-sixth red flower, moving through his beautiful jungle in the company of twenty-five other red flowers. Or was I just a bit of the jungle itself? I could not make up my mind.

The difficulties we encountered in the finale of the first act were typical of the production as a whole. The three boys have just led Tamino to Sarastro's temple, which has three doors. 'I venture boldly to enter,' sings Tamino. 'My intentions are noble and pure. So tremble, you cowardly villain, for my duty is to rescue Pamina.' Twice he is refused entry, but when he knocks on the third door, a priest emerges, known as the Speaker. 'Where are you going, bold stranger? What do you seek in this holy chamber?' But the speaker could not come out on this occasion, for Chagall had merely painted the door on the drop. Rennert explained the problem to him. Chagall thought for a moment, then took a pair of scissors and cut the door open. Of course, it could not be used as a door, so there was nothing for it but to replace it with a proper wooden door, through which the priest might emerge.

I was very pleased with Papageno's feathered costume, except for the tail, which hung down rather sadly behind me. We were standing in front of the mirror in the costume department. 'You are triste, Monsieur Prey?' asked Chagall. 'Why?'

'The tail looks so depressing,' I explained. Chagall fetched the original design and examined it, nodding thoughtfully and pursing his lips. With a few strokes of his pencil, he drew the tail-feathers so that they stuck out rather cheekily. That was the answer. He sewed a small leather support across the base of the tail-feathers, which made them stick up in the air. The effect was just right, except that now I could no longer sit down.

'A fascinating show!'—'A visit to the Met is as good as a visit to a museum of modern art'—such was the reaction of the press. In my opinion, all the best elements in the production were summed up most effectively in a comment of Rennert's: 'Chagall's symbols and allegories create an illusion, thereby leading the audience into a magical realm, which lies somewhere between dream and reality.'

My participation in this production was a great personal triumph for me, indeed the greatest I ever experienced in America. For this I owe much to the work of Chagall, and to the wonderful symphony of colour which he created around the theme of Papageno. The artist himself was in raptures. After the *première* he hugged me and said, 'Monsieur Prrey, you arr Mozaarrr!'

CHAPTER 15

At the top of my profession

Recitals and guest appearances

In 1967 I appeared in my own television show, entitled *Schaut her, ich bin's* ('Look, it's me'), which soon became very popular, with viewing figures not far short of those of sports programmes. Of the many guest appearances I made, one of the most memorable was in *The Barber of Seville* at the 1968 Salzburg Festival. Luigi Alva's Count Almaviva was simply stunning, especially in the more florid passages, while Fernando Corena proved equally brilliant as Bartolo. All three of us recently appeared together in the same opera again, in February 1980, but this time in Vienna, with Alberto Erede conducting. Such reunions are always joyful occasions. The conductor in the Salzburg production was the youthful Claudio Abbado, who became world-famous overnight. The inexhaustible imagination of Jean-Pierre Ponnelle made for a really exciting performance. I believe all the soloists excelled themselves, and it was certainly a high point in my career, though for some strange reason the production ran for only a very short time in the Salzburg Festival.

In the autumn of the same year I made a guest appearance at the *Teatro Colon* in Buenos Aires. I also made a number of new recordings, of which I shall mention only two. The first was a recording of *The Marriage of Figaro* in March 1968, under Karl Böhm, with Mathis, Janowitz, Troyanos, Fischer-Dieskau and Lagger. My role was no longer that of the Count, but that of Figaro himself. I later sang yet another low baritone role, as Plumkett in Flotow's opera *Martha*. I made this recording together with Anneliese Rothenberger and Nicolai Gedda.

Easter 1969 was the occasion of a much-acclaimed per-
formance of Haydn's *Creation* in Salzburg, with Herbert von
Karajan conducting. Gundula Janowitz sang soprano with
quite astonishing brilliance. In May I took part in Vaclav
Kăslik's television production of *Così fan Tutte* under Karl
Böhm, with Gundula Janowitz, Christa Ludwig, Olivera
Miljakovic, Luigi Alva and Walter Berry. Then, in September,
I had the honour of singing Schumann's *Dichterliebe* at the
inaugural concert of the Alice Tully Hall at New York's Lincoln
Center. In December 1969, I was the first German to sing the
title role in Rossini's *Barber of Seville* at La Scala, Milan, in
Italian of course.

What else should I mention? In 1970, I was back singing
Papageno at the Met. In the summer of 1971, I again
experienced the incredible enthusiasm of Japanese audiences.
My itinerary included Tokyo, Yokohama and Osaka. In the
winter of 1971, I made my debut at the Lyric Opera in Chicago,
again in Rossini's *Barber*.

Since the early seventies, my recital tours of the United States
have become a kind of tradition. My concerts in New York's
Carnegie Hall always form the high point of these tours. Unlike
the Met, this wonderful concert hall has been preserved in its
original form, and it would be a tragedy if it were ever to be
pulled down. With a seating capacity of nearly 3,000, it still
preserves an atmosphere of intimacy. However, the Carnegie
Hall is plagued with financial problems, as it receives no grants
from the state.

How much does a recital at the Carnegie Hall cost? Only
recently, the rent of the hall, together with staffing and other
extras, would have cost as much as $4,000 and publicity, which
is very expensive in America, would have cost a further $6,000,
making $10,000 all told, not to mention the accompanist's fee.
At that time a concert ticket cost around four to five dollars in
New York. Costs and ticket prices have both risen in the
meantime, and under these circumstances a concert organiser
can consider himself lucky if he makes a profit at all.

Solo recitals are thus extremely risky, and by no means as

profitable as they might seem. However, the record industry makes up for this. In the seventies I made a name for myself singing German folk songs on record. In 1970 Philips engaged me to do eight LPs, including ninety-six folk songs altogether. They were beautifully arranged for choir and orchestra by Fried Walter, a sensitive musician and a talented composer, who was the musical director at RIAS Berlin. We count the Walters amongst the closest of our friends. I can think of no one with a better understanding of instrumentation. 'Friedchen,' I always tell him, 'you could write a concert for piccolo and vacuum-cleaner and it would still sound fantastic.'

Planning tours

I always have my diary with me and it often contains the short entry 'Lange'. This refers to Christian Lange, who has been my secretary for many years, and who also has the onerous task of working out the details of my itinerary. This he carries out by letter, telegram and telephone. He is thoroughly familiar with my requirements, but the job is still rather like a cross between a military campaign and a Chinese puzzle.

Doctor, family and friends have all advised me to take more care of my health and to lighten the work-load. At all events, periods of rest must always be planned into the timetable. Geographical considerations must also be taken into account. If, for example, I had a recital in Munich on the 11th March, followed by a second one in Stockholm on the 13th and a third one in Vienna on the 15th, naturally I would object strongly.

My timetable is planned provisionally a good three years in advance. It normally takes eighteen months before ninety per cent of engagements are firmly booked, after numerous preliminary discussions, negotiations, telephone calls, cancellations and reinstatements. Herr Lange eventually comes to see me, and presents me with a full chronological list of engagements. We will naturally have discussed all the details in the course of the past year, but it will be my first opportunity to see the complete timetable for myself. Bärbel also takes a full part in these proceedings.

Here is an example from 1975. Up to and including the 3rd of January, I am singing at the Munich State Opera. On the 5th we set sail on the *MS Europa*, where I am due to give a concert on board.

'And what if it's rough? I'll get cramp in my legs.'

They bring out the stabilisers for the concert, but I still get cramp. We travel to Jamaica via Puerto Rico, Haiti, Antigua, St Thomas and other islands... ten days of golf works wonders!

Tanned and rested, we arrive in New York on 28th January. There is a press conference that evening, but the next day is free. On the 30th we begin rehearsals for a *Winterreise* recital at Carnegie Hall, which is to my knowledge the first ever televised concert to be broadcast live from the Carnegie Hall.

What about February? The Carnegie Hall recital takes place on 1st February. On the 2nd I sing in the Tully Hall, on the 3rd at Yale University. On the 4th I am back in the Tully Hall, on the 5th in Houston and on the 6th in Boston.

'This is far too much,' says Bärbel.

For the remainder of the month I am recording in Munich: *Carmina Burana* for television, with Jean-Pierre Ponnelle; then a record of Pfitzner songs for the Philips collection.

In March there is not a single free day. The first week is spent on recordings. There is a Bach concert in Munich on the 10th. On the 11th I begin a tour of Germany: Karlsruhe on the 12th, Wiesbaden on the 13th, Frankfurt on the 15th and 16th, Neuss on the 18th, Osnabrück on the 19th, Münster on the 20th, Bach cantatas in Bremen on the 21st, Kassel on the 23rd. From the 24th to the 28th, there are rehearsals for *La Traviata*, then there is *The Marriage of Figaro* on the 29th, followed by *The Magic Flute* on the 31st, all in Hamburg. The next holiday is in May.

My thoughts wander to Amrum, and to our holiday cottage by the sea... There is not much travelling to do in April. 'Look, Bärbel. We're in Hamburg for the whole month.'

Lange goes into greater detail: 'Just one or two odd exceptions. A recital in Hanover on the 6th, one in Lübeck on the 15th, one in Kiel on the 22nd and one in Berlin on the 27th.

Apart from that it's just rehearsals, with three *Magic Flutes*, five *Traviatas* and one *Figaro*.

'There's a space on 10th April,' I say. 'We might be able to fit another recital in there.'

'Here we go again!' says Bärbel.

'But we've set aside the whole of May for a holiday on Amrum.'

'What's this then?' asks Bärbel. '10th May departure, 11th May in London?'

'Oh yes,' I explain. 'I've just got a Lieder recital at the Royal Festival Hall. But I can get away on the 12th, and I'll be back on Amrum again by evening.'

'A fine holiday!'

The first half of June is pretty well booked up. We are in Austria from the 2nd to the 12th: in Klagenfurt on the 2nd, Graz on the 4th, Vienna on the 6th, Linz on the 8th, Innsbruck and Hohenems on the 10th. On the 14th we are in Strasbourg. I also have a firm booking in Schleissheim on the 22nd. We begin recording *Zar und Zimmermann* for television on 16th June. But I am free from the 30th onwards.

'Look, Bärbel, we can have another fortnight on Amrum.'

'Only a fortnight?'

'It's the only way. I've got a concert in Bad Reichenhall on the 18th, and then it's time for the Munich Festival.'

'But Hermi,' protests Bärbel. 'The children will be on holiday by then, and you promised... '

'Well, what else can I do? On 27th July there's a concert with Karl Richter in Ottobeuren; on the 28th we start rehearsing *Così* in Salzburg; on the 29th I'm singing in a Sunday concert on television; then on 5th August there's the *Così première* at the Small Festival Theatre.' (I'm very much looking forward to that!) 'Then there's my Salzburg recital with Hokanson on the 7th, and *Così* on the 8th, 18th, 23rd and 28th. And the period from the 9th to the 17th has to be kept free for TV recordings. What's that on the 21st?'

'A reception with the *Landeshauptmann* [provincial administrators] of Salzburg,' explains Lange.

The programme continues with rehearsals for Mahler's 8th

Symphony with Bernstein on the 25th, leading up to a concert on the 30th and a film recording in Vienna from 1st to 4th September. We have not yet fixed the dates for Lieder recitals in Munich, Marburg and Austria. I can see another gap in the timetable.

'Look, Bärbel. We can take another fortnight's holiday from 11th September. I say, Herr Lange, what about that recording of Schönberg and his contemporaries, which I'm supposed to be doing with Michael Krist and the Vienna School? Can't we somehow squeeze that in between 9th and 17th August?'

'But you've got TV recordings then,' says Bärbel.

'I've booked four days in October for the Vienna School,' explains Lange.

'Good. Those songs are really tricky. What else have we got in October?'

'First there's a recording of *Fledermaus* with Carlos Kleiber,' says Lange. 'There's a recital in Stuttgart on 8th October, and then it's back to *Fledermaus*. You're singing in Frankfurt on the 13th, and you're invited to a reception at the Hammerschmidt Villa on the 15th; you're giving a recital in Hilden on the 16th, followed by a Beethoven recital in Salzburg on the 18th; then from the 19th to the 22nd there's that recording with Krist that you mentioned; it's *The Magic Flute* in Munich on the 23rd, followed by a gala performance for the Red Cross in Pforzheim on the 25th; then it's off to East Berlin, for a recital on the 27th and *The Barber* at the State Opera, *Unter den Linden*, on the 29th; and after that you're off to the Soviet Union.'

The Russian tour is very interesting this time, and includes four recitals: Moscow on 31st October, Riga on 2nd November, Tallin on the 4th and Leningrad on the 6th. It is not far from there to Stockholm for a concert on the 7th. There are more television recordings in Hanover on the 9th, followed by a recital in Hamburg on the 10th. I stay on in Hamburg for two performances of Brahms' *Requiem* at St Michael's Church, and return to Munich to sing in *La Traviata* on the 13th. There are two more performances of Brahms' *Requiem*, one in Freiburg on the 15th and the other in Frankfurt on the 16th. I return to Munich on 18th November to start rehearsals for *The Barber*. I

interrupt these to give a recital in Heilbronn on the 20th. There
are two performances of *The Barber* on 26th November and 2nd
December. They are followed by a recital on 16th December,
and Mendelssohn's *Paul* with Richter from the 17th to the 22nd.
There might possibly be one or two more engagements in
Munich over the festive season. At all events, I am due to sing at
La Scala on 30th December.

'Well, that's quite enough,' says Bärbel.

Things do not always work out as planned. Anyone who has
built a house knows how different it looks from the architect's
original plan. However, I note in retrospect that we kept to our
1975 schedule with virtually no changes of plan.

Light baritones are no longer in demand

I am really a sort of one-man business: 'Hermann Prey, Musical
Productions Ltd. Planning, production, delivery, sales and
administration: Hermann Prey.'

I do have agents abroad, who give me advice, make new
contacts and prepare contracts, but everything else is left to me.
All this depends on my own energy and imagination, and
especially on my vocal chords.

Every engagement involves a series of deliberations. For
example, I have recently been considering whether to extend
my repertoire, and if so in what way. Should I resurrect a role I
have not sung for years, such as Marquis Posa in Verdi's *Don
Carlos*? Why not, after all?

Although I had considerable success with this role during my
years in Hamburg, I was already aware that it did not really suit
my voice. The same is true of all Verdi's dramatic baritone roles:
Macbeth, René, Simone, Luna, Rigoletto, Amonasro. There
used to be a term for my particular lyric baritone voice:
Kavaliersbariton. This type of voice was suited, not only to Mozart
roles, but also to many typically German roles, such as Peter
Michaelow in *Zar und Zimmermann*, the Count in *Wildschütz* and
Kühleborn in *Undine*, all of them by Lortzing. Other such roles
include King Solomon in Goldmark's *Queen of Sheba*, Petrucchio

in Goetz' *Taming of the Shrew*, the musician in Humperdinck's *Königskinder*, and the hunter who turns out to be Prince Regent in Kreutzer's *Nachtlager von Granada*; also the title role in Marschner's *Hans Heiling*, and to a certain extent Hamlet in Ambroise Thomas' opera of that name. Alas, these once-popular roles are hardly ever performed in any of our major opera houses today, apart from the *Volksoper* in Vienna and the Gärtnerplatz Theatre in Munich. How many times have I discussed this problem with my wife or with friends? Bärbel and I sometimes even dream about it.

'I dreamed,' she once said, 'that you sang Mackie Messer in the *Residenztheater* on Thursday, Cherubini's *Water Carrier* in the Gärtnerplatz Theatre on Friday and *Wolfram* in the National Theatre on Saturday.' A few days later, I read in the *Süddeutsche Zeitung* that August Everding had become director of all three theatres. 'Bärbel,' I said, 'maybe your dream wasn't so far from the truth!'

Recital programmes

I take the greatest care when choosing a recital programme. There is quite a science involved in selecting the right sequence and combination of songs. The programme must be chosen to suit a variety of tastes. Concerts may be in small towns such as Bad Reichenhall, in larger towns such as Detmold and Kiel, or in big cities such as Munich or Hamburg. The programme must also be acceptable all over the world, be it in London, Paris, Berlin, Vienna, Zürich, Tokyo or New York. After a particularly successful recital, I always wish I could have given it in my beloved home town of Berlin. Much as I love to sing there, I only rarely have the opportunity of doing so. It was a great joy, therefore, to be able to sing Figaro in Berlin at the beginning of this year. The conductor was Karl Böhm, and the cast also included Julia Varady and Barbara Hendricks in the female roles, and Walton Grönroos as Count Almaviva, standing in for Fischer-Dieskau at very short notice. The production was an enormous success.

What is my idea of a really good programme? The first priority is not to expect too much, either of oneself or of the audience, not to be too ambitious, and not to sing too much. I often came to grief on this point in the early years. It is also essential to create a programme which is well balanced as regards both length and content, for the audience wish to enrich their musical experience without becoming too exhausted in the process. So two sessions of 35 to 40 minutes apiece are quite sufficient.

Many of those who come to my recitals are unfamiliar with Lieder. It is quite possible that they have seen me on television, and have come to see and hear me in the flesh. They will notice that my programme contains a number of 'difficult' songs. The printed programmes for my concerts do not normally contain the words of the songs; it disturbs my concentration when the audience have their noses in their programmes. I try to sing in such a way that every word can be understood. In my opinion, visual communication between singer and audience is of vital importance. It is only by looking at me as I sing that my songs can be fully understood.

I love to devote a whole recital to one of the great Lieder composers, and to present an evening of Beethoven, Schubert, or Schumann. For example, I might sing Schumann's *Kernerlieder* in the first half, followed by *Dichterliebe* in the second. Schubert's *Winterreise* will of course occupy a whole evening. It is possible to divide a *Winterreise* programme in half, thus providing for an interval. However, although an interval is otherwise preferable, I like to perform *Winterreise* without interruption, as this helps to preserve the unity of the work.

I have always been generous with encores, though this will depend very much on the mood of the audience. The more ecstatic the audience, the more I am able to give. In Salzburg I once gave a whole hour of encores!

I sometimes choose a theme for a recital. For example, I am fond of presenting ballad evenings. In this I have a certain affinity with Wolfram von Eschenbach in Wagner's *Tannhäuser*. I often think of myself as a minnesinger, a troubadour or a hidalgo. Eight hundred years ago, I might well have wandered

around on foot from castle to castle, carrying my harp. I am very fond of walking, so the life would probably have suited me.
Here is one of my favourite programmes:

> Franz Schubert Three ballads by Johann Wolfgang von Goethe
> *Erlkönig* ('The Erl-King'), D 328
> *Der König in Thule* ('The King of Thule'), D 367
> *Der Sänger* ('The singer'), D 149
>
> *Ballad* by Friedrich von Schiller
> *Der Taucher* ('The diver'), D 77
>
> Carl Loewe Three nordic ballads
> *Archibald Douglas*, op. 128 (Th. Fontane)
> *Herr Oluf* ('Lord Oluf'), op. 2,2 (J. G. Gerder)
> *Odins Meeresritt* ('Odin riding on the waves'), op. 119
> (A. Schreiber)
>
> Three ballads by Johann Wolfgang von Goethe
> *Der getreue Eckart* ('Faithful Eckart'), op. 44,2
> *Hochzeitslied* ('Wedding song'), op. 20,1
> *Erlkönig*, op. 1,3

This programme has a certain element of symmetry: it begins with Schubert's famous setting of *Erlkönig*, and ends with Loewe's lesser-known version of the same Goethe ballad. Loewe was only a year older than Schubert, and they both composed *Erlkönig* at about the same time in their youth. If one listens carefully, one is forced to admit that the Loewe version is just as exciting as that of Schubert, with rhythms which seem to anticipate the *Ride of the Valkyrie*.

The choice of Schiller's ballad, *Der Taucher*, is an unusual one as Schubert's setting is extremely long. It occupies twenty-four pages of music in my edition, and takes the same number of minutes to perform, which is probably the reason why it is so rarely sung.

When I give a whole series of recitals, I often like to juxtapose two composers. For example, the combination of Pfitzner and Strauss proved highly successful at the 1970 Salzburg Festival. Schumann and Strauss have also been very popular together, in a recital consisting of Schumann's *Kernerlieder*, followed by a selection of Strauss songs.

I often devote a whole evening to a particular poet, such as

Goethe, Heine or Eichendorff. I might, for instance, sing some of
Schubert's Goethe settings in the first half and some of Wolf's in
the second half.

Schubert is without doubt central to my work as a recitalist.
The greatest of all the Lieder composers, he has always held a
special fascination for me. I once made up a programme entitled
A life in song for one of my American tours. The choice of songs
was intended to show the intellectual and emotional development of Schubert's life. The first group of songs represents his
search for God, and the second describes love and parting. The
third part talks of resignation and alienation from the world,
while the fourth looks forward to death and transfiguration. The
programme looked like this:

I

Der Pilgrim, D 494 (Schiller)
Sehnsucht ('Longing'), D 636 (Schiller)
Ganymed, D 544 (Goethe)
Die Allmacht ('Omnipotence'), D 852 (Pyrker)
Die Sterne ('The stars'), D 939 (Leitner)

II

An die Leier ('To the lyre'), D 737 (Bruchmann)
Der Blumenbrief ('The flower-letter'), D 622 (Schreiber)
Alinde, D 904 (Rochlitz)
Rastlose Liebe ('Restless love'), D 138 (Goethe)
Willkommen und Abschied ('Welcome and farewell'), D 767
   (Goethe)

(interval)

III

An die Entfernte ('To the distant one'), D 765 (Goethe)
Sehnsucht ('Longing'), D 879 (Seidl)
Im Frühling ('In the spring'), D 882 (Schulze)
Über Wildemann ('About Wildemann'), D 884 (Schulze)
Erster Verlust ('First loss'), D 226 (Goethe)

IV

Fahrt zu Hades ('Journey into Hades'), D 526 (Mayrhofer)
Totengräber's Heimweh ('The homesick grave-digger'), D 842
   (Craigher)
Im Abendrot ('At sunset'), D 799 (Lappe)
Schwanengesang ('Swan-song'), D 318 (Senn)
Nachtstück ('Night-song'), D 672 (Mayrhofer)

My favourite, however, is my own extended version of Schubert's *Schwanengesang*, the series of fourteen songs which were published posthumously by Haslinger. The collection includes seven poems by Ludwig Rellstab, six by Heinrich Heine and one by Johann Gabriel Seidl. I decided to supplement the *Schwanengesang* with some more Seidl songs, in order to create a whole evening's recital. I therefore added four more Seidl texts to that of *Taubenpost*. The programme begins with the Seidl songs, which form the first half together with the Heine songs. Then I sing the seven Rellstab songs after the interval.

Five songs based on poems by Johann Gabriel Seidl

Im Freien ('In the open air')
Sehnsucht ('Longing')
Der Wanderer an den Mond ('The wanderer addresses the moon')
Am Fenster ('At the window')
Die Taubenpost ('The pigeon post')

Six songs based on poems by Heinrich Heine

Der Atlas ('Atlas')
Ihr Bild ('Her portrait')
Das Fischermädchen ('The fisher girl')
Die Stadt ('The town')
Am Meer ('By the sea')
Der Doppelgänger ('The wraith')

(interval)

Seven songs based on poems by Ludwig Rellstab

Liebesbotschaft ('Message of love')
Kriegers Ahnung ('A warrior's forebodings')
Frühlingssehnsucht ('Springtime longings')
Ständchen ('Serenade')
Aufenthalt ('Sojourn')
In der Ferne ('In the distance')
Abschied ('Farewell')

All four of the Seidl songs which I added are set at night. *Im Freien* is not often performed. It is full of feeling and has a gentle accompaniment, and is highly appropriate as an opening song, with its broad legato phrases setting the mood for the whole evening. The gentle moonlit landscape gives way to the icy chill of *Sehnsucht*. The poet stares up through ice-covered window-panes at the clear night sky, while the stars remind him of his loved-one. The staccato notes in the bass presage the frozen tears in *Winterreise*.

The next song is about a wanderer who talks to the moon. The ponderous minor chords give way to the major, as though the moon were shedding a comforting ray of light. The wandering philosopher is indicated by the two-four walking rhythm typical of Schubert's 'wanderer' songs.

This is followed by one of my favourite songs, *Am Fenster*. The piano introduction is in the mixolydian mode, the seventh of the mediaeval modes. The ancient harmonies seem to me to conjure up a picture of a small-paned window, covered in ivy and lit up by the silvery moon. All these moon songs are shot through with longing, longing for one's homeland, for love and for rebirth. Nowhere is this more clearly expressed than in Seidl's *Taubenpost*. A man lies dying, while bright music floats in through the open window. Perhaps it is the wedding music for his girl, who is now marrying someone else. We can hear a flute, a fiddle and the plucking of a double bass. Bedridden, he sends out a homing pigeon to tell her of his longing. The serene harmonies in the piano are in stark contrast to the wistfulness of the melody, creating an effect which is both unusual and fascinating.

The six Heine songs follow, finishing dramatically with *Der Doppelgänger* immediately before the interval. The Rellstab songs which form the second part of the programme include a number of well-loved songs, such as *Liebesbotschaft* and *Ständchen*. The last song is appropriately called *Abschied* ('Farewell').

I shall now devote a whole chapter to the Heine songs, which are in many ways the most demanding of all Schubert's songs.

CHAPTER 16

Schubert's Heine legacy

My early love for the poet

I know of no other verses I would rather sing than those of
Heinrich Heine. My father used to keep a volume of his poetry
on the second shelf of his bookcase, so I came to read Heine long
before any of my class-mates. As a Jew, Heine was taboo at the
Grey Monastery during the Third Reich. They could not ignore
his famous *Lorelei* poem, given its status as a folk song, but they
even got round this by calling the poem anonymous.

Leafing recently through the second volume of his collected
works, I discovered the following poem, which I learned as a boy
and still know by heart today.

> *Wie rasch du auch vorüberschrittest,*
> *Noch einmal schautest du zurück*
> *Der Mund, wie fragend, kühngeöffnet,*
> *Stürmischer Hochmut in dem Blick.*
>
> *O, dass ich nie zu fassen suchte*
> *Das weisse flüchtige Gewand!*
> *Die holde Spur der kleinen Füsse,*
> *O, dass ich sie nie wiederfand!*
>
> *Verschwunden ist ja deine Wildheit,*
> *Bist wie andern zahm und klar,*
> *Und sanft und unerträglich gütig,*
> *Und ach, nun liebst du mich sogar.*

As you swiftly walked past,
You cast back one glance,
Your insolent mouth opened in a question,
With an expression of angry pride.

Oh, that I may never try to grasp
Your white gown as it passes!
Oh, that I may never again find
Your beautiful little footprints!

Your anger has disappeared,
You are as gentle and serene as the others,
So soft, so insufferably kind,
And now you even love me!

I found this poem quite enchanting, perhaps because the picture which Heine created of his beloved corresponded to my own idea of feminine beauty. I have since come to love all of Heine's poetry. I particularly like the way he can represent melancholy, emotion, beauty, suffering and grief, all within the space of a few lines. I love the gentle humour of his verse, and the way he can use a single phrase to reveal hidden meanings. I was eighteen when I first discovered that Schubert had set some of Heine's poetry to music. I wanted to sing them straight away, but Harry Gottschalk warned me that they were the most difficult of all Schubert's songs. Just as Rome had not been built in a day, he thought it best for me to wait, and was quite right in this.

To my mind, Heine's humour remains as fresh today as it ever was. This is in sharp contrast to the rather serious tone of the romantic composers such as Schubert, Schumann, Mendelssohn and Brahms, who were inspired to set his verse to music. All of them preferred to choose poems which were gentle and charming, or sad and emotional, avoiding his more satirical verses. Those who only know Heine from the song literature can hardly be aware of the more humorous side of his character, and of the way he loved to make fun of others.

Schubert would have witnessed the sensational first publication of Heine's early poetry, which appeared in 1823, entitled *Lyrisches Intermezzo* ('Lyrical Interlude'). Robert Schumann was later to set many of these to music. This was followed in 1826 by *Reisebilder* ('Travel Scenes'), which included a cycle called *Heimkehr* ('Home-coming'). Then, in 1827, he published the complete collection of his youthful works, entitled *Buch der Lieder* ('Book of Songs'). It was only a year later, shortly before the composer's death, that Schubert sent six settings of Heine's verse to his publisher, Tobias Haslinger. Of all the 250 poems which Heine had published, Schubert had chosen six from the *Heimkehr* cycle. The song titles are shown in brackets.

No. 8 *Du schönes Fischermädchen (Das Fischermädchen)*
    16 *Das Meer erglänzte weit hinaus (Am Meer)*
    18 *Am fernen Horizonte (Die Stadt)*
    22 *Still ist die Nacht (Der Doppelgänger)*
    25 *Ich stand in dunkeln Träumen (Ihr Bild)*
    26 *Ich unglücksel'ger Atlas (Der Atlas)*

Heine only uses titles to refer to ballads or epic poetry. The lyric poetry to be found in *Heimkehr* does not carry any titles, only numbers. It is impossible to tell whether the titles of Schubert's songs stem from the composer himself, or from the mercenary-minded Tobias Haslinger, who was fond of titles. It was he who gave the name *Schwanengesang* to Schubert's posthumous collection. Schumann, on the other hand, did not invent his own titles, but used the first line of any poem where no original title was available. Needless to say, the title *Dichterliebe* did not come from Heine.

Schubert's Heine legacy is very small when compared to the twenty-four Heine songs which Schumann composed. Of the ninety or so poems to be included in Heine's *Heimkehr* collection, Schubert appears for some strange reason only to have gone as far as number twenty-six. There is no obvious reason why he should have confined himself to the earlier poems. Given that he was introduced to Heine's verse by friends, it is conceivable that he was given an incomplete set. Or, perhaps, he was planning to write more songs at the time he died. Whatever the case, one thing is clear: Schubert chose only the saddest poems, which corresponded to his own mood of melancholy and despair.

I normally sing these songs in the order in which Haslinger originally published them, though I have often wondered whether to change this. After all, it was not necessarily the order that Schubert intended. He was no longer around at the time they were published.

In choosing the keys for these songs, I have attempted to make the transitions as smooth as possible harmonically, in order to preserve the unity of the collection. I sing *Ihr Bild* in its original key of B flat minor, *Das Fischermädchen* in G major, *Die Stadt* in B minor, *Am Meer* in B flat major, and *Der Doppelgänger* in B flat minor. G, B flat and B are all related. *Der Atlas* is the only exception, being in F sharp minor, which gives the interpretation a certain dramatic impetus.

The Six Songs

Der Atlas

Ich unglücksel'ger Atlas! eine Welt,
Die ganze Welt der Schmerzen muss ich tragen,
Ich trage Unerträgliches, und brechen
Will mir das Herz im Leibe.

Du stolzes Herz, du hast es ja gewollt!
Du wolltest glücklich sein, unendlich glücklich,
Oder unendlich elend, stolzes Herz,
Und jetzo bist du elend.

Unhappy Atlas that I am! I must carry
A whole world full of suffering;
I must bear what is unbearable,
And my heart wants to break within me.

Proud heart, this is what you wanted!
You wanted to be happy, infinitely happy,
Or infinitely miserable, proud heart!
And now you are miserable.

The rhythm of this poem is extremely complicated, rather like a recitative. Only a master like Schubert could set it in conventional three-four time.

Heine's description of Atlas' superhuman struggles is in many ways reminiscent of the artistic temperament, one moment shouting for joy, the next in the depths of despair. Schubert was familiar with these tensions, as I am also.

The song is in three parts, the first and last being in the sharp

key of F sharp minor (a flat key in the original), while the middle
section is in the flat key of B flat major (a sharp key in the
original). There are no gentle transitions between them,
Schubert merely juxtaposes them like three blocks hewn out of
granite. The texture of the accompaniment is similarly jagged
and rock-like.

(Orig. version in G minor / B major / G minor)

1. Teil   2. Teil   3. Teil

Above this, the melody moves sharply up and down, like the
jagged outline of a mountain range.

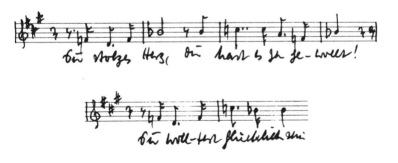

The heavy octaves in the bass rise up like a clap of thunder, and I
feel as though transported by invisible powers. *Der Atlas* is in
many ways Schubert's most intensely personal song, just as it is
Heine's most intensely personal poem.

Ihr Bild	Her portrait
Ich stand in dunkeln Träumen,	Dreaming darkly, I stood
Und starrt' ihr Bildnis an,	And looked at her portrait,
Und das geliebte Antlitz	And the face I loved
Heimlich zu leben begann.	Took on a life of its own.
Um ihre Lippen zog sich	Her lips formed into
Ein Lächeln wunderbar,	A wonderful smile,
Und wie von Wehmutstränen	And her eyes glistened
Erglänzte ihr Augenpaar.	As if with melancholy tears.
Auch meine Tränen flossen	My tears also flowed
Mir von den Wangen herab—	Down from my cheeks—
Und ach, ich kann es nicht glauben,	Alas, I cannot believe
Dass ich dich verloren hab'!	That I have lost you!

The beginning of this song is highly descriptive. The sad unison figure, beginning on the piano alone, but continuing with the voice, gives a vivid impression of the poet's dark dreams as he stares bleakly at her portrait. As soon as her face lights up, however, the piano also takes on a new life.

The song reminds one of the 13th song of Schumann's *Dichterliebe* cycle, *Ich hab' im Traum geweinet* ('I wept in my dream'). In both songs, the piano comments on what the singer is saying. In Schumann the poet weeps in his dream, while in Schubert the portrait smiles and weeps at one and the same time. This is so typical of Heine!

Schubert's music continues to swing wildly between sadness and joy, between minor and major. I try to bring this out in the tone-colour of the voice, for example in the phrase *zog sich ein Lächeln wunderbar* [but not too much, for the mood keeps changing unexpectedly]. The listener must be kept guessing as the music wanders to and fro between major and minor. A good example is the piano interlude between the second and third stanzas, which ends on a bare fifth. What key are we in? B flat major or B flat minor?

Das Fischermädchen

Relatively speaking, this is the happiest of the six Heine songs, but only at first glance. For even this song is ultimately unhappy in tone.

Das Fischermädchen	The fisher-girl
Du schönes Fischermädchen, *Treibe den Kahn ans Land;* *Komm zu mir und setze dich nieder,* *Wir kosen Hand in Hand.*	Beautiful fisher-girl, Bring your boat into shore; Come and sit beside me, and We will hold hands together.
Leg an mein Herz dein Köpfchen, *Und fürchte dich nicht zu sehr;* *Vertraust du dich doch sorglos* *Täglich dem wilden Meer.*	Lay your head on my heart, And do not be afraid; You boldly entrust yourself To the wild sea every day.
Mein Herz gleicht ganz dem Meere, *Hat Sturm und Ebb und Flut,* *Und manche schöne Perle* *In seiner Tiefe ruht.*	My heart is just like the sea, With its storms and its tides, And there in its depths lies Many a beautiful pearl.

Ironic humour is difficult to express in music. For me it is the pedantic rhythm of this song which gives some indication of the poet's ironic intentions. What is the meaning of the siciliano rhythm which pulses through every single bar of the song? Does it represent the rocking of the boat, or the playing of the waves, or merely the boldness of the young suitor's advances? The piano never stops:

Das Fischermädchen is rather like Ernesto's serenade from Donizetti's opera *Don Pasquale*, in which the chorus sustains a continuous barcarolle accompaniment. This point should be borne in mind when deciding on the tempo for this song, which can so easily be sung too fast. If this happens the diction will suffer. For such beautiful music to be fully effective, it is essential that every syllable be heard and understood.

At the beginning of the second stanza, it is important to suppress the natural rhythm of the melody. If the *an* is stressed too much, it makes nonsense of the meaning: *Leg* **an** *mein Herz dein Köpfchen...* ('Lay your head *on* my heart...')

(Orig. version in A flat major)

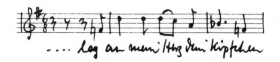

Perhaps Schubert wrote it in a hurry. Inexperienced singers might do well to sing it like this:

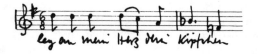

Though the song is called *Fischermädchen*, it is not really about the fisher-girl, but about the young suitor who is trying to win her favours. It is a serenade, but not in the usual sense. Don Giovanni, for example, would have told her that her lips were as sweet as honey. This suitor merely sings of his own virtues, in the hope that she will find them acceptable. She would be better advised to stay in her boat.

We are not told if the fisher-girl accepts the young man's advances. If she were so imprudent as to do so, the consequence might well be that of the later song, *Am Meer*, for the gentle metaphors contain a hidden threat. 'My heart is as stormy as the sea. If I am to woo you, you will have as much to cope with as a boat on the sea. You must dive very deep to find the pearls which I have to offer.'

This is only one of many interpretations. What is so fascinating about Heine is his ambiguity. This song appears on the surface to be no more than a harmless flirtation. The sea is gentle, the waves splash softly, and the two young lovers make eyes at each other. Yet we sense the underlying passion, which could break out at any time.

Schubert's music is no less ambiguous, as it flits about between major and minor, between light and shade, continually slipping from one key to another. Schubert wishes to show us how lovers can waver between joy and despair. It is a state which can go on for ever. For in all these songs, with the one exception of *Ihr Bild*, the piano introduction and the postlude are identical. The song is like an unending round, on reaching the end, one is tempted to return to the first verse and repeat the whole song.

Die Stadt

This song in some ways reflects Schubert's taste for the macabre. Poems 18 and 19 of *Heimkehr* are both about a town. Schubert might well have chosen number 19, where Heine has his tongue firmly in his cheek as he muses on the injustice of love. Note that he makes a pun on the word *Tor*, which has two meanings: 'gate' and 'fool'.

Die Stadt	The town
Sei mir gegrüsst, du grosse,	Greetings to you, great
Geheimnisvolle Stadt,	Town full of secrets,
Die einst in ihrem Schosse,	Who once held my sweetheart
Mein Liebchen umschlossen hat.	Within your womb.
Sagt an, ihr Türme und Tore,	Tell me, you towers and gates,
Wo ist die Liebste mein?	Where is my sweetheart?
Euch hab' ich sie anvertrauet,	I entrusted her to you,
Ihr sollet mir Bürge sein.	You were to be my guarantors.

Unschuldig sind die Türme,	The towers are innocent,
Sie konnten nicht von der Stell',	For they could not move
Als Liebchen mit Koffern und	When lovers with boxes and
Schachteln	cases
Die Stadt verlassen so schnell.	Leave the town in such haste.
Die Tore jedoch, die liessen	But the gates would let
Mein Liebchen entwischen gar still;	My love slip quietly away;
Ein Tor ist immer willig,	For a fool is always willing
Wo eine Törin will.	When a girl is foolish too.

However, Schubert's town looked quite different. He preferred the endless despair of poem number 18.

Am fernen Horizonte	On the distant horizon,
Erscheint, wie ein Nebelbild,	There appears the foggy image
Die Stadt mit ihren Türmen,	Of the town with its towers,
Im Abenddämm'rung gehüllt.	Veiled in evening twilight.
Ein feuchter Windzug kräuselt	A damp gust of wind ruffles
Die graue Wasserbahn;	The grey waters,
Mit traurigem Takte rudert	As with melancholy strokes
Der Schiffer in meinem Kahn.	The boatman rows my boat.
Die Sonne hebt sich noch einmal	The sun rises again
Leuchtend vom Boden empor,	In splendour from the earth,
Und zeigt mir jene Stelle,	And shows me the place
Wo ich das Liebste verlor.	Where I lost my beloved.

Like the text of *Am Meer*, this poem appears to begin peacefully, and keeps its tragedy a secret until the very last line. In it Heine employs some of his favourite poetic devices—the hovering twilight as the day turns to night, the mysterious fog, and the unfathomable depths of the sea. Schubert summons all his creative powers to capture the mood of this imagery. There is a vivid arpeggio figure which runs through the whole piece. This chord is nothing new in itself, but the way Schubert used it was then, and still remains, quite unique. He repeats it all of 17 times, accentuating the second and third beats. It sounds like the strokes of the boatman's oar.

(Orig. version in C minor)

The boatman rows sadly towards the town. Schubert leaves the harmonies deliberately ambiguous, we have no way of knowing whether the music is modulating into G sharp, B, D or F (A, C, E flat or F sharp in the original). The sound is impressionistic, ambiguous and full of foreboding. Schubert wrote the piece in C minor, the key which is traditionally used for a funeral march. The water theme is interspersed with contrasting chordal passages with firmer harmonies.

The end of the song remains unresolved, yet another unusual feature of this highly original song. Indeed, Schubert was anticipating by many years the techniques of the impressionist composers.

Am Meer

Das Meer erglänzte weit hinaus
Im letzten Abendscheine;
Wir sassen am einsamen Fischerhaus,
Wir sassen stumm und alleine.

Der Nebel stieg, das Wasser schwoll,
Die Möwe flog hin und wieder,
Aus deinen Augen liebevoll
Fielen die Tränen nieder.

Ich sah sie fallen auf deine Hand,
Und bin aufs Knie gesunken;
Ich hab' von deiner weissen Hand
Die Tränen fortgetrunken.

Seit jener Stunde verzehrt sich mein Leib,
Die Seele stirbt vor sehnen;
Mich hat das unglücksel'ge Weib
Vergiftet mit ihren Tränen.

By the Sea

The sea shone far and wide
In the last light of evening;
We sat at the lonely fisherman's cottage,
Silent and alone.

The fog came up, the waters rose,
The gull flew hither and thither,
And the tears fell lovingly
From your eyes.

I saw them fall on your hands,
And I fell to my knees;
From your white hands
I drank up the tears.

Since then my body has wasted away,
And my soul has been dying from longing;
The poor wretched woman
Has poisoned me with her tears.

The first bar of *Am Meer* is just as unconventional as the last bar of *Die Stadt*. All previous songs, including those of Mozart, Beethoven *and* Schubert, had begun quite firmly in the tonic. *Am Meer* begins in stark contrast to this, with a neapolitan sixth followed by a dominant seventh.

Very slow

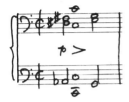

I noticed when I was studying *Rigoletto* that Verdi unconsciously employs exactly the same device at several points during the opera, particularly at moments of high drama.

Rigoletto

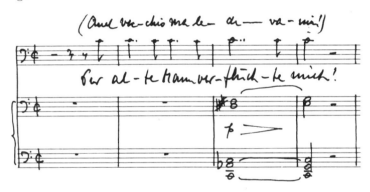

I often like to get an impression of a song from the visual effect of the notes on the page. I find I can learn an enormous amount from the pattern they form, depending on whether they are few and far between, or else densely packed together. This is particularly true of an original manuscript. *Am Meer* illustrates this point rather well, as it fills exactly two pages of music, and is symmetrical in form, so that the second page is very similar to the first. The first page depicts various natural phenomena—the evening sun, reflected in a glassy sea; the billowing, steamy fog, the rising tide, and the wild flapping of the gulls. The second page describes a soul tortured by longing.

The song makes heavy demands on legato technique, as the

voice forms long phrases above a hymn-like accompaniment. The music is in the major, and conjures up a picture of the peaceful, shimmering sea. Then the scene becomes more sombre, with a shivering pianissimo in the piano. There follows a crescendo, in which the music rises to a climax and then wanes again. Peace and tranquillity return, but the beauty is tainted by grief. Poisonous tears from loving eyes—a paradox so typical of Heine!

Der Doppelgänger

Still ist die Nacht, es ruhen die Gassen,
In diesem Hause wohnte mein Schatz;
Sie hat schon längst die Stadt verlassen,
Doch steht noch das Haus auf demselben Platz.

Da steht auch ein Mensch und starrt in die Höhe,
Und ringt die Hände vor Schmerzensgewalt;
Mir graust es, wenn ich sein Antlitz sehe—
Der Mond zeigt mir meine eigne Gestalt.

Du Doppelgänger, du bleicher Geselle!
Was äffst du nach mein Liebesleid,
Das mich gequält auf dieser Stelle
So manche Nacht in alter Zeit?

The Double

The night is still, the streets are asleep;
My beloved once lived in this house;
She has long since forsaken the town,
But the house still stands here just as before.

And a man stands there, staring upwards,
Wringing his hands and racked with pain;
I shudder to see his face,
For the moonlight reveals my own likeness.

You spectre, you pale companion!
Why do you mock my lovelorn grief,
And the pangs I suffered in this very place,
So many nights in times gone by?

The air still rings with the veiled harmonies of *Am Meer*, and the miserable sphinx with her poisoned tears; the piano begins with four stark chromatic chords.

(Orig. version B minor) Very slow

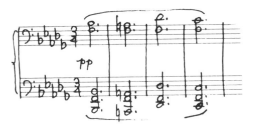

These form the first chords of a ten-bar chaconne theme, which is repeated, with slight variations, as many as six times during the course of the piece. Indeed, the chaconne nearly forms the sum total of the accompaniment, which is a highly original idea for a song.

I am reminded here of Robert Schumann. According to his biographer, it was a repeated note in his head—an A, I believe—which portended his eventual insanity. This must have been a dreadful torture for a composer. I always think of poor Schumann when I hear the first four chords of *Der Doppelgänger*, not because of the chaconne theme itself, but on account of the repeated F (F sharp in the original) which it contains within it. Though hidden in the accompaniment, it is always there, and returns as many as fifty times in all. This agonising ostinato determines the whole musical form of the piece.

The melody also turns about the same F and is repeated sixty times in all, forming nearly half of all the notes to be sung. In the first stanza in particular, the voice scarcely leaves this note, venturing a mere third above it and a fifth below. Only in the second stanza does the voice move into the upper register. It rises stepwise to a top F on the words *vor Schmerzensgewalt* ('racked with pain'), and reaches a top F sharp on the word *Gestalt* ('likeness'). The excitement in the poem is reflected in the tension of the music.

At the beginning of the final stanza, the chaconne theme

gathers speed as it rises chromatically. It winds upwards, but
continues to hang on the F. On the word *äffst* ('mock') the music
modulates unexpectedly from B minor to D minor. The effect is
shattering as the horror of this ghastly scene is summed up in one
simple chord of D minor. I take great care to perform the song in
strict time right up to the beginning of the accelerando.

Note the treble forte which Schubert placed under the word
manche in the last line. Treble forte occurs only twice in any of
Schubert's songs: once in Opus 1, *Erlkönig*, on the word *Gewalt*
('strength')—and here in *Der Doppelgänger*, one of his last
published works. It is remarkable that he should have written
his two loudest notes, one at the beginning and one at the end of
his composing life. Between them he produced a massive output
of more than one thousand published works, including operas,
symphonies, piano pieces, chamber works, sacred music and
over six hundred songs, all within the space of fifteen years. The
music must have poured from his pen. Not even an experienced
copyist could have written it all down within so short a period.

CHAPTER 17
Rehearsals and performance

What makes a good accompanist?

When you give as many as forty to fifty recitals a year, it is of paramount importance to choose the right accompanist, or rather pianist. The term accompanist is a deceptive one, as it makes the pianist seem less important than he really is. Singer and accompanist form an inseparable unit. I have worked with a variety of musicians in the course of a long career, so I know how vital the accompanist is to the standard of the performance.

It is unusual for singers to collaborate with world-class soloists and when this does happen it is normally for some special purpose. It might be in the context of a festival, or for some commemorative concert or recording. For example, I recently recorded some Liszt songs together with Alexis Weissenberg, winner of the Liszt Academy Prize in Budapest. We got on marvellously from the outset. The same was true of a performance I made with Friedrich Gulda Schumann. Indeed, we responded to one another spontaneously, without any of the initial communication problems which sometimes occur. I also enjoyed performing with Alfred Brendel, with whom I shared a passion for Schubert. At the time, Alfred was still on the threshold of his meteoric rise to fame. We both benefited greatly from working together.

Whether such partnerships work or not depends very much on the adaptability of the individuals concerned. The pianist must take account of the fact that the singer, who is intimately acquainted with the song literature, cannot be expected to interpret the songs in a way which goes against some of the basic insights which he has gained. The pianist must therefore recognise this, even to the extent of subduing his own instincts in cases of severe disagreement, for the sake of the performance.

Who have been my most frequent partners over the years? First Gerald Moore, who, alas, no longer performs in public. He has retired to his house in the country, where he now devotes himself to writing books. Geoffrey Parsons and Irwin Gage both work exclusively as accompanists, which is unusual these days. It is unfortunate that both of them are so much in demand, as it means they are permanently booked up. They work year in, year out, with a variety of singers, to whom more are added every year. They know the song literature inside out, and have years of experience, not only of Lieder, but also of the singers who sing them! In short, they are in their element on the accompanist's stool, and as such are irreplaceable.

I very much enjoy performing with Günther Weissenborn. A man with forty years' experience as an accompanist, he has played for such illustrious singers as Tiana Lemnitz, one-time star at the Berlin Opera, Jaro Prohaska, Erna Berger, Walther Ludwig, Peter Anders, Nicolai Gedda, Rita Streich and Dietrich Fischer-Dieskau—as many as three generations of singers! I have Weissenborn to thank for introducing me to the beautiful songs of Hans Pfitzner, which sadly are still very much neglected.

Another stage-partner of mine is Wolfgang Sawallisch, with whom I perform once or twice a year if I am lucky. I rarely perform with Karl Engel these days, which is a great shame. However, Leonard Hokanson still plays regularly for me, and for this I am very grateful. Two recent additions to the circle are Michael Krist and Helmut Deutsch. These last three are none of them typical accompanists, as all of them are involved in other activities, such as conducting, teaching and solo performances. Leonard Hokanson considers it extremely important to remain a good all-round musician, after the model of his teacher Arthur Schnabel. Hokanson performs not only as a soloist, but also as a member of an ensemble, and in particular with the Odeon Trio, a group which he himself founded. He also teaches at the Frankfurt Conservatoire. For me Hokanson is the ideal accompanist, as he works with no other singer, and has to adapt himself only to me. It was he who coined the phrase 'It is art that conceals art'. An interpretation often appears to come easily and spontaneously, and for this reason the listener will often attribute it to the inspiration of the moment. Nothing, however, could be further from the truth, for it is the result of long and protracted discussions. The two performers will have gone so closely into every detail that between them they will have created a new and composite interpretation.

Problems of tempo must be solved together. The great Lieder composers managed without metronome markings, so that questions of speed are very much left to the interpreter. How, for example, should one distinguish between *mässig* ('*moderato*'), *etwas geschwind* ('somewhat fast') and *ziemlich geschwind* ('fairly fast') in the context of a cycle such as Beethoven's *An die ferne Geliebte* or Schubert's *Winterreise*? Tempi are a matter of taste. I may have an exact conception of the speed I want, but I must always be ready to discuss and, if necessary, to accept, a contradictory opinion. Trying to keep to the tempi which have been chosen is another matter again. A good example of this is *Kriegers Ahnung*, the second song from Schubert's *Schwanengesang* cycle, which requires a gradual *accelerando*, from *nicht zu langsam* ('not too slow'), through *etwas schneller* ('somewhat faster'), eventually reaching *geschwind, unruhig* ('fast, excited').

We must also discuss dynamics. Here the pianist must follow the singer's lead with regard to volume levels. The pianist can distinguish a whole variety of nuances at any point on the keyboard by the merest adjustment of the touch, while the singer is of necessity more limited in his capabilities. His pianos and pianissimos must be clearly heard from the back row of the gallery, which can be as far as seventy yards away. To make the voice carry this far is one of the most difficult things a singer has to do, and the pianist must adjust and make allowances for this. The answer to the problem lies, quite literally, in his finger-tips.

Playing forte is not without its problems either. There are some pianists who can play forte, or even fortissimo, without drowning the singer. Alas, not every pianist can achieve this.

It is often the poem itself which determines the dynamics of a song. Many pianists dispute this, considering the text to be of secondary importance. As instrumentalists, they are chiefly interested in the music. In some places, however, it would be disastrous to ignore the words. There is, for example, a song by Brahms, the first line of which runs, *Wir wandelten, wir zwei zusammen, ich war so still und du so stille.* ('We walked, the two of us together; I was so quiet, and you were so quiet.') The instructions are contained in the words of the poem, and it is up to both singer and pianist to carry them out.

The piano introduction to Brahms' song, *Wie bist du, meine Königin*, is another example in point. It is not enough here simply to play the notes in a soft legato. Only by reading the words does the meaning of these bars become clear:

> *Wie bist du, meine Königin,*
> *durch sanfte Güte wonnevoll!*
> *Du lächle nur, Lenzdüfte wehn durch mein Gemüte*
> *wonnevoll.*

> (My queen, how blissful your gentle charms have made you! Only smile, and the scents of spring will waft blissfully through my soul.)

The word *wonnevoll* ('blissful') is repeated nearly a dozen times in all, and is the key to the whole musical treatment of the work. Every bar must 'ooze' with feelings of bliss, and it is important that the piano introduction should be played in the same 'blissful' manner. Indeed, the feeling is contained within the rising melodic figure.

Adagio (molto espressivo e dolce)

It is a herculean task for the pianist to try to communicate this 'bliss' within so short a fragment of melody. Perhaps a slight rubato on the first quaver of each bar will help, or maybe he should sing the word to himself as he plays it: bli-issful, bli-issful, bli-issful, bli-i-iss-ful! It is certainly not easy.

Prima la musica or prima la parola?

I personally find the words of Lieder just as interesting as the music, so much so that I have neglected a number of songs in the past, merely because I could not make anything of the text.

It is not easy for a composer to find a poem which corresponds to the ideas in his head. This was no problem for the medieval minnesingers, who wrote their own words for their songs. Most people know that the minnesingers lived in the twelfth and thirteenth centuries, but not many have any idea what *minnesang* was or what it sounded like. When, therefore, I began recording my large song collection in the early seventies, it seemed logical to start with a *minnesang* by Walther von der Vogelweide. The collection thus spans a period of eight centuries altogether.

It is difficult for us in the twentieth century to appreciate the internal beauty of the *minnesang*, because, unlike Schubert's, the melody will not stand up on its own. In the *minnesang*, the vocal line is no more important than the various aspects of the text, such as the versification, the metre and, especially in the songs of the troubadours of Provence, the alternation between masculine and feminine endings. The *trouvères* of central and northern France performed what were known as *Groslais*, consisting of as many as 150 verses. The singer would improvise during the performance, in a manner similar to the modern 'jam-session'. The bard might well enhance his performance with a number of spontaneous ornamentations and decorations.

It must have required a well-developed sense of musical form to achieve such beauty and symmetry. The songs were not composed for the uneducated listener. *Minnesang* was, after all, very much the preserve of the nobility; it was not created by the common people, neither was it intended for them.

By the end of the fourteenth century, these musical bards were already a thing of the past. The art of poetry had become divided from that of music. There were a number of reasons for this. Firstly, the art-form of the mediaeval epic poem had reached a stage where it could no longer develop any further. Secondly, new instruments were appearing, which offered the opportunity, hitherto unknown, of playing music as an ensemble—the advent of polyphony. This also enabled musicians to find new audiences elsewhere. One notable exception was that of the Mastersingers, who revived the *minnesang* tradition in the middle of the sixteenth century. They, however, were not so much interested in creating something new as in preserving the ancient tradition, and their music did not stand the test of time.

Since then, the composition of songs has taken on quite a different form. The composer will go through a number of poems and select the one which most inspires him, or which he considers most suitable. In the nineteenth century, composers preferred to choose the poetry of their contemporaries, which often tended to have a rather monotonous metre. The first of a pair of lines usually had one more syllable than the second, as in Eichendorff's *Mondnacht*. In other cases, all the lines of the poem had the same number of syllables, as in *Waldgespräch*, also by Eichendorff. The poetry itself had changed in its emphasis. For the minnesinger, the structure of the verse was of paramount importance, but for poets such as Uhland, Lenau, Eichendorff, Mörike and Heine, it was the content of the verse which took precedence. Moreover, they composed poetry without the least intention of setting it to music. Some of them even tried to prevent this from happening. Goethe, for example, never came to terms with Schubert's settings of his poems. In this he was probably influenced by his musical mentor, Carl Friedrich Zelter, who also went out of his way to ensure that Goethe's friendship with Loewe was nipped in the bud.

As the poems did not always fit into the musical forms which composers wished to use, they often took the liberty of 'editing' the poetry, repeating odd phrases, and sometimes whole lines. Occasionally they might even go so far as to change the wording.

There are one or two places in the literature where I tend to stumble over the words, at least in my mind. This is usually because the words and the music do not quite fit. There is, for example, a place in Brahms' *Von ewiger Liebe* ('Of eternal love'), where I never really feel quite at home. The first stanza of Wentzig's poem goes like this:

> *Dunkel, wie dunkel in Wald und in Feld!*
> *Abend schon ist es, nun schweiget die Welt.*
> *Nirgend noch Licht und nirgend noch Rauch,*
> *Ja, und die Lerche sie schweiget nun auch.*

> How dark it is in the woods and the fields!
> It is evening, and the world is silent.
> There is no more light and no more smoke—
> Yes, even the lark is now silent.

If the poem were recited, the speaker would probably give extra stress to the word *ja*. In my opinion, Brahms does not fit this word very well into the music, for some strange reason, he tacks it on to the previous line. Perhaps he did not quite know what to do with it.

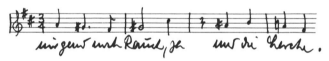

I am always tempted to sing it like this:

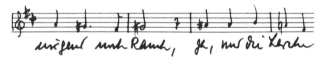

—or even to leave out the *ja* entirely:

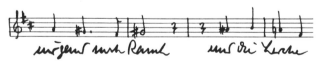

At all events, I always have to concentrate very hard to sing it as the composer intended.

Two of the best 'marriages' of words and music are Robert

Schumann's song-cycles Opus 39 and 48. They are based on poems by Eichendorff and Heine, and are known as his *Eichendorffflieder* and *Dichterliebe* cycles respectively. I have no idea which of the two I find the more captivating: Eichendorff with his poetic appreciation of nature, or Heine with his melancholy symbolism.

The chief protagonist in the Eichendorff cycle is the moonlit forest of the old German fairy tales. In *In der Fremde*, for example, the lonely young man wallows in nostalgia beneath the rustling trees of a lonely forest; it is in the forest that the nocturnal wanderer encounters the Lorelei witch; *Mondnacht* gives a mysterious picture of the forest rustling and blossoms shimmering in the moonlight; the tree-tops shudder in the *phantastische Nacht* of *Schöne Fremde*; forests surround the stone knight in his ancient castle; in *Zwielicht*, there are hunters wandering through the forest; *Im Walde* describes a wedding as it passes through the forest; finally, the last poem, *Frühlingsnacht*, talks of migrant birds flying over the wood.

The flower is to Heine what the forest is to Eichendorff. In the beautiful month of May, the buds are all open, and flowers spring up where the poet's tears fall; he loves the rose and the lily with passionate joy; he plunges his soul into the lily's cup; Our Lady is surrounded by flowers in the cathedral at Cologne; the little flowers know 'how sorely my heart is wounded'; on the bright sunny morning, the flowers whisper to one another and look on the poet with sympathy; in his dreams, his beloved gives him a cypress wreath; bright flowers bloom in the golden light of evening in that land of bliss. These words, these pictures and symbols, give life and breath to the music, just as the music gives life and breath to the words.

Perhaps I am so fond of the German *lied*, simply because the poetry moves me as much as the music.

CHAPTER 18

After the performance

Just one moment, please

After a performance, Bärbel is usually the first person to come to my room. Fortunately for me, most artists' rooms are well-hidden in the labyrinth of corridors behind the concert hall or opera house. They are thus difficult, or even impossible, for autograph hunters to reach, but Bärbel knows how to find me. She stands guard at the door while I am changing. If someone knocks on the door, she pops her head out and says, 'Would you wait just one moment, please.' We later retire with friends to some local hostelry, or maybe to a small party which someone is giving. Wherever we are, I am usually desperate for a beer by this time. We are rarely in bed before half past one, which is one of the unfortunate side-effects of an artistic career.

'It's a shame,' I say as we go to bed.

'What's a shame?' asks Bärbel.

'We've got to know so many nice people. That history professor who was sitting opposite me, he told me all sorts of interesting things about the Aztecs. And his wife was very nice.'

'And what's a shame about that?'

'It's just that we'll probably never see them again. You meet people, you have a nice conversation and you really get to like them, but then you never see them again.'

Bärbel tries to comfort me. 'I expect lots of people find that. It's not easy to make friends at our age.'

'You can say that again! We simply never have time to make friends. It's like this: the more people know Hermann Prey, the fewer people I know. It gets worse and worse.'

'You've got your family. But there again, you're always too busy with your work to be interested in your children and their problems.'

'What's that got to do with me? It's up to them to sort out their own problems. After all, they're old enough.'

'Let's stop this. Turn the light out. It's ten to two.'

The next morning, Bärbel is already up and about, emptying drawers and cupboards and packing my dinner-jacket. I shut my eyes and start ruminating. I must be mad, tearing about from place to place, camping out in hotel-rooms, and I've forgotten what home cooking tastes like. I am feeling tired and depressed. The waiter brings the breakfast up to our room, but I cannot be bothered to get up, I would rather stay in bed for good.

'Bärbel, what's the name of this hotel?'

'Park Hotel,' says Bärbel from the bathroom.

'In Aachen? Is there a Park Hotel in Aachen?'

'But we're not in Aachen. We were in Aachen the day before yesterday.'

The day before yesterday? I could have sworn I was in Aachen. I decide not to ask Bärbel where we are, because I would rather work it out for myself, but for the life of me, I cannot remember where we are. Last night's applause is still ringing in my ears, but I have no idea which town it was that gave me such a marvellous reception. I try to remember the concert hall, the way the seats were arranged, the lighting, and the corridor to the green-room. But in vain.

'Up you get,' calls Bärbel. 'We're supposed to be away from here by half past ten at the lastest.'

Away from here? But where are we? Where are we going?

'Aren't you feeling very well?'

No, I am feeling dreadful.

'What's the matter?' asks Bärbel.

'My head's swimming,' I reply. 'I think I'll have to call the whole thing off.'

'You've overdone it again. I could see it coming.'

I eventually pull myself together and haul myself out of bed. The circus moves on, and there is another concert that evening.

Such moments of doubt are often followed by glowing successes. You might think I was in top form, but I have learned to read the writing on the wall, and have no illusions about my present state of health. I also know it is my own fault as I have a tendency to take on far too much. The moment I see a space in my diary, I ring up Christian Lange and say, 'Herr Lange, we've still got room for a . . . ' In 1977, I managed to get into such a state that I had to take a whole six months off.

On we go to Kiel, to Strasbourg, to London, to Paris or maybe to Rome. We are always glad to be on our way back to Munich, which has been our home since 1961. Last night's conversation is continued in the car:

'Now I'm going to spend exactly two days in Munich. I'll deal with the post, have a chat with Herr Lange, sort out that business about the folk song record and get the car serviced, and then I'm off to Feldbrunn.'

Bärbel is biting her lip.

'Come on, say something!'

'What do you expect me to say? You've got it all worked out. Anyway, I've got plenty to do in Munich, and quite apart from that, I want to spend a few days with the children. The ZDF [Germany's second TV channel] doesn't arrive in Feldbrunn until next Thursday. Of course I'll have to be there by then, but that still leaves me with a whole four days at home. I intend to take full advantage of them.'

'But I don't want to stay in Munich.'

'Then you'll have to go up to Feldbrunn on your own. You're always complaining that we know so many people but don't have any real friends. Tell me, how do you expect to make friends if you're never at home and they never find you in?'

Home sweet home

Seventeen years ago, we bought two houses either side of a meadow just outside Munich. I prefer to keep the address a secret, because we sometimes have unwelcome visitors. One Sunday, for example, the doorbell rang at nine in the morning.

A completely unknown lady was standing at the gate. The only reason she did not come into the garden was that Unica, our dog, had dashed out to the gate, in spite of a leg injury, and was barking loudly at her. Angela, the housemaid, came back with the news that she had come from a distance, was a great fan of mine, and had to speak to me personally. I sent down a message to the effect that Herr Prey never received anyone unannounced, and never at nine o'clock on a Sunday morning. I put on my dressing gown and peeped out of the window. Angela was speaking to the lady, who began to gesticulate wildly, pointing to a paper bag she was holding. Angela reappeared, saying that the woman was becoming very insistent. She had come specially from Ravensburg or Klagenfurt or somewhere, and would not leave until she had seen me and given me two pounds of apples from her garden. Unica was barking furiously. Our elder daughter Annette was just coming out of the kitchen with the tea. 'Well,' she said, 'let's hope that's the end of her.' Just then the telephone rang. Our younger daughter Fränzi answered it and said that it was Claudio Abbado from London.

I took the receiver with a smile, expecting some new and interesting offer. 'Hello Claudio... no, you didn't wake me...' But that was the last I heard, for at that moment Unica followed Angela into the house, sat down by the phone and started barking again. I put my hand over the receiver and shouted, 'Get this animal out of here!' Bärbel, Annette, Franziska and Angela descended on the dog; peace returned, and at last I could hear what Claudio was saying. I was disappointed to learn that it had nothing to do with music. It was about a house in London, which I was hoping to rent during the weeks of my forthcoming visit to Covent Garden. It belonged to a friend of Claudio's, who unfortunately needed it for himself. This meant that I would have to look elsewhere. Feeling rather disgruntled, I put the phone down, only to hear the doorbell ring again. This set Unica barking. 'Hasn't she gone yet?' I shouted. My wife threw down her knife and fork and stormed out of the house, with Unica barking at her heels. Our son Florian called out sleepily from upstairs; he wanted to know what the row was all about. At last Bärbel came back with the apples, but not before she had received another volley of abuse. There have been occasions when eventually I have been forced to go and 'present' myself.

I have already mentioned our two houses. My wife and I live in one of them, together with our three children. Annette is twenty-four, Fränzi is nineteen and Florian is twenty-two. I have so far said very little about my children, probably because I could not hope to do them justice. My wife and I never stop talking about our children, and not a day goes past without our mentioning them. I could produce a whole book about them, though they would have to write the second half themselves to give their side of the story. They have grown up now, and will have their own opinions on the matter. I am pleased to say that all of them have artistic gifts. They all paint very well, each with an individual style. My elder daughter Annette has at last decided on a career, and has been going to drama school for the last nine months. I recently saw her in a studio performance of Max Mell's play, *Jeanne d'Arc*, and was greatly impressed by her powers of expression. My younger daughter Franziska loves to work with wood. She is training as a cabinet-maker, and hopes eventually to restore antique furniture.

Florian is studying music and singing. He recently sang the difficult Bach Cantata, *Der Friede sei mit dir* ('Peace be unto you'). I could never have sung it so beautifully at his age. I appreciate how much he has benefited from growing up in a musical family. Even so, it will certainly not be easy for him as my son. He is also working as a general dogsbody for the children's photographer, Herbert Achternbusch.

My parents-in-law live in the house on the other side of the meadow. Not only has my father-in-law helped me a lot in business matters, but he and his wife brought up our children while Bärbel and I were on tour. They are still there today, and will always help out if they are needed.

Our house in Munich is just right for us. The hall is full of souvenirs, and leads into a living room which looks out onto the garden. My studio is to the right. I never stay very long in the living room and as soon as I have heard the latest news on the television, I retire to my studio. I have just come back from a recital tour, but there is still a lot to be done. I have to work out a new recital programme and refresh my knowledge of an old opera role of mine in which I am soon to make a guest appearance. I often have an entirely new role to study, which at the time I am writing is that of Beckmesser.

I work best in complete isolation. As soon, therefore, as circumstances allow, I slip off to our lovely little chalet in Lietzental, Upper Bavaria. It is made of wood, has a shingle roof, and smells deliciously of pinewood. It is just the right size, having four rooms leading off a central corridor: a living room with a fireplace, a bedroom, a smaller room with bunk beds and, most important of all, a comfortable kitchen/dining room, where we spend most of our time. Bärbel is a marvellous cook, and it is lovely to sit in the kitchen and breathe in the delicious cooking smells. The room looks out onto the green, wooded valley and the tall pines which remind me of my grandfather's villa in Berlin. It is the ideal place to recover from the stresses of life.

We have another small house not far from this retreat. It consists of one room only, and serves as my studio. It has two enormous advantages in this respect: firstly, there is no telephone; secondly, the door is so difficult to open that the uninitiated intruder will always think it is locked, even when it is not. I can work here without the slightest disturbance.

My friend Peter Karger has a small hut about six miles from here, to which he retires for similar reasons. A dentist, he has kept my teeth in order for the last twenty years. We would meet there in all weathers to go on long rambles, and this would give us the chance to talk together, to relax and to recover our equilibrium. I have other friends who are fond of hiking. For instance, Fritz Hoffmann, Peter and I once planned a cycling tour in September 1981. We had intended to cycle from Feldbrunn as far as Nebel on the island of Amrum, a journey of some eight hundred miles in all. We had already planned the route, ninety per cent of which runs along country lanes. In the event we will start at five every morning and given an average speed of roughly six miles per hour, we can manage just over forty miles a day. This means that we can easily make it to Amrum in three weeks.

In addition to a good cape, I shall take a set of good maps

with me, so that I can follow the route exactly. Large-scale Ordnance Survey maps are the most accurate, and they almost show the individual trees. I can imagine the sort of thing I might say: 'Well, lads, this path goes on for two point seven kilometres, then we come to a hill which looks down on Kloppenhausen and its castle. A path branches off to the town, and exactly one hundred metres to the left is an oak which is four hundred years old.' It will be enormous fun if it works out.

CHAPTER 19

An audience of millions

While I was working in Hamburg in the mid fifties, I used to come past the same fruit stall every day on my way home from the opera. Every now and then I would stop to buy a few oranges, grapes or mandarins. The woman who worked at this fruit stall was unusual in that she always had classical music on her radio. One day I could hear the *Fidelio* Overture, so I asked her if she liked Beethoven. At first she was taken aback, but then she laughed loudly and said, 'Of course. I've always liked that sort of thing.'

'Why don't you come to our opera?'

She gawped at me. 'What, me! Come to the opera? All those posh people? That'll never do for the likes of me.'

'That's where you're wrong,' I said. 'It's different these days. Anybody who likes opera can go.'

She passed me my bag of fruit and giggled. 'Me at the opera? Pull the other one!'

Just before Christmas I managed to get hold of a couple of complimentary tickets. One of them I gave to my friend Wolfgang, and the other one to the lady at the fruit stall. I told Wolfgang, 'On your left you'll find my old fruit-seller. You must tell me if she likes the opera.'

The seat on Wolfgang's left was unfortunately empty. I wanted to save the poor woman the embarrassment of having to make excuses, so I simply did not mention the matter to her again. She must have been afraid of going in. At the time I never dreamed the day would come when people could watch music being played in their own homes. Three years later, when I first appeared on television, singing six songs from *Winterreise*, I could not help thinking of my old friend at the fruit stall.

It is the middle of January 1979. The entry in my diary for the second half of January is 'ZDF'. This is the abbreviation for the *Zweites Deutsches Fernsehen*, West Germany's second national television channel. I was due to appear with them in a programme entitled 'Christmas with Hermann Prey', which was to be broadcast almost a year later, on New Year's Eve 1979. I really love television work, and always look forward to the recordings, even though they can be gruelling.

Bärbel is still in Munich. As planned, I have come up to Feldbrunn alone, in order to make a few 'takes' at our idyllic little retreat in the Lietzental.

It is a quarter to eight in the morning, and it is still cold in our little wooden chalet. The heating does not go on until eight o'clock. Only rarely does the telephone ring before eight, but anything can happen when you are working with the ZDF. Sure enough, just at that moment the phone rings. I jump out of bed, run through into the living room and answer the phone. It is Bärbel.

'What's the matter? You *are* coming?'

'Yes, I am. But the ZDF isn't coming today. They've just rung up, but we have to go to Berbling tonight.'

'For the takes in the church? When are we supposed to be there? Would you ring them up and ask them? I don't want all that kerfuffel with the make-up again. And if possible, they should try and heat the church.'

'You'd better talk to them yourself.'

'No, whenever I ring them they start umming and ah-ing and end up making even more changes. Do please come soon. There's no more room in the kitchen. And bring Traumhel with you. Yesterday I burnt my right thumb and forefinger . . . What? No, it's nothing serious, but at the moment I couldn't manage a piano recital.'

Bärbel arrives at half past eleven, and I am happy again. Within half an hour, the kitchen is back in order and full of cooking smells. I no longer need to slip off to the village to eat.

The picturesque little village of Berbling lies in Upper Bavaria, just north of the Autobahn between Munich and

Salzburg. It boasts a small hostelry, which serves the most delicious country food. It is also a place of pilgrimage for art lovers, with its beautiful baroque church of the Holy Cross, which is where the filming is to be done. It is getting dark as we arrive in Berbling. The church seems to have awoken from its hibernation and is lit up, so that it can be seen from some distance away. The camera team have parked their vehicles in the forecourt; the machines and generators are all humming away; in the corner of the churchyard the floodlights are ready to be switched on; the unwary visitor is liable to trip over clusters of wires.

I am used to this atmosphere of frenzied activity. I have hardly arrived in Berbling when I hear the familiar call, 'Please, Herr Prey...' I await further instructions. 'Please, Herr Prey, the "mask" is waiting for you.'

In the German theatre, the word 'mask' does not mean the kind of mask worn at the German Shrovetide carnivals, or by English children at Hallowe'en. It refers to the person who does the make-up, whether it be the Egyptian make-up for Radames or the grey paint to be sprayed on for Germont. The person to carry out this task should be equable by nature and capable of understanding the feelings of an actor who is about to face the public.

Television make-up staff have a number of extra problems to deal with. Once, for example, I was filming for an opera. The recordings lasted several weeks, and I had to be made up at 7.15 every morning. The 'mask' included a beard, known in the profession as *Sauerkohl* (another word for sauerkraut). After a time, this produced a painful rash, which proved excruciating for both of us.

On this occasion, the make-up man is waiting at the local inn, where the ZDF have booked a private room. Bärbel and I greet him as an old friend. I sit down at an improvised make-up table and put my face in his capable hands. The costume designer is not required on this occasion, as I am to appear in an ordinary suit. We are in the middle of making up when the proprietress comes in with the food and beer we have just ordered. I look in the mirror and see Bärbel enjoying her meal. At last everything is ready and I am allowed to start eating my sausage, but at that very moment the door flies open. 'Herr Prey, please come for your take.'

I cross the churchyard and enter the church, which is freezing cold. For some reason it could not be heated. The twenty or so television staff are wrapped up in duffle-coats. They blow on their hands and rub them, flex their elbows and generally keep moving about so as to keep their blood circulating. 'Herr Prey,' says someone in a hoarse voice, 'please go to the altar.' I obey and place myself in the spotlight, thinking to myself, if only I had worn my fur-lined boots!

It would be impossible to sing in such a cold church. I imagine the organ is frozen up too. Today the pre-recorded music is to be played through from a tape recorder, while I attempt to mime to the sound of the loudspeakers. Synchronising lip movement and sound in this way is an art in itself.

I have studied the score and directions thoroughly. I know when the organ is about to begin, and to be ready with a rapt expression of prayerful devotion. Soon Hermann Prey's voice comes over the loudspeaker: *Ich steh' an deiner Krippen hier, Herz Jesulein, mein Leben...* ('I stand here by your crib, Jesu my heart, my life...'). On the word 'crib', I turn my head to the left and gaze at a trumpeting cherub in the niche behind the pulpit. The camera follows my gaze... 'Stop.' The music dies away with an ominous rumble. Something has gone wrong. They have mounted the camera on runners in order to follow my movements, but it has somehow got stuck, perhaps the runners are iced up. The technicians flock round the camera, looking like a tribe of eskimos. Their discussions show a decided resemblance to a rugby scrum. It is a chance for me to blow on my hands and rub them, and to flex my elbows, and eventually we start the take again.

Quiet! Clapperboard! Camera! Sound! The organ plays— rapt expression of prayerful devotion—*Ich steh' an...* Stop. Amen to all that. Two of the spotlights have gone out. The familiar voice intones, 'Herr Prey, please don't move, the bulbs will be replaced at once.' Sure enough, in no time at all they are screwed into place. 'Herr Prey, your take, please.' The

spotlights refuse to go on and the voice orders, 'Check the cable.'
Two of the plugs have fused. Somebody has trodden on the
cable, but at least both the plugs are intact. 'Herr Prey, your
take, please.' Quiet! Clapperboard! Sound! The organ plays—a
rapt expression of prayerful devotion—*Ich steh' an deiner
Krippen*... This time we get as far as the third line, at which
point the director interrupts. 'I want a close-up here.' The
camera is rolled away again. The director and cameraman have
a somewhat heated discussion, so there is a short break. Then the
voice repeats, 'Herr Prey, your take, please.'

We manage at last to shoot a few feet of film. Then we have to
transfer to a new set. The hoarse voice announces a quarter of an
hour's break and I retire to the private room. In the meantime
the beer has become warm and the sausage cold. I have brought
some reading matter with me. I read a little and chat with
Bärbel and the make-up man, who also works in the theatre.
Make-up staff can always tell you a lot about what is going on in
the theatre world. Exactly ten minutes later, the door opens.
'Herr Prey, please...'

We work up to midnight in Berbling. The next day the show
will move on to Kufstein, where we are to do a few takes in the
market place and in front of the famous organ, the *Heldenorgel*.
The Kufstein authorities have kept up all their Christmas
lighting for our benefit. As with most outdoor recordings, there
will be a host of difficult modifications and lighting problems to
be dealt with. We must also make allowances for spectators, who
are liable to hold up proceedings. The takes will probably last
until two or three o'clock in the morning.

'Goodbye then, everybody. Come on, Bärbel. I'm tired out
and frozen to death. Let's go. I must have a hot shower.'

'But not too hot, or you won't be able to sleep.'

'What of it? I'm going to spend the whole night standing by
the crib and smiling.'

'Yes, smiling, to an audience of millions.'

CHAPTER 20

Zu neuen Taten

A musical adventure

My fiftieth birthday was on 11th July 1979, and I celebrated it on the island of Amrum, together with fifty friends and neighbours. A year and a half passed after that during which I worked on this book and made new plans for the future. The decade to come is to be the most varied and eventful period of my life. There is a quotation from *Götterdämmerung* which has become my own personal motto: *Zu neuen Taten* ('To new exploits'). It is thus appropriate that Wagner should be my next musical adventure, though not the Wagner of *Götterdämmerung*. For, to be honest, I am not especially interested in singing the role of Gunther. Rather, I have decided after long consideration, to supplement my repertoire with the role of Sixtus Beckmesser, town clerk in *The Mastersingers of Nuremberg*. It is my first new Wagner role since 1959, when I first sang Wolfram with Wieland Wagner in Hamburg. It is also an unusual role for a lyric baritone like myself. My Beckmesser debut was at the Bayreuth Festival Theatre in the summer of 1981, under the direction of Wolfgang Wagner.

For a long time before the festival I took my piano score of *The Mastersingers* on all my tours, both at home and abroad. The part must be studied extremely thoroughly. I was pleased to discover that the *tessitura* is relatively high and thus well-suited to my particular voice. The part of Beckmesser would appear to be fairly straightforward from an acting point of view, but as a character role it was something quite new to me. Apart from the rather unsuccessful serenade in the second act, and the even more catastrophic solo in the singing contest, there is nothing in the part which remotely resembles an aria. His part is always moving about. However, it is for this very reason that I was so fascinated by the role. *The Mastersingers of Nuremberg* is without doubt the most approachable of all Wagner's operas. For it is not about gods, heroes or saints, but about simple everyday folk with all their strengths and weaknesses. What is more, Wagner has given Beckmesser some very amusing lines to sing.

I cannot explain why I waited so long before plucking up the courage to sing this role. It probably has something to do with the fact that I have always identified with youthful roles such as Papageno, Guglielmo and Figaro, or with more mature roles such as the Count in *Figaro* and Wolfram in *Tannhäuser* which meant that I found it difficult at first to put myself in the role of a 'loser' such as Beckmesser. However, my sense of comedy has helped me to work my way into the part.

It was Monday, 8th December 1980 and as I wrote I was sitting in Room No.416 at the Hotel Imperial in Vienna. Through the window I could see the handsome façade of the Vienna Music Society's headquarters, which has taken on a special significance for me today. For in only a few hours' time I was to be received into honorary membership of the Company of Friends of Music in Vienna.

'I must pop down to the Kärntner Strasse,' said Bärbel, 'I've got some shopping to do. I'll leave you to rest in peace.'

'Have you seen my *Mastersingers* score anywhere?'

'I thought you wanted to work on your book.'

'Yes, of course I do. But I want to write a bit about *The Mastersingers*.'

'It was on your bedside table this morning. Wait a minute... Here under these letters... No, it isn't here either... '

'Would you just have a look in the bathroom?'

'Ah, here it is, by the side of the bath.'

Beckmesser was with me, wherever I went.

My Beckmesser: a real gentleman

When I wrote this, there were eight more months to go before

46. When I met Bärbel it was love at second sight. This, our very first picture, was taken in 1951.

47. Bärbel has travelled with me on tour for more than twenty years. I could never cope without her, but together we can survive the hardships of a nomadic existence. This picture

was taken during a two-month tour starting from Vienna, which took us to Moscow, Tokyo, San Francisco, New York, Dublin, and finally back to Munich.

48. The United States have almost become our second home.

49. There are some really romantic spots in Toronto, even in winter.

50. There are hardly any communication problems with Japanese children.

51. I can only relax properly when I am free of all professional worries. The best

place for this is our cosy little thatched cottage on the North-Sea island of Amrum. Alas, we cannot spend as much time here as we would like.

52. At the *Nationaltheater*, Munich, which was formally re-opened in November 1963, twenty years after it had been destroyed in the Second World War.

53. About sixteen years ago, we moved to a house just outside Munich, together with our three children, (from left to right) Annette, Franziska and Florian. We have made this our permanent home.

54. On a family cruise to Istanbul, with (from left to right) Fränzi, Annette and Florian. All of them have grown up and are now completely independent.

55.   I owe a debt of gratitude to my parents-in-law, Erich and Wally Pniok, for without them Bärbel could never have come with me on tour. When we went away, they always came to look after both house and children.

56.   I need absolute peace and quiet when preparing for recitals. My study is the best place for this, though it rarely looks as tidy as it does in this picture.

my Beckmesser debut, so it would have been rash of me to talk of an interpretation which had not yet been fully worked out. However, of one thing I am certain: my Beckmesser was not to be some mindless Nuremberg lout. Sixtus Beckmesser is the only one of all the singers to have a Latin Christian name. The only intellectual amongst a group of common artisans, such as Veit, Kunz, Konrad, Fritz and Hans, he is something of an outsider, and lives up to his name. He has apparently been to a classical school, where he studied Latin and Greek with more success than I ever did. As town clerk, he occupies a position of considerable responsibility. Anyone who has dealings with the city chancery must first apply to Beckmesser. In short, he is a gentleman worthy of respect.

Mastersingers contains some of the best dialogue that Wagner ever wrote. Hans Sachs and Sixtus Beckmesser have some particularly good lines, which are a real pleasure to perform. There is a marvellous example at the beginning of the opera, when Beckmesser presents himself to the masters and public: *Immer bei Sachs, dass den Reim ich lern' von blüh' und wachs!'* ('With Sachs I always hear the same words about blooming and growing!'). This is the comedy of *The Mastersingers* in a nutshell.

I hoped to be able to present Beckmesser in a serious light, as a gentleman worthy of Eva's hand, to whose suit her father Pogner has no objections apart from age. Beckmesser, clever as he is with tabulature, is unlucky in matters of the heart. He is quite up to composing a master-song, can distinguish between the different note lengths, and we assume he can sing well. For otherwise he would not have been accepted as a mastersinger, let alone chosen as *Merker* or 'rule-judge'. He is the sort of person who can achieve great feats in private, but goes to pieces totally in public. Hence the great débâcle in the singing contest.

I wanted to take care to sing Beckmesser's song entry as beautifully as possible, even when he starts to muddle up the words. I shall also try to demonstrate how he suffers from stage-fright without ever realising what nonsense he is singing.

Is the town clerk as wicked as Sachs makes him out to be? Or does the cobbler judge him too harshly in his eagerness to make things easy for Stolzing? I take the latter view. In the scene in which Beckmesser hides what he thinks to be Sachs' song in his pocket, he is not acting from greed, but from sheer desperation, terrified lest Sachs will pip him to the post with his unexpected song entry. In the mistaken belief that this will expose Sachs as Eva's suitor, he brings out the piece of paper and tries to give it back to him. His exaggerated relief when he hears that Sachs has no intention of courting Eva during the contest seems to me to be quite in keeping with a man who is clumsy and unsure of himself in matters of the heart, and who feels threatened by the competition of his rivals. The same applies to his instinctive dislike of Stolzing. For these reasons, I intended to present Beckmesser, not as someone ridiculous, as is so often the case, but as the unfortunate victim of fate.

In this connection, it has been argued that Wagner made Beckmesser into a figure of fun expressly in order to ridicule the powerful Viennese music critic, Eduard Hanslick. If Wagner himself is to be taken at his word, such suggestions must definitely be rejected. According to his autobiography, the composer was surprised that such speculations should ever have arisen. He writes, 'My visit here (i.e. to Vienna) began with a rather odd incident. As so often happens these days, I was asked to read my *Mastersingers* text aloud to the Standhartner family. As Herr Hanslick was a friend of mine, it seemed appropriate that he should be invited to the occasion. We noticed how pale and silent this formidable critic became during the reading. After I had finished, he could not be persuaded to stay, but took his leave in a decidedly irritable fashion. My friends all agreed that he must have understood the opera to be a lampoon directed against himself and felt insulted that we should have invited him to the reading. After that evening, the critic became noticeably cooler towards me, and later became openly hostile.'

New territory

Wagner's *Mastersingers* is not the only new role which I then intended to sing in the near future. I had further plans to move out of my normal range of light baritone roles. The first of these to come was Mandryka in *Arabella* by Richard Strauss in the autumn of 1982, closely followed by Alban Berg's *Wozzeck*. Both were to be sung under Claudio Abbado in Vienna, and would be difficult but exciting challenges. Another new project of mine concerned Wagner's first youthful opera, *Das Liebesverbot*, which is based on Shakespeare's play *Measure for Measure* and was first performed in 1836. We planned to present it at the National Theatre in Munich, on the 13th of February 1983, the centenary of the composer's death.

I have yet another adventure in store. Gyula Trebitsch, the film producer, had asked me to take part in a feature film which will last a whole evening. What was special about this was that I was to take on, not one, but two main roles. The script was by Robert Stromberger, and was entitled *Mein Bruder und ich* ('My brother and I'). It is the story of twin brothers with ambitions as singers, one of whom is more successful than the other. The plot contains a number of surprises, and is in the form of a musical comedy.

The success of this film would depend very much on the director, Klaus Peter Witt, who is an expert in the use of all modern recording techniques. He also would have the task of leading me, an opera singer, albeit one with television experience, through a whole evening's worth of film which includes both musical and verbal entertainment. There would presumably be scenes in which I would act with myself, so to speak. I hoped there would also be filming techniques which would allow me to embrace myself!

A word of thanks to the people of Vienna

It is the 9th of December 1980. I am back in my hotel room in Vienna. Sitting at my desk, I gaze through the window at the home of the Vienna Philharmonic, and think of the unforgettable events of the previous night. It was almost exactly twenty-five years ago, on 2nd December 1955, that I sang my first *Winterreise* in the Brahms Room of the Vienna Music Society. Since then I have appeared there on as many as fifty occasions. Yesterday I was accorded the honorary membership of the Company of Friends of Music in Vienna. I was formally received by their president, Prof. Dr Horst Haschek, on the basis of a unanimous decision by their General Meeting. This is a great honour for me, and I see it as the greatest triumph of my artistic career.

The honour which has been bestowed on me carries with it enormous obligations. The first person to be so honoured was Ludwig van Beethoven in 1826. The list of honorary members to be elected in the subsequent 150 years consists mostly of famous composers, outstanding conductors and instrumentalists. Composers include Felix Mendelssohn in 1837, Hector Berlioz in 1846, Robert Schumann in 1852, Johannes Brahms in 1876 and Anton Bruckner in 1891; in this century, Richard Strauss in 1916, Hans Pfitzner in 1926, Paul Hindemith and Igor Stravinsky in 1952, and Carl Orff in 1979. Some of the conductors to have been so honoured are Hans Richter, Wilhelm Furtwängler, Bruno Walter and Arturo Toscanini; instrumentalists include Clara Schumann, Joseph Joachim, Pablo Casals and Wilhelm Backhaus. There are not many singers. The last to be so honoured was Hermann Winkelmann in 1907, seventy-three years ago. Winkelmann had been Vienna's most celebrated tenor at the turn of the century, and had sung the title role at the first performance of Wagner's *Parsifal* in Bayreuth.

Prof. Haschek said in his address, 'It requires much dedication to achieve the apparent ease with which his singing always inspires us. Yet it requires more than great talent and vocal training to achieve such depths of expression, which are only made possible through deep spiritual insights. We most sincerely hope that Hermann Prey will sing for us as often as he possibly can. It will be a great joy to invite him to Vienna on frequent occasions.'

Then it was the turn of the General Secretary Albert Moser to announce that, thanks to the financial backing of the City of Vienna, the Company of Friends of Music would be able to realise a project which for many years has been very close to my heart: a performance of the complete works of Schubert in chronological order. Following a previously unsuccessful attempt in Hohenems in Vorarlberg, the project is now to be carried out in Vienna. It is the fulfilment of a dream, for which I am extremely grateful to the people of Vienna.

I am certain that the project will be successful, and hope that many of the Company of Friends of Music will thus become acquainted with some of the composer's lesser-known works. We were to begin in the late autumn of 1983 with his youthful works. Solo and chamber works would be performed in the Brahms Room, orchestral items in the great hall. All the performances would take place on or near the 19th November, the anniversary of Schubert's death.

'Then we'll be back here in the Imperial,' I said to Bärbel, 'in the same room. And I'll finish the proceedings with *Die schöne Müllerin*, *Winterreise* and *Schwanengesang*. That'll be the end of the Schubertiad and Hermann Prey will stop.'

Bärbel looked at me sceptically. 'But in twelve years' time you won't even be sixty-five. And you've always said you'll still be singing *Winterreise* when you're seventy-five!'

'And I will!' I laugh. 'When I'm seventy-five I'll stage my come-back!'

DISCOGRAPHY

There are many recordings of Hermann Prey available in Germany and in other European countries and specialist record dealers should have the information and be able to obtain them. The following are available in Great Britain and in the United States of America.

Great Britain

LITURGICAL

J. S. BACH: Mass in B minor*
Cantatas 32, 57, 61, 128, 158, 173.
Christmas Oratorio
Mass in F major
Mass in A major.
PUCCINI: Messa di gloria

OPERA

FLOTOW: Martha (extracts)*
HUMPERDINCK: Die Königskinder
LORTZING: Der Wildschutz
Zar und Zimmermann*
MILLOCKER: Der Bettelstudent*
Gasparone

MOZART: Cosi fan tutte*
       Le Nozze di Figaro*
       Der Zauberflöte*
ORFF: Die Kluge
PUCCINI: Madama Butterfly
ROSSINI: Il Barbiere di Siviglia*
J. STRAUSS: Die Flerdermaus*
R. STRAUSS: Ariadne auf Naxos*
         Capriccio*
SUPPÉ: Boccaccio
WEINBERGER: Schwanda the Bagpiper.

SYMPHONIC

MAHLER: Symphony No. 8.*

LIEDER

LISZT: (with Alexis Weissenberg, piano). Es muss ein wunderbares sein; Ein Fichtenbaum steht einsam; Nimm einen Strahl der Sonne; Die Vatergruft; Anfange wohlt ich fast versagen; Der du von dem Himmel bist; Lasst mich ruhen; Morgens steh ich auf und frage; Uber allen Gipfeln ist Ruh; Die drei Zigeuner; Blume und Duft; Wer nie sein Brot mit Tränen ass; Die Fischerstochter: Drei Sonaten von Petrarca

BEETHOVEN: (with (Wolfgang Sawalisch, piano). An die Hoffnung; Adelaide; Six Songs op.48; Maigesang; Marmotte; Das Blumschen; Wunderholt; Neue Liebe; Neues Leben; Aus Goethes Faust; Wonne der Wehmut; Sehnsucht.

BRAHMS: (with H. Deutsch, piano). Wie bist du, meine Königen; Von ewiger Liebe; Die Mainacht; An die Nachtigall; Sonntag; Der Gang zum Liebschen; Dein blaues Auge; Sehnsucht; Meine Liebe is grun; Senerade; Minnelied; Meerfahrt in Walsseinsamkeit; Wir wandeln; Wie Melodien zieht es mir; Ständschen; Salamander.

*Also available in U.S.A. (*see note under U.S.A*)

SCHUBERT: (with H. Deutsch, piano). Der Sänger; Seensucht; Rastlose Liebe; Der Fischer; Meerestille; Der König in Thule; Der Schatzgraber; Erlkönig; Promotheus; Ganymed; An Schwager Kronos; Versunken Heheimnes; An die Entfennte; Willkommen und Abschied; Der Musensohn; Lieberhaber in allen Gestalten; Am Flusse; Trinklied; Heidenroslein; Erster Verlust; An den Mond; Wanderss Nachtlied.

(with K. Engel) An Sylvia; im Abendrot; Erlkönig (coupled with Margaret Price & J. Lockhart (piano) and others).

OPERATIC ARIAS

(with Berlin Deutsche Oper) Arias from operas by Kreutzer, Lortzing, Marschner, Nessner, Wagner.

United States of America

*Titles marked with an asterisk above are available in the U.S.A. but under different labels. The following are also available in the U.S.A

LITURGICAL

J. S. BACH: St. John Passion
BRAHAMS: German Requiem
MOZART: Canons 2-12

OPERA

BEETHOVEN: Fidelio
KORNGOLD: Die tote Stadt

PFITZNER: Palestrina
SCHUBERT: Alfonso und Estrella
WEBER: Der Freischütz
　　　　Oberon

LIEDER

SCHUBERT: Goethe Lieder (with Elly Ameling)

PHOTO CREDITS

Clive Barda, London: No. 35. Bavaria Verlag, Gauting: No. 29. Karl Bayer, Garmisch: No. 41. Bild am Sonntag, Hamburg: No. 51. Peter Bischoff, Bremen: No. 50. Ilse Buhs, West Berlin: No. 40. dpa, Dusseldorf: No. 47. Hanns Hubmann, Munich: No. 52. Keystone Press Service, Hamburg: No. 42. Siegfried Lauterwasser, Uberlingen: No. 22. Lars Looschen, Munich: No. 10. Max-Reinhardt-Forschungs-und- Gedenkstätte, Salzburg: No. 24. Werner Neumeister, Munich: No. 9. F. Peyer, Hamburg: No. 7, 8, 56. Photo Fayer, Vienna: No. 39. Photo Ellinger, Salzburg: No. 14, 17, 31, 32, 36, 37. Paul Sessner, Dachau: No. 24. Stern, Hamburg: No. 18, 30. Suddeutscher Verlag, Munich: No. 13. Felicitas Timpe, Munich: No. 16, 20, 21, 27. Sabine Toepffer, Munich: No. 11, 12, 38, 43. H. Zabel, Hamburg: No. 15. Hajo Zitzelsberger: No. 53. ZDF, Mainz: No. 48. All others come from private collections.

INDEX